My Book

This book belongs to

Name: _____

Cover Design by :
MATH-KNOTS LLC

First Edition :
January, 2019

Author:
Gowri Vemuri

Questions: mathknots.help@gmail.com

This book is dedicated to:

My Mom, who is my best critic, guide and supporter.

To what I am today, and what I am going to become tomorrow,

is all because of your blessings, unconditional affection and support.

This book is dedicated to the

strongest women of my life ,

my dearest mom

and

to all those moms in this universe.

G.V.

www.math-knots.com

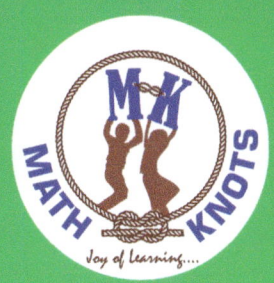

What is CogAT ?

The Cognitive Ability Test® (CogAT) test measures thinking and analytical skills in young children from K-12, in various sections of Verbal, Quantitative and Non-Verbal. Many counties and states conduct this test to identify kids for CogAT serves as one of the basic measures to identify the Gifted and Talented pool for accelerated educational programs in many counties and states.

Cognitive skills are the skills the brain uses to think, learn, read, remember, pay attention, and solve problems. Kids develop these skills as part of their growing up. Our book helps kids, in channelizing their skills.

As Einstein said "Education is not the learning of facts, but the training of minds to think". We want to bring joy of learning while channelizing the young minds thinking to reach their optimum potential. Students get familiarized with various strategies, tips and techniques thus improving their thinking abilities. All our tests are created in a multi-color, kid friendly format. For each test is based on theme for the students to have a little fun as they learn. As the students get familiarize with testing format, their vocabulary also builds up.

Our tests give an edge and simulate the testing pattern, in such a way that child feels very comfortable when they take the test in their schools.

Various counties and states apply multiple criteria for selecting kids for gifted or Advanced Academic programs and CogAT is one of the basic criteria. CogAT comprises of the following three main categories

- Verbal Section
- Quantitative Aptitude
- Non-Verbal Section.

Our Practice tests are based on the following:

Verbal Section:

Students are tested in the areas of vocabulary, comprehension of ideas, and the relation between various words. The test comprises of the below three sub sections/tests.

1. Verbal Classification

Three words that are alike in some way and form a group are given to the students, along with four choices to choose. One of the four choices don't belong to the group. Student has to identify the odd man and bubbles the correct option in the bubble sheet.

5 www.math-knots.com

2. Sentence Completion

A sentence is given to the student with four picture options. Student uses the vocabulary and comprehension skills and choses the right picture that makes the best sense in the sentence. Student bubbles the correct option in the bubble sheet.

3. Verbal Analogies

The student is given three words. The first two words go together. The third word goes with one of the answer choices. The student is asked to choose the word that goes with the third word the same way that the second word goes with the first. Student bubbles the correct option in the bubble sheet.

Quantitative Aptitude Section:

The Quantitative Aptitude sub sections tests the student's abstract reasoning, quantitative reasoning, analytical and problem-solving skills. The test comprises of the below three sub sections/tests.

1. Quantitative Relations/Number Analogies

Figures in the first row belong to each other in a certain way. Student is expected to identify the number analogy in the first row. The figures in the second row follow the same analogy as the first row. Student analyzes and thinks through to find the right choice from the given four options. Student bubbles the correct option in the bubble sheet.

2. Number Series

Series of beads are given on various strings /rods. Student identifies the number series and figures out the beads on missing rod/string. Student bubbles the correct option in the bubble sheet.

3. Equation Building /Number Puzzles

A number equation is given in a kid friendly format. Student solves for the number that goes in the place of the question mark. Student bubbles the correct option in the bubble sheet.

Non-Verbal Section (Spatial Reasoning):

The Nonverbal Battery comprises of the most unique problems to students. The questions on these tests are based on geometric shapes and figures. The tests require visualization, thinking and analytical abilities. The test comprises of the below three sub tests.

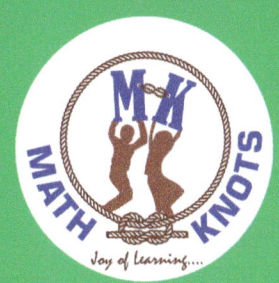

1. **Figure Classification**

The student is given three figures that are a like in some way. Four answer choices are given to choose from and one of the choices belong to the given group in a certain way. Students analyzes the figures to choose the right option and bubbles the correct option in the bubble sheet.

2. **Figure Analogies/ Figure Matrices**

Figures in the first row belong to each other in a certain way. Student is expected to identify the figure analogy between figures in the first row. The figures in the second row follow the same analogy as the first row. Student analyzes and thinks through to find the right choice from the given four options and bubbles the correct option in the bubble sheet.

3. **Figure Analysis/Paper Folding**

A Square, Rectangle or any shape figure is folded once or more as shown in the figure. Holes are punched to the folded figure and opened completely. Students are expected to think through on how the figure will look like after opening it up and bubbles the correct option in the bubble sheet.

Book Includes, detailed solutions and tips, that will help kids do well in the **CogAT test.**

Do Visit our website www.math-knots.com for more products and also for our online subscription.

Math-Knots ------- Joy of Learning

INDEX

www.math-knots.com

INDEX

www.math-knots.com

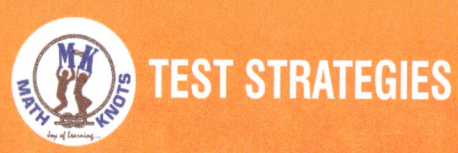
Start from the middle of right choice and fully fill the bubble completely.

Wrong

A 　　　B ◯　　　C ◯　　　D ◯

Wrong

A ◯　　　B ◯　　　C 　　　D ◯

Wrong

A ◯　　　B ◯　　　C 　　　D ◯

Partial Filled Bubble is not correct.

Correct

A ◯　　　B ◯　　　C ⬤　　　D ◯

PREPARATION FOR THE TEST

1. To simulate the testing format, a parent or an adult shall read the questions to the student to answer the practice test sets.

2. Student need to have a pencil and an eraser.

3. Student need to make sure they are bubbling the circles in the right way.

Before the testing date.

1. Make sure the child has a good nights sleep and a good breakfast.

www.math-knots.com

www.math-knots.com

TEST - 1

VERBAL SECTION

VERBAL CLASSIFICATION

Lets Start the Test...

www.math-knots.com

Sample

Three words are related in a certain way. Four options are given. Identify the choice that does not belong to the group ?

One	Two	Three	
Six	Eight	Five	Gate
A ◯	B ◯	C ◯	D ◯

Solution : D

Three words in the question belong to one group. One of the four choices doesn't belong to the same group. Identify and bubble the correct choice. In the given question all three in first row are words as well as numbers in words. Lets take a look at the answers. All choices are words but three are numbers in words and one other word gate, which is incorrect.

www.math-knots.com

All the questions in verbal classification test 1 are to be answered following the below question (instruction).

Three words are related in a certain way. Four options are given. Identify the choice that <u>does not belong</u> to the group ?

1. Australia   Africa   Asia

North America   London   Europe   Antarctica

A◯   B◯   C◯   D◯

2. Cottage   Bungalow   Farm House

Palace   Manor   Villa   Portico

A◯   B◯   C◯   D◯

3. Ear   Hand   Leg

Heart   Lower Limb   Nail   Cheek

A◯   B◯   C◯   D◯

4. Arithmetic   Fractions   Decimals

Geometry   Algebra   Mathematics   Calculus

A◯   B◯   C◯   D◯

5. Dollar   Pound   Dinar

Peso   Rupee   Money   Euro

A◯   B◯   C◯   D◯

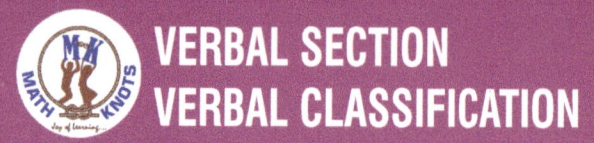
6.   **Adorned**   **Ornate**   **Elaborate**

Showy   Fancy   Beautify   Dull

A◯   B◯   C◯   D◯

7.   **Honey**   **Amber**   **Gold**

Mustard   Teal   Banana   Lemon

A◯   B◯   C◯   D◯

8.   **Boar**   **Bull**   **Dog**

Duck   Buck   Rooster   Tiger

A◯   B◯   C◯   D◯

9.   **Prism**   **Cube**   **Cylinder**

Cone   Sphere   Pyramid   Pentagon

A◯   B◯   C◯   D◯

10.   **Look**   **Scan**   **Glimpse**

View   See   Wink   Gaze

A◯   B◯   C◯   D◯

 www.math-knots.com

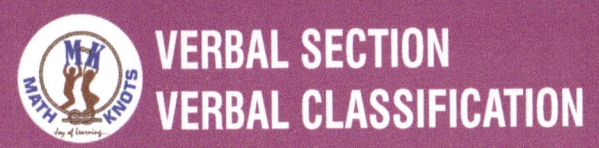
11. **Friendship** **Affection** **Harmony**

Closeness   Intimacy   Fondness   Animosity

A ◯   B ◯   C ◯   D ◯

12. **Ring** **Watch** **Bangle**

Armlet   Tiara   Wristband   Charm

A ◯   B ◯   C ◯   D ◯

13. **Actress** **Hero** **Actor**

Performer   Artist   Heroine   Producer

A ◯   B ◯   C ◯   D ◯

14. **Earth** **Venus** **Moon**

Milky way   Sun   Neptune   Jupitar

A ◯   B ◯   C ◯   D ◯

15. **Apple** **Mango** **Cherry**

Orange   Potato   Plum   Grapes

A ◯   B ◯   C ◯   D ◯

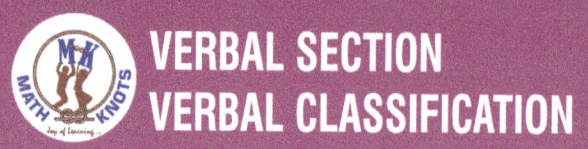
16.　**Cricket**　　**Flea**　　**Beetle**

Scorpion　　Bug　　Hopper　　Insect

A ◯　　B ◯　　C ◯　　D ◯

17.　**Perfect**　　**Present**　　**Future**

Past Future　　Progressive　　Interrogative　　Future Simple

A ◯　　B ◯　　C ◯　　D ◯

18.　**Chlorine**　　**Neon**　　**Sulphur**

Nitrogen　　Iodine　　Radon　　Lead

A ◯　　B ◯　　C ◯　　D ◯

Lets Start the Test...

www.math-knots.com

Sample

Look at the question with the Tennis Ball. Maya is trying to solve the below brain teaser. "Rik has more stamps then Ryan. Ryan has more stamps than Luke. Who has more stamps ?" Bubble the correct option.

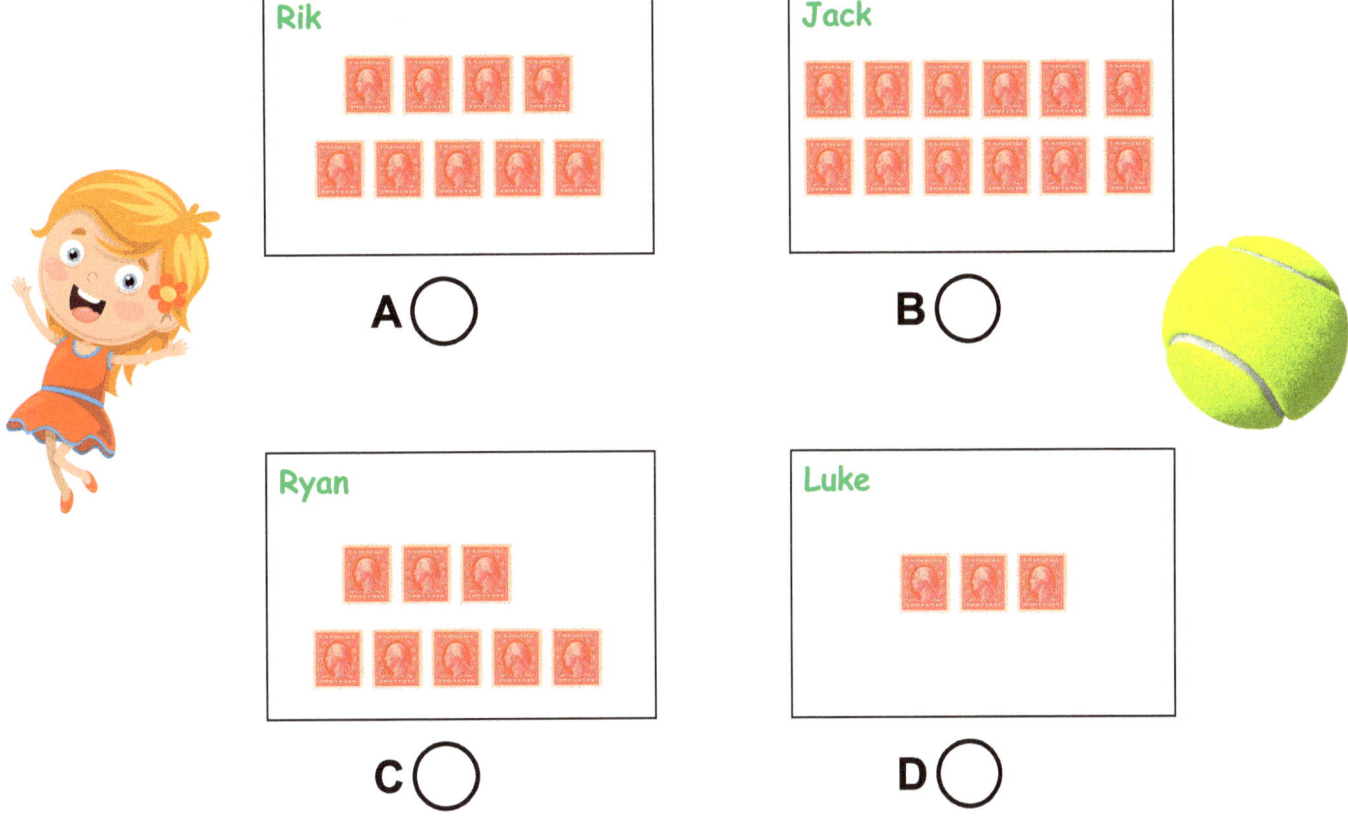

Solution : A

The Correct choice is A. The question doesn't compare with what Jack has.

Rik has the most stamps.

Rik > Ryan > Luke

www.math-knots.com

www.math-knots.com

Q-1

Look at the question with the Square. Help Anne to find out which of the below options do not belong to the same group. Identify the correct picture and help her to bubble the right choice.

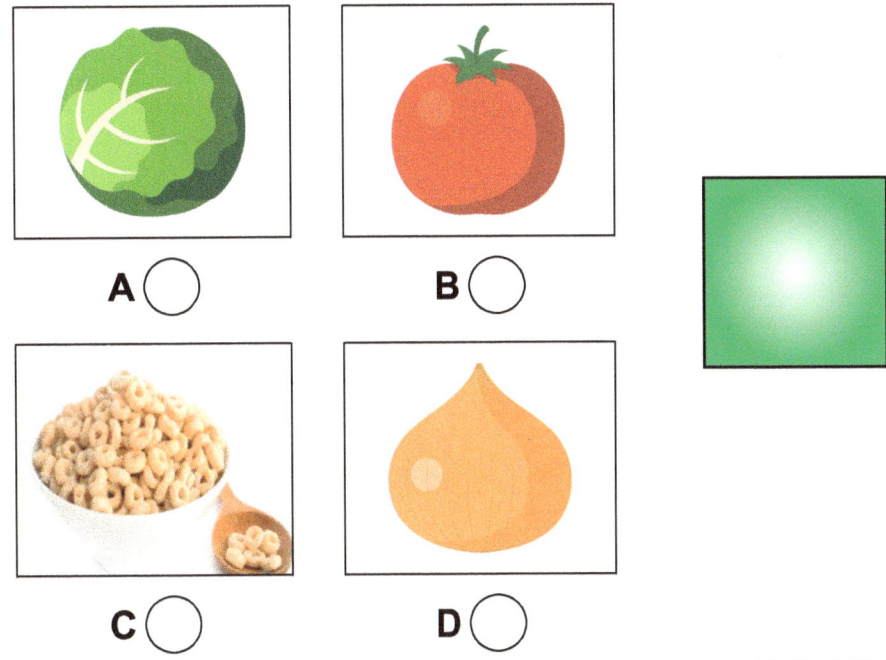

A ◯   B ◯

C ◯   D ◯

Q-2

Look at the question with the Diamond. Jack is trying to solve the below brain teaser. Can you please help him to solve? "Sam weighs less than Tom and Tom weighs less than Tim. Who weighs most?" Identify the correct solution and help him to bubble the right choice.

Tom   Harry

A ◯   B ◯

Sam   Tim

C ◯   D ◯

www.math-knots.com

Q-3

Look at the question with the Pentagon. Help Lola to find out which of the below can fly. Identify the correct picture and help her to bubble the right choice.

A ◯　　　　**B** ◯

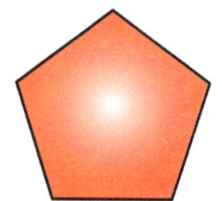

C ◯　　　　**D** ◯

Q-4

Look at the question with the Triangle. Kyla's daughter Beth comes home with fever from school. Which of the below do you think Kyla needs to find out the temperature. Identify the correct picture and help her to bubble the right choice.

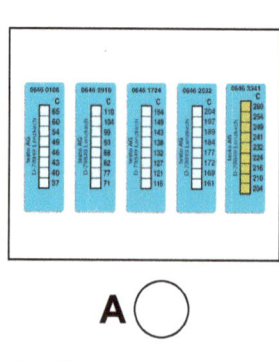

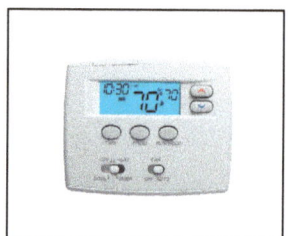

A ◯　　　　**B** ◯

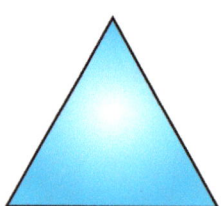

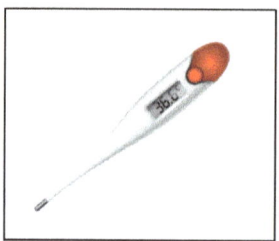

C ◯　　　　**D** ◯

www.math-knots.com

Q-5

Look at the question with the Septagon. Ricky's friend Sam's favorite Sport uses a bat which has a mesh. Help Ricky to find his friends favorite sport.Identify the correct picture and help him to bubble the right choice.

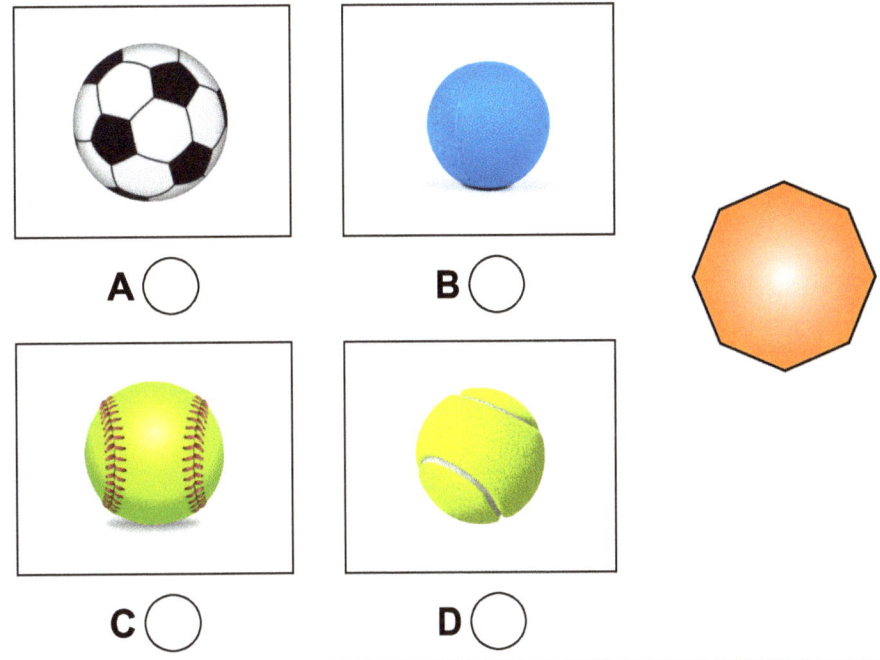

A ◯   B ◯

C ◯   D ◯

Q-6

Look at the question with the Hexagon Mia is standing facing west and then she makes a right turn and then again, a right turn. Which direction is Mia facing now? Identify the correct picture and help her to bubble the right choice.

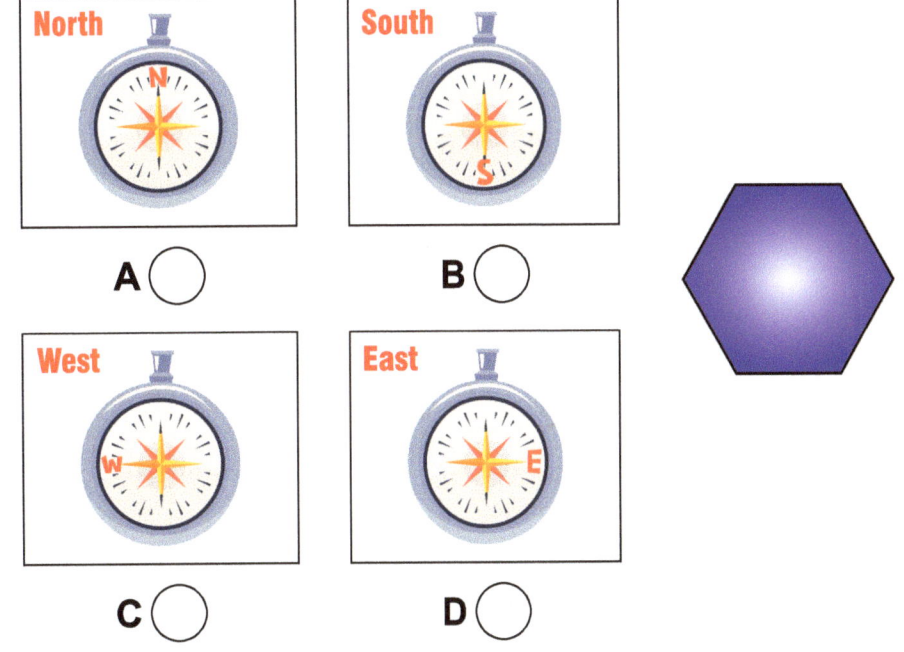

North   South

A ◯   B ◯

West   East

C ◯   D ◯

     www.math-knots.com

Q-7

Look at the question with the Octagon. Mary is working on her science project. Topic give to the class is Fruits and Vegetables. She wanted to know which vegetables grow under the ground. Which of the below vegetable grows under the ground? Identify the correct picture and help her to bubble the right choice.

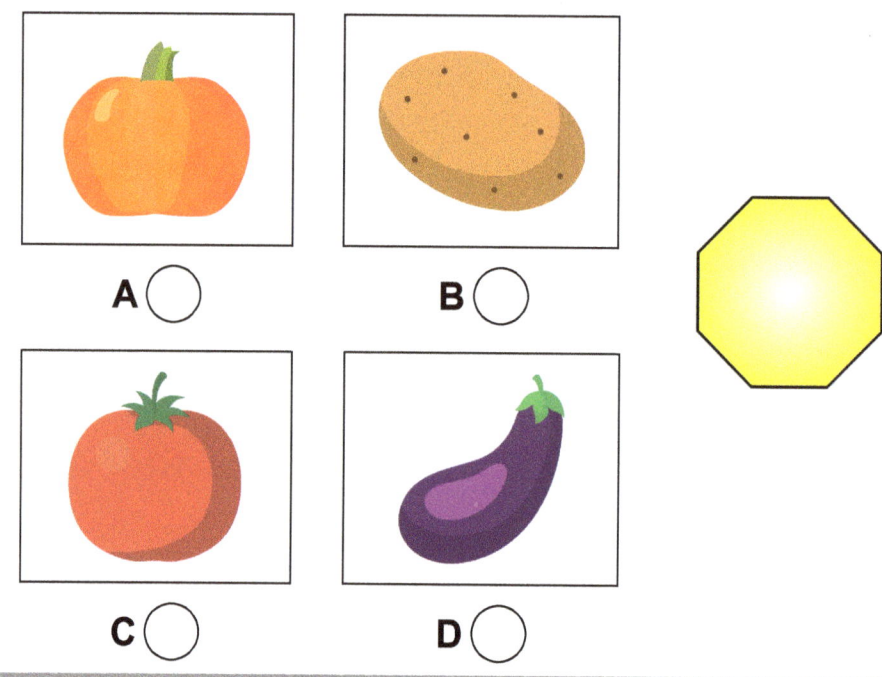

A ○   B ○

C ○   D ○

Q-8

Look at the question with the Trapezoid. Raksha bakes a lot of cookies for her school bake sale. She wants to sell them by pounds. Which of the below does she need to take with her for the bake sale. Identify the correct picture and help her to bubble the right choice.

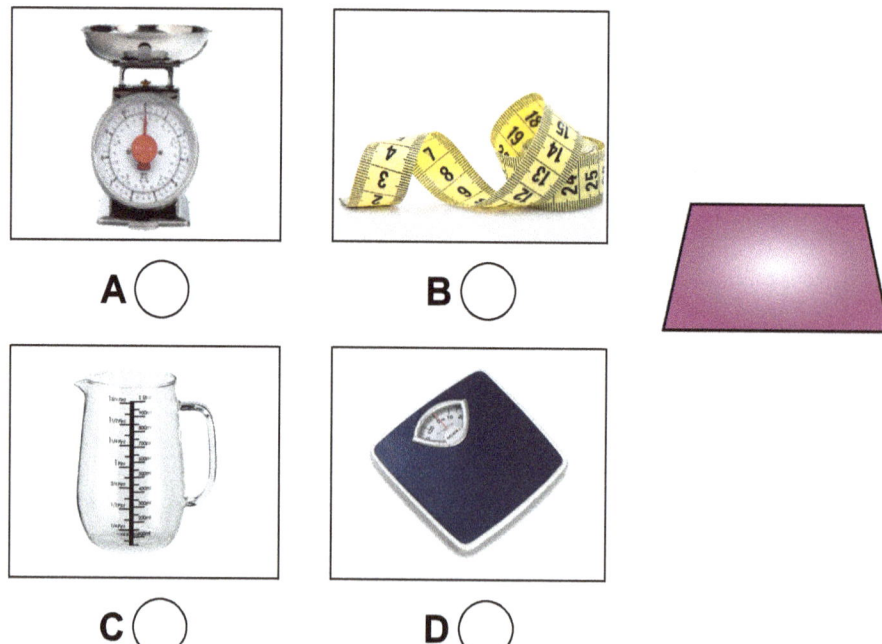

A ○   B ○

C ○   D ○

www.math-knots.com

Q-9

Look at the question with the Parallelogram. Lisa goes to the store to buy her school supplies. She is looking for something with which she can't write or draw with it. Which of the below options is she looking to buy? Identify the correct picture and help her to bubble the right choice.

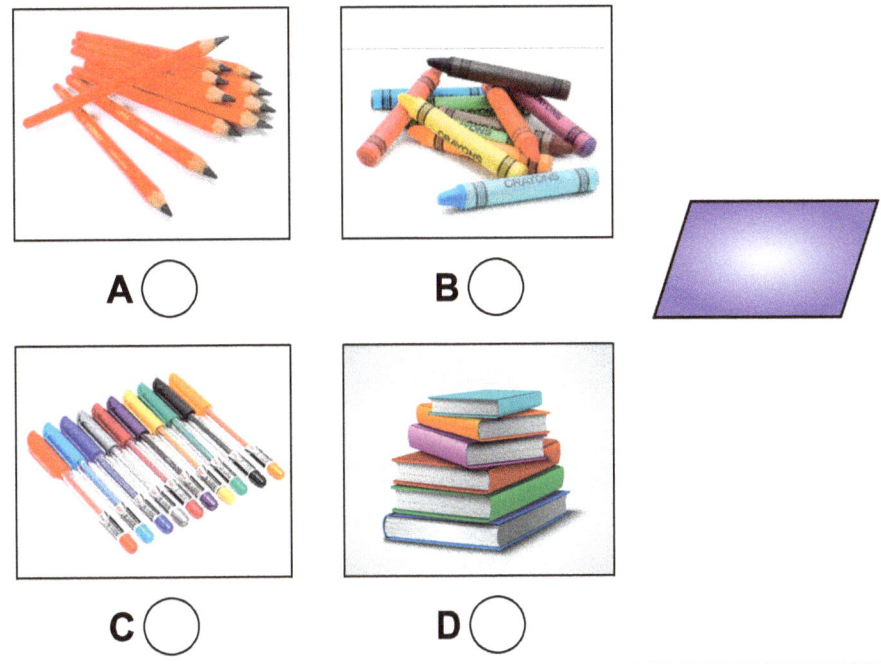

A ◯   B ◯

C ◯   D ◯

Q-10

Look at the question with the Oval. Ben went to the Zoo with his class today. He is looking to connect the color of Zebra to the given four choices as below. Identify the correct picture that resembles the same. Help him to bubble the right choice.

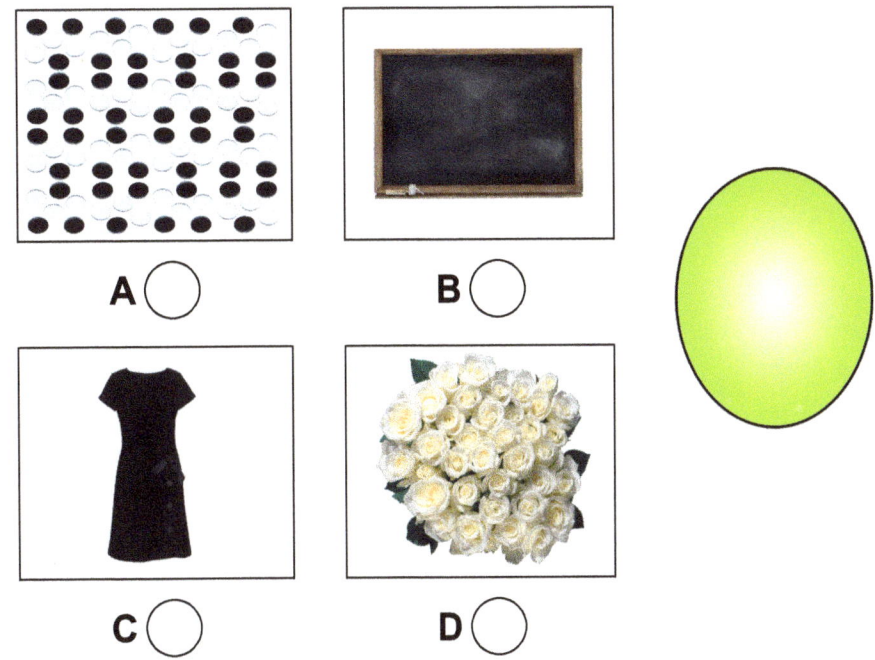

A ◯   B ◯

C ◯   D ◯

www.math-knots.com

Q-11 Look at the question with the Heart. Ryan is learning about various sounds in his science class. Which of the following rings? Help him to identify the correct picture and to bubble the right choice.

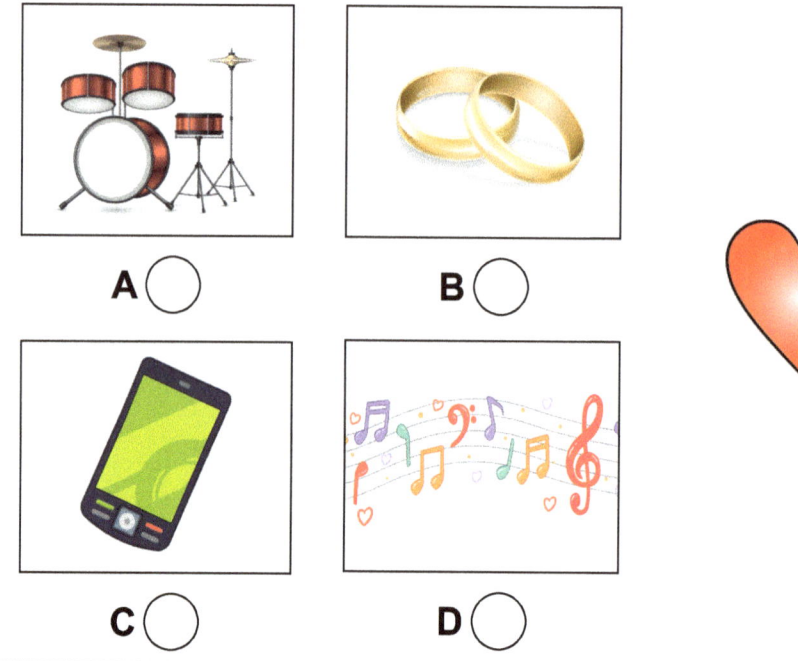

A ◯   B ◯

C ◯   D ◯

Q-12 Look at the question with the Snow Flake. David is trying to solve the below brain teaser. "Octagon has more sides than Pentagon. Pentagon has more sides than Square. Which figure has most sides?" Identify the correct solution and help him to bubble the right choice.

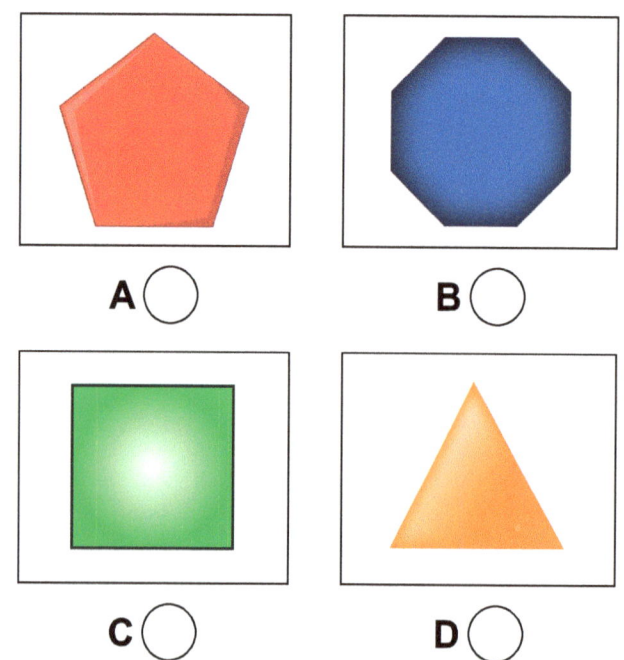

A ◯   B ◯

C ◯   D ◯

www.math-knots.com

Q-13

Look at the question with the Plus Sign. Oded is learning about electricity in his science class. Which of the following choices does not need electricity to operate? Help him to identify the correct picture and to bubble the right choice.

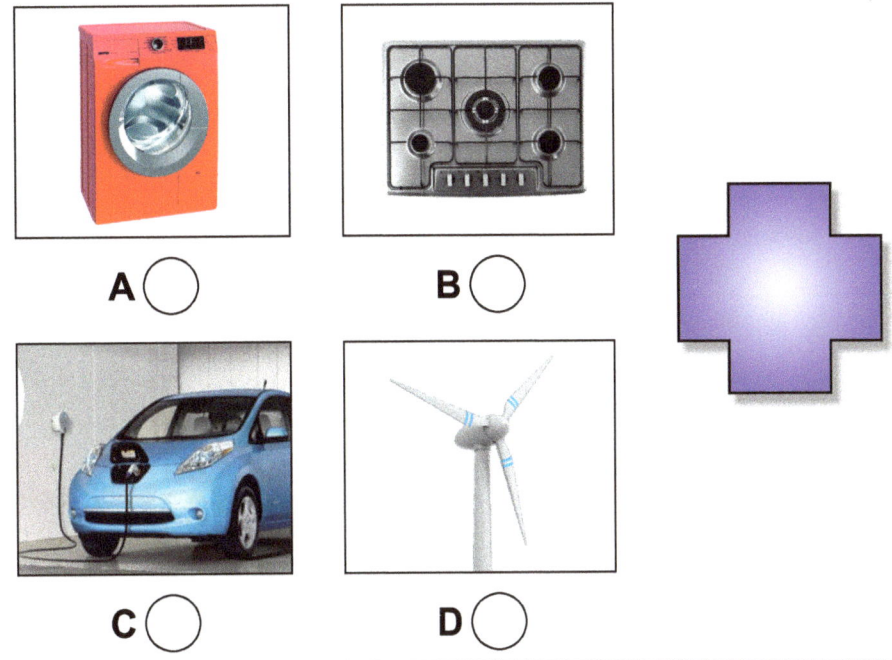

A ◯   B ◯

C ◯   D ◯

Q-14

Look at the question with the Smiley. Urmi wakes up from sleep and feels her mouth is smelling badly. So, what do you think she needs now? Help her to identify the correct picture and to bubble the right choice.

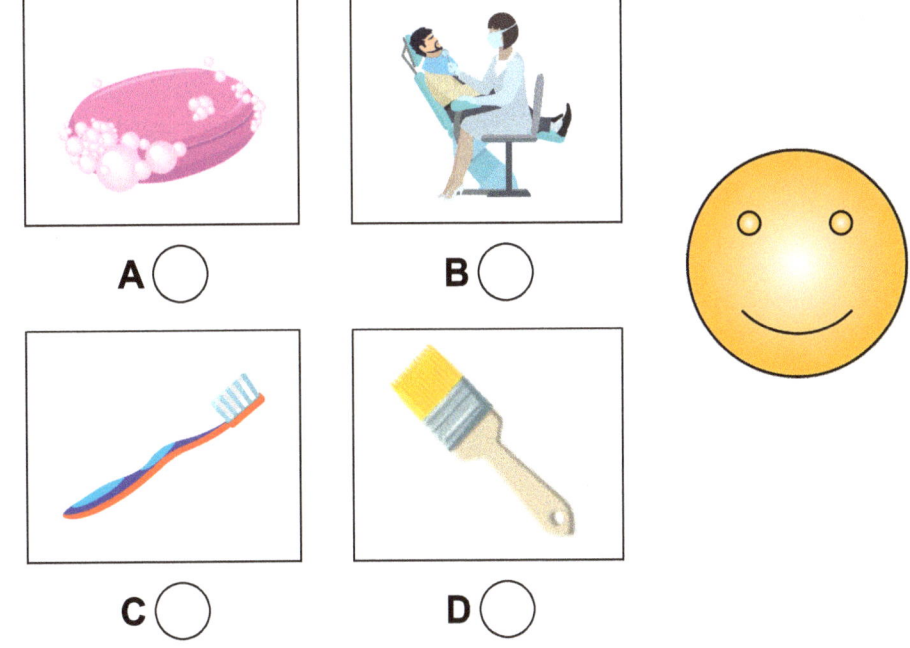

A ◯   B ◯

C ◯   D ◯

www.math-knots.com

Q-15

Look at the question with the Moon. Ken wants to build a writing table for his 5-year-old daughter. He goes to the store to buy the necessary tools. what do you think he shall buy from the below options? Help him to identify the correct picture and to bubble the right choice.

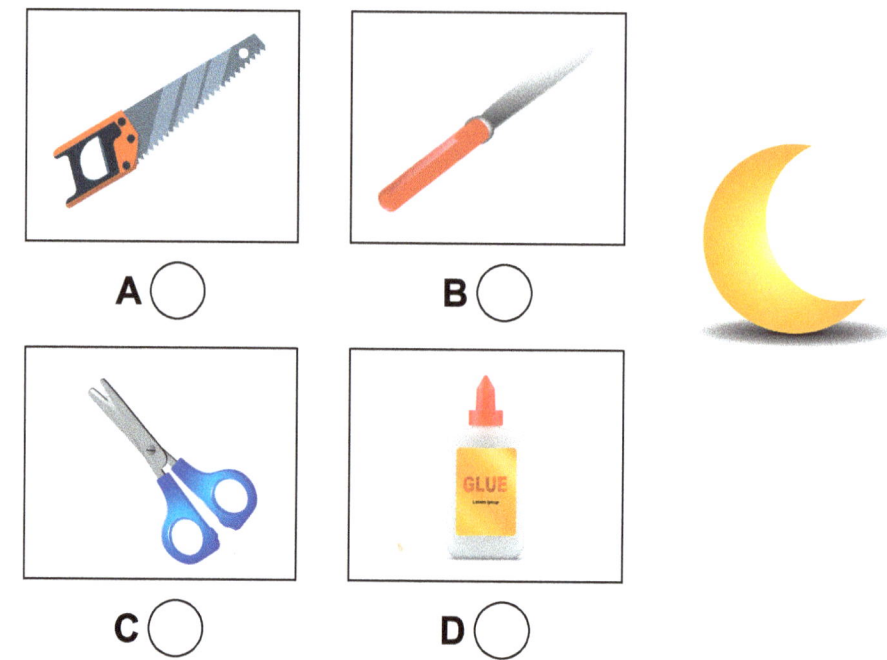

A ◯   B ◯

C ◯   D ◯

Q-16

Look at the question with the Stars. Jia loves to play her music by modulating air flow. Help her to choose the right instrument from the below. Help her to identify the correct picture and to bubble the right choice.

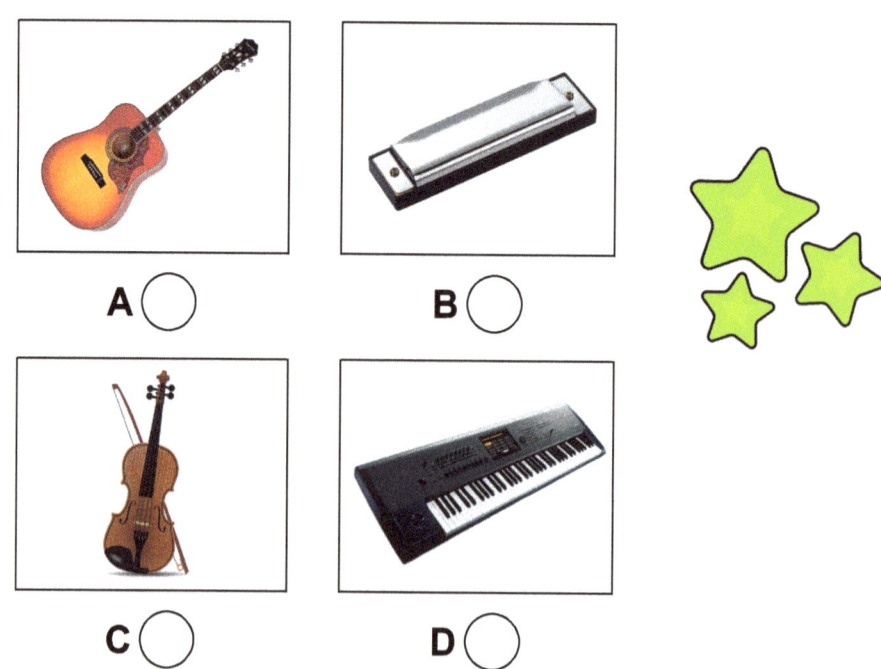

A ◯   B ◯

C ◯   D ◯

www.math-knots.com

Q-17

Look at the question with the Clouds. Jane loves Berries and she uses lots of berries in her cereal every day morning. Which of the below fruits do you think Jane doesn't eat in her cereal? Help her to identify the correct picture and to bubble the right choice.

A ◯   B ◯

C ◯   D ◯

Q-18

Look at the question with the Cylinder. Lara is learning about various holidays. Help her to find which of the below does not represent St. Patricks day. Identify the correct picture and help her to bubble the right choice.

A ◯   B ◯

C ◯   D ◯

TEST - 1

VERBAL SECTION

VERBAL ANALOGIES

Lets Start the Test...

www.math-knots.com

Sample

The first two words are related in a certain way as the next two words. Identify the missing word.

Clouds : White :: Sky : ?

Bold	Blue	Silver	Yellow
A ◯	B ◯	C ◯	D ◯

Solution : B

First analogy is color of the clouds which is white. Color of sky is blue.

Right choice is B.

Student needs to think through how the first two are related and then relate it to next analogy in the same way. Bubble the correct option.

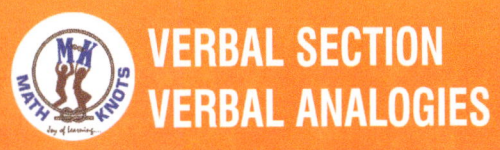
All the questions in verbal analogies test 1 are to be answered following the below question (instruction).

The first two words are related in a certain way as the next two words. <u>Identify the missing word.</u>

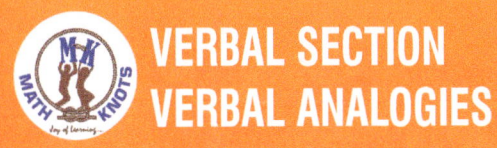

1.   Sunglasses : Summer :: Gloves :   ?

Winter   Fall   Autumn   Spring

A◯   B◯   C◯   D◯

2.   Donkey : Stable :: Goat :   ?

Kennel   Burrow   Pen   Coop

A◯   B◯   C◯   D◯

3.   10 : Number :: A :   ?

Consonenent   Writing   Language   Alphabet

A◯   B◯   C◯   D◯

4.   Pentagon : 5 :: Quadrilateral :   ?

7   4   5   3

A◯   B◯   C◯   D◯

5.   Gold : Yellow :: Tree :   ?

Green   Orange   Red   White

A◯   B◯   C◯   D◯

       www.math-knots.com

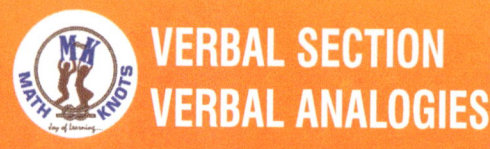
6.   Thermometer : Temperature :: Rain Gauge :   ?

Humidity   Wind   Precipitation   Sky

A◯   B◯   C◯   D◯

7.   Wings : Birds :: Fins :   ?

Birds   Sparrow   Ladybug   Fish

A◯   B◯   C◯   D◯

8.   Thankgiving : November :: Memorial Day :   ?

May   December   April   February

A◯   B◯   C◯   D◯

9.   Up : Down :: Right :   ?

Corner   Below   Above   Left

A◯   B◯   C◯   D◯

10.   Cow : Calf :: Cat :   ?

Spider ling   Kitten   Foal   Ducklet

A◯   B◯   C◯   D◯

www.math-knots.com

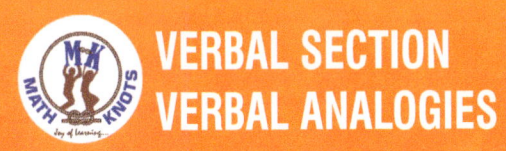
11.   **Insects : 6 legs :: Octopus : ?**

8 legs   5 legs   10 legs   12 legs

A◯   B◯   C◯   D◯

12.   **Medicines : Pharmacy :: Food : ?**

Book Store   School   Restaurant   Office

A◯   B◯   C◯   D◯

13.   **Ship : Water :: Train : ?**

Road   Sky   Sub Way   Track

A◯   B◯   C◯   D◯

14.   **Telescope : Magnification :: Accelerometer : ?**

Acceleration   Voltage   Survey   Magnetic Field

A◯   B◯   C◯   D◯

15.   **Christmas : Christmas Tree :: July Fourth : ?**

Turkey   Green   Labor Day   Fire Crackers

A◯   B◯   C◯   D◯

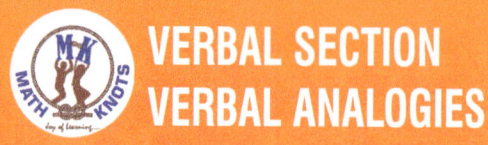
16.   Green : Spinach :: Orange :   ?

Tomato   Carrot   Peppers   Banana

A ◯   B ◯   C ◯   D ◯

17.   Zebra : Stripes ::   Lady Bug :   ?

Dots   Solid color   Zig Zag   Lines

A ◯   B ◯   C ◯   D ◯

18.   Hurricanes : Ocean :: Tornado :   ?

Storm   Waves   Land   Sky

A ◯   B ◯   C ◯   D ◯

TEST - 1

QUANTITATIVE APTITUDE

NUMBER ANALOGIES

Lets Start the Test...

www.math-knots.com

Sample

Look at the question with the Parrot. Two boxes in the first row are related in a certain way which is similar to two boxes in the second row. Ken is trying to fill the bubble under the correct option. Help him to select from options A, B, C, and D.

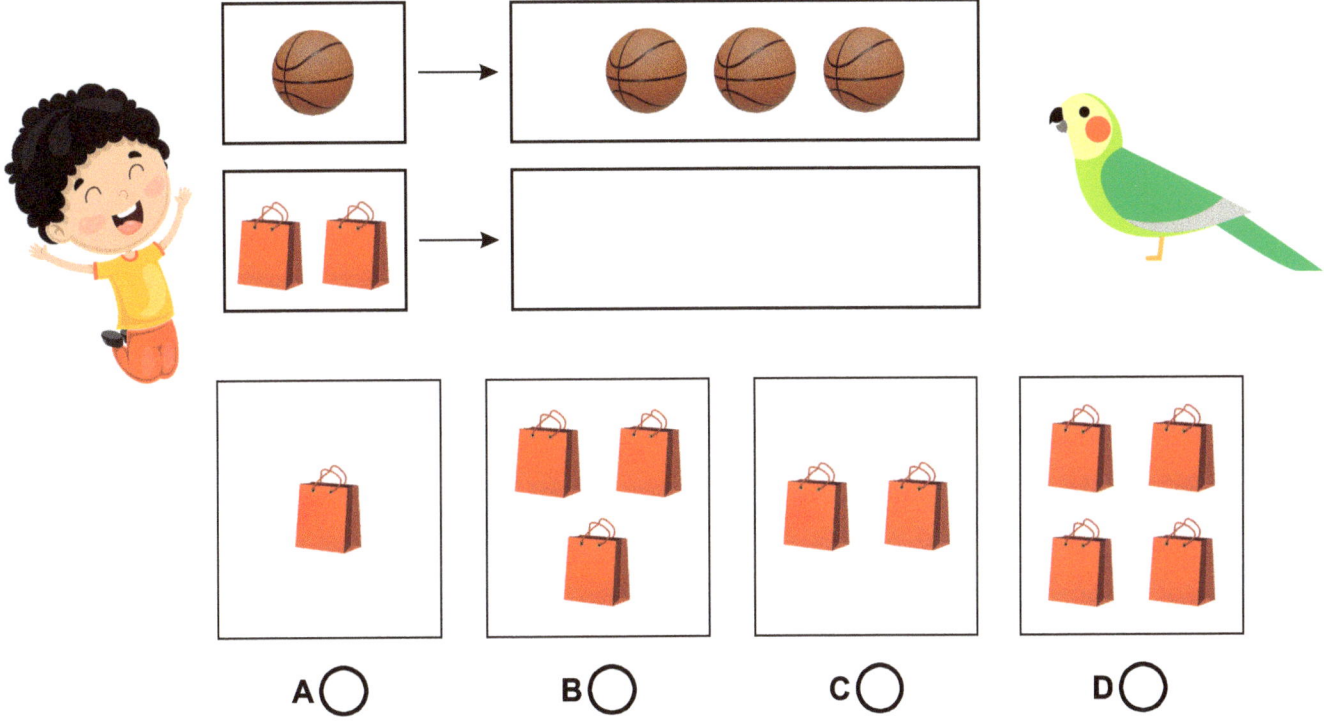

Solution : D

In first row, one ball to three balls [(1+2) adding two more]

In second row, two bags by adding two more will become four bags.

The analogies can be formed by adding or subtracting a certain number meaning increasing or decreasing by a certain quantity. Students needs to understand the right analogy and bubble the correct option.

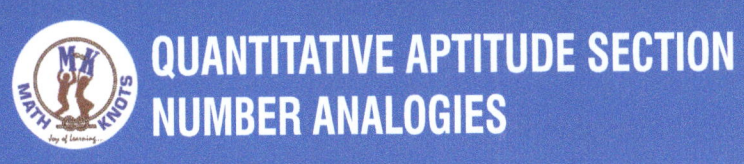

Q-1

Look at the question with the Game Console. Two boxes in the first row are related in a certain way which is similar to two boxes in the second row. Sam is trying to fill the bubble under the correct option. Help him to select from options A, B, C, and D.

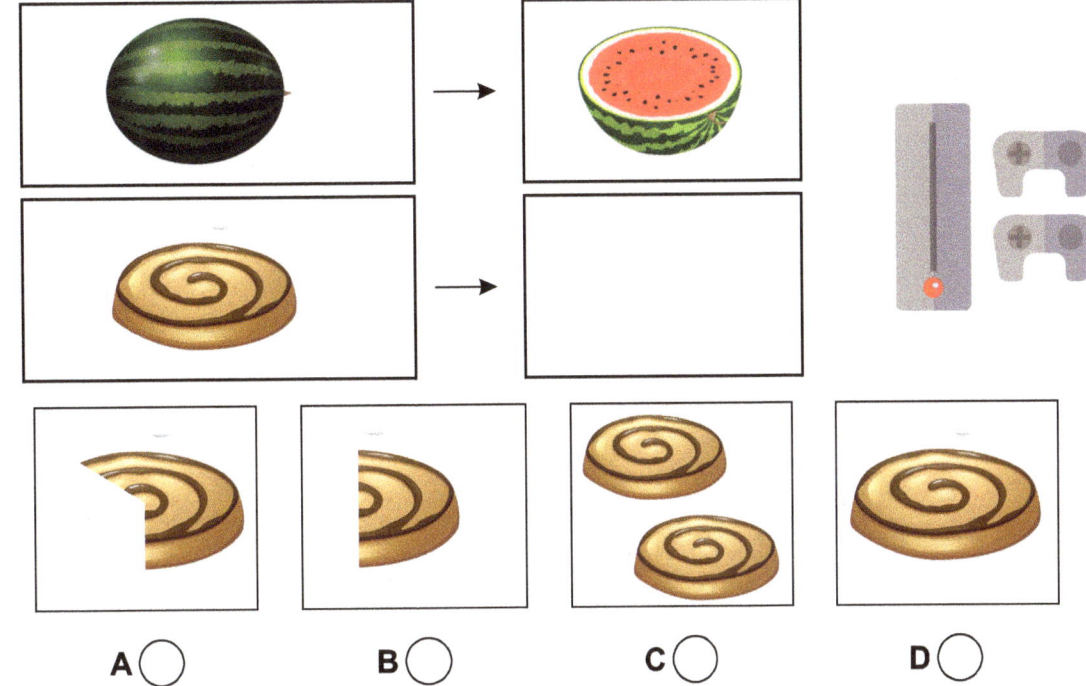

A◯ B◯ C◯ D◯

Q-2

Look at the question with the Smart Watch. Two boxes in the first row are related in a certain way which is similar to two boxes in the second row. Mary is trying to fill the bubble under the correct option. Help her to select from options A, B, C, and D.

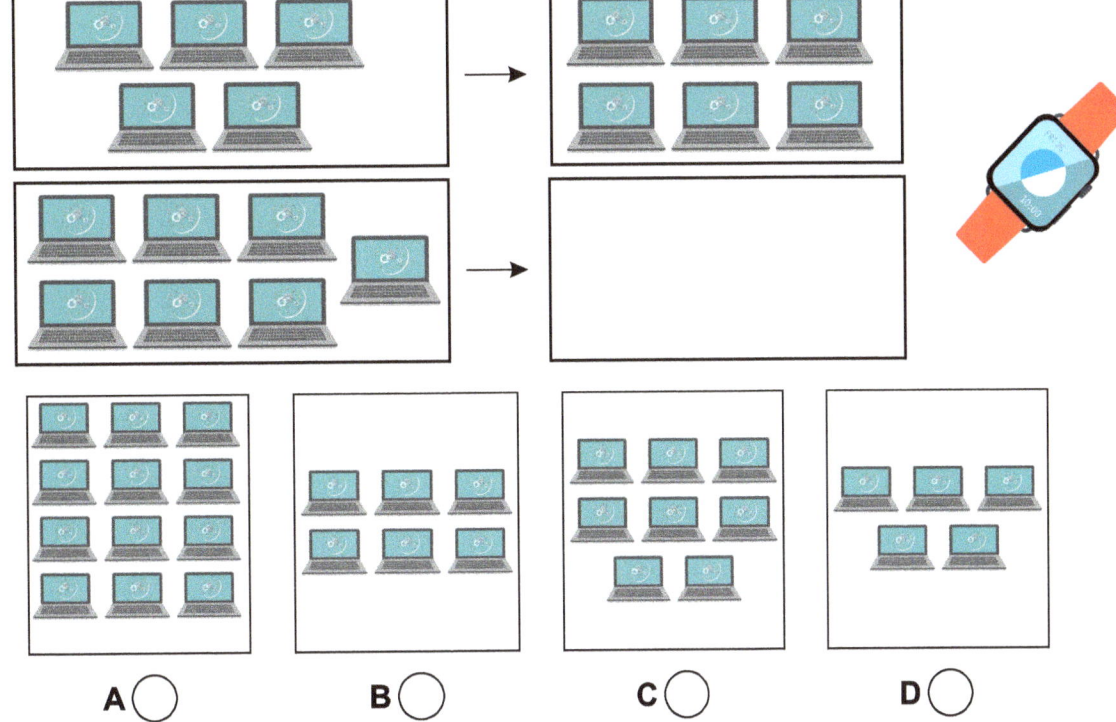

A◯ B◯ C◯ D◯

www.math-knots.com

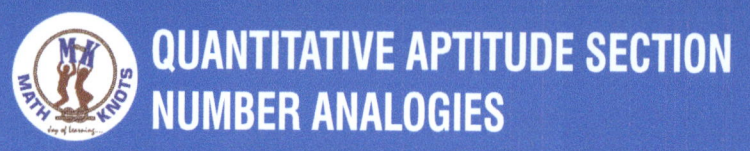
Q-3

Look at the question with the Head Set. Two boxes in the first row are related in a certain way which is similar to two boxes in the second row. Feona is trying to fill the bubble under the correct option. Help her to select from options A, B, C, and D.

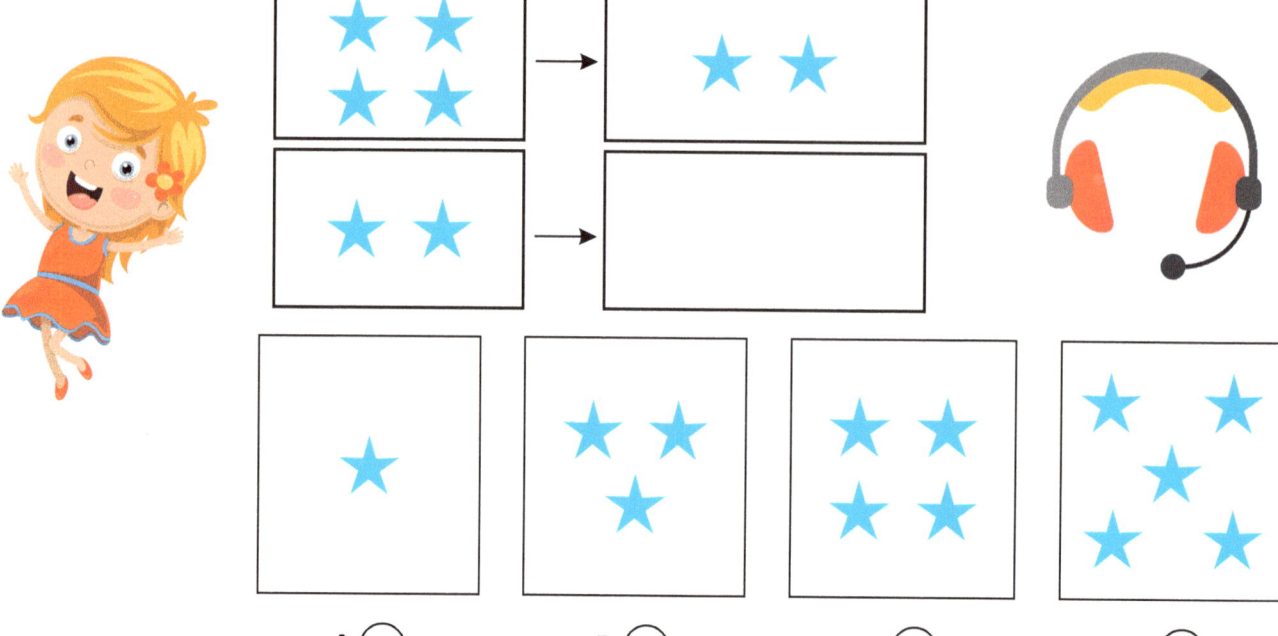

A ◯   B ◯   C ◯   D ◯

Q-4

Look at the question with the UPS. Two boxes in the first row are related in a certain way which is similar to two boxes in the second row. Robert is trying to fill the bubble under the correct option. Help him to select from options A, B, C, and D.

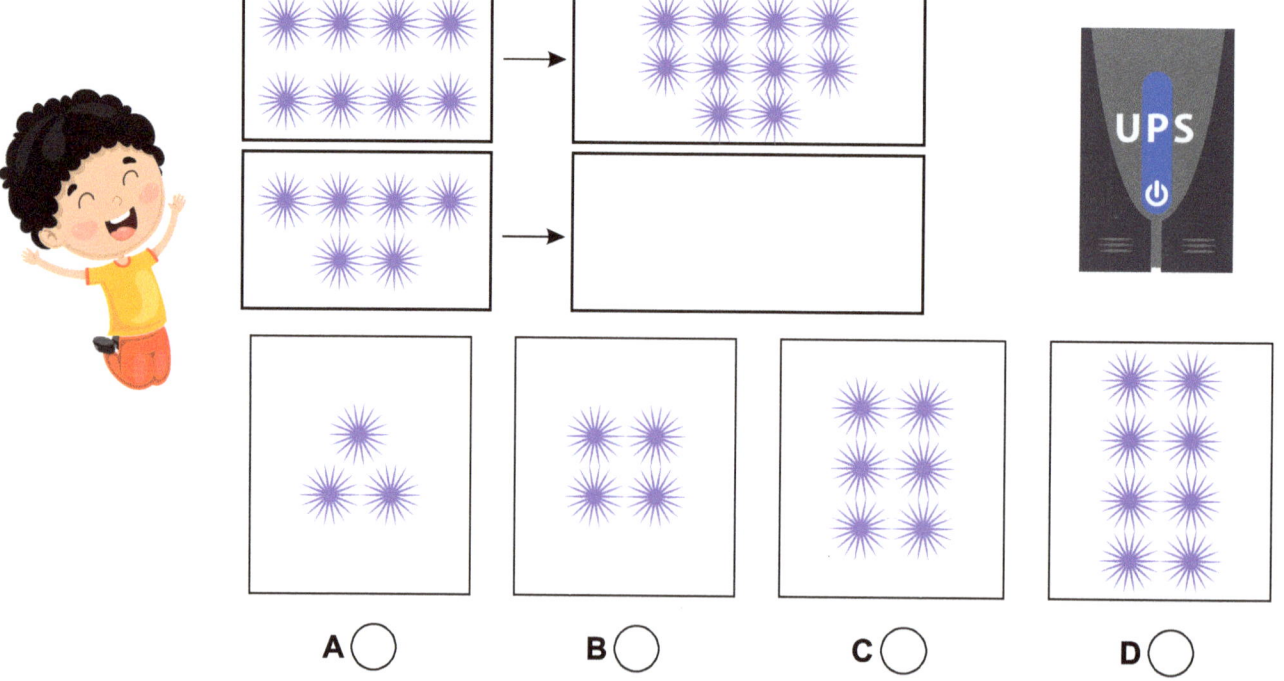

A ◯   B ◯   C ◯   D ◯

www.math-knots.com

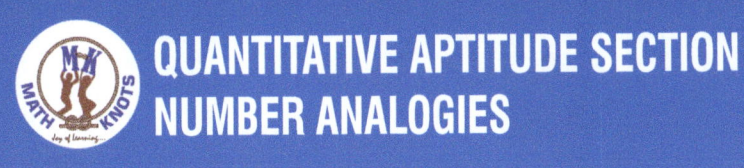

Q-5

Look at the question with the Kindle. Two boxes in the first row are related in a certain way which is similar to two boxes in the second row. David is trying to fill the bubble under the correct option. Help him to select from options A, B, C, and D.

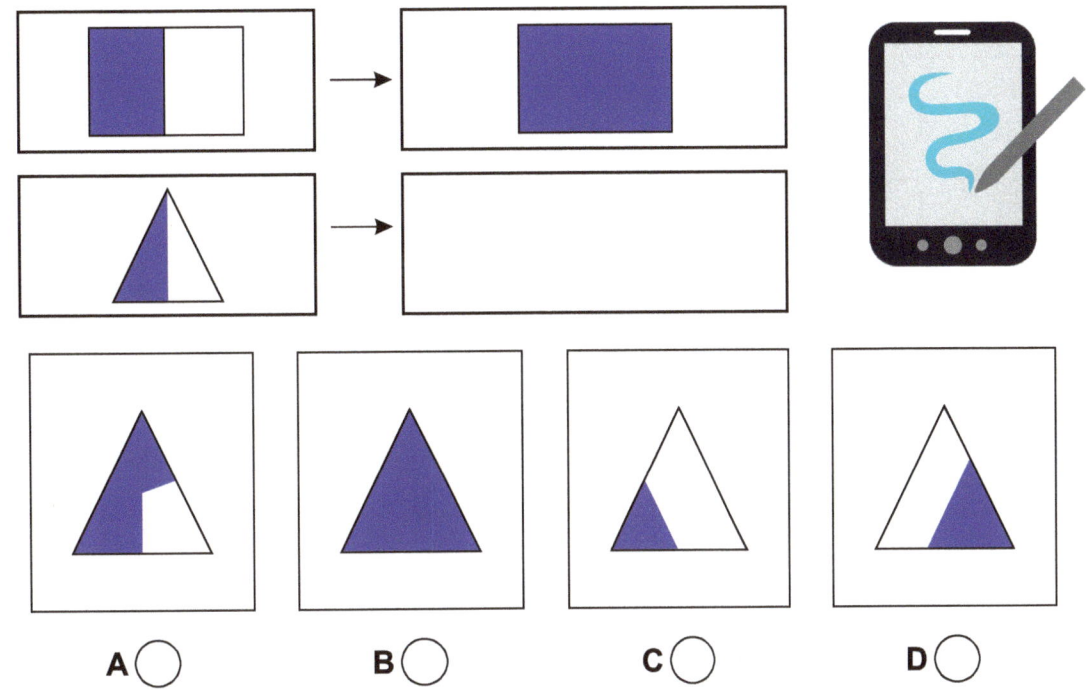

A◯ B◯ C◯ D◯

Q-6

Look at the question with the Mouse. Two boxes in the first row are related in a certain way which is similar to two boxes in the second row. Sofia is trying to fill the bubble under the correct option. Help her to select from options A, B, C, and D.

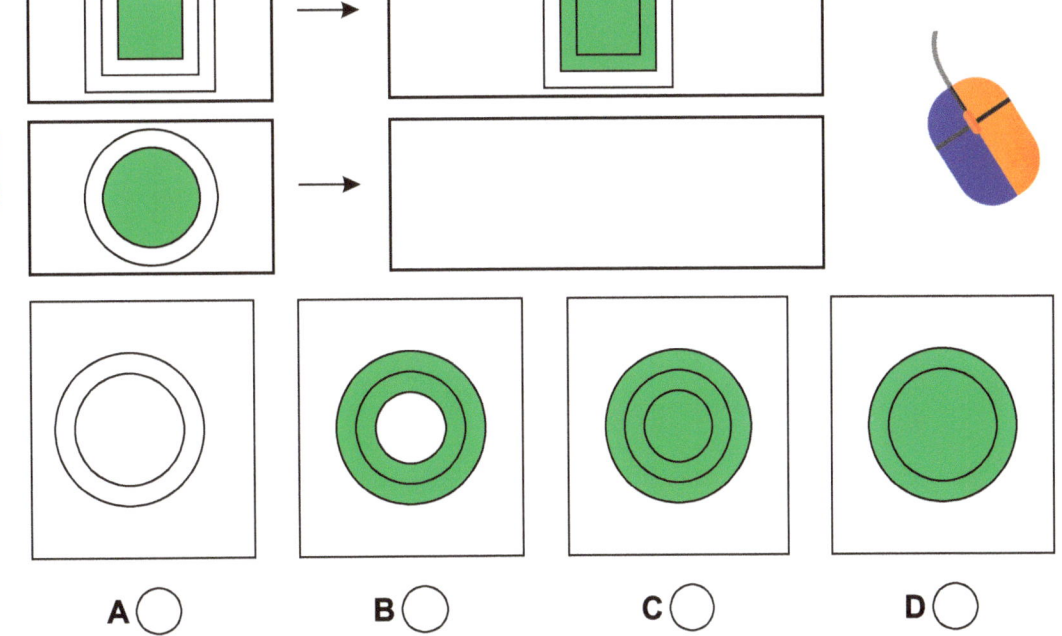

A◯ B◯ C◯ D◯

www.math-knots.com

Q-7

Look at the question with the Scanner. Two boxes in the first row are related in a certain way which is similar to two boxes in the second row. Ava is trying to fill the bubble under the correct option. Help her to select from options A, B, C, and D.

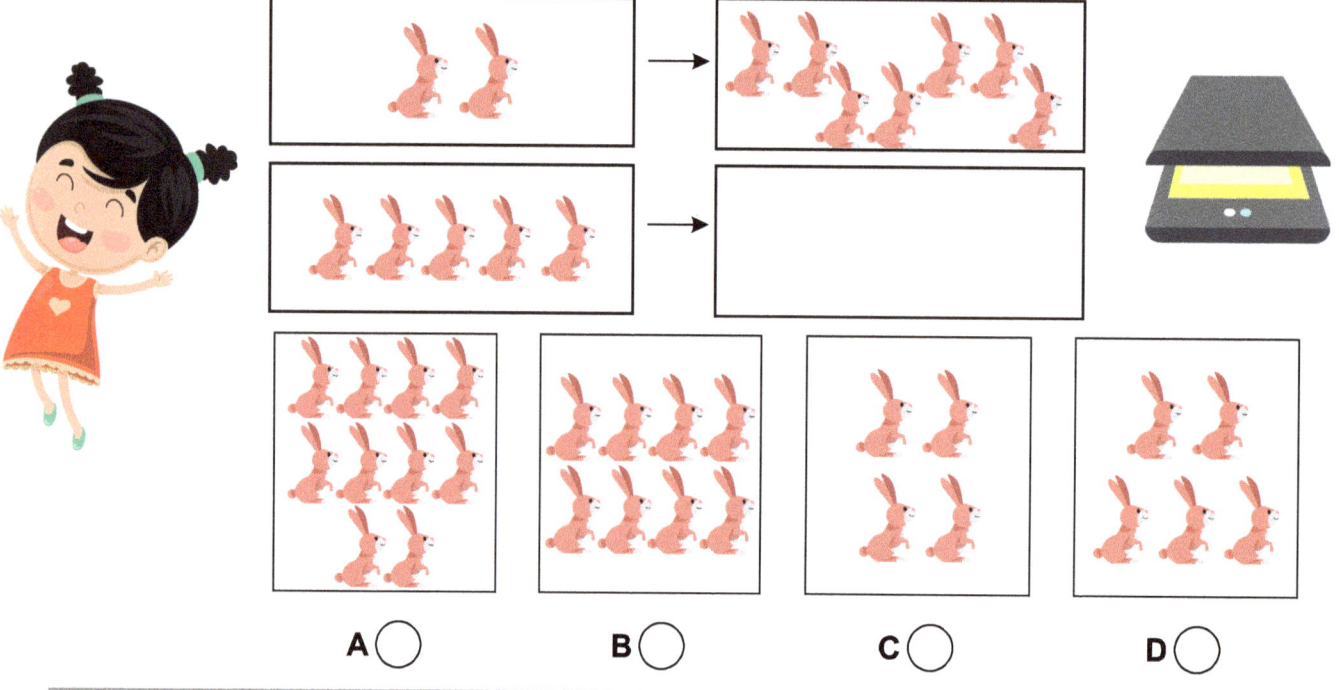

A ◯   B ◯   C ◯   D ◯

Q-8

Look at the question with the Printer. Two boxes in the first row are related in a certain way which is similar to two boxes in the second row. Johnson is trying to fill the bubble under the correct option. Help him to select from options A, B, C, and D.

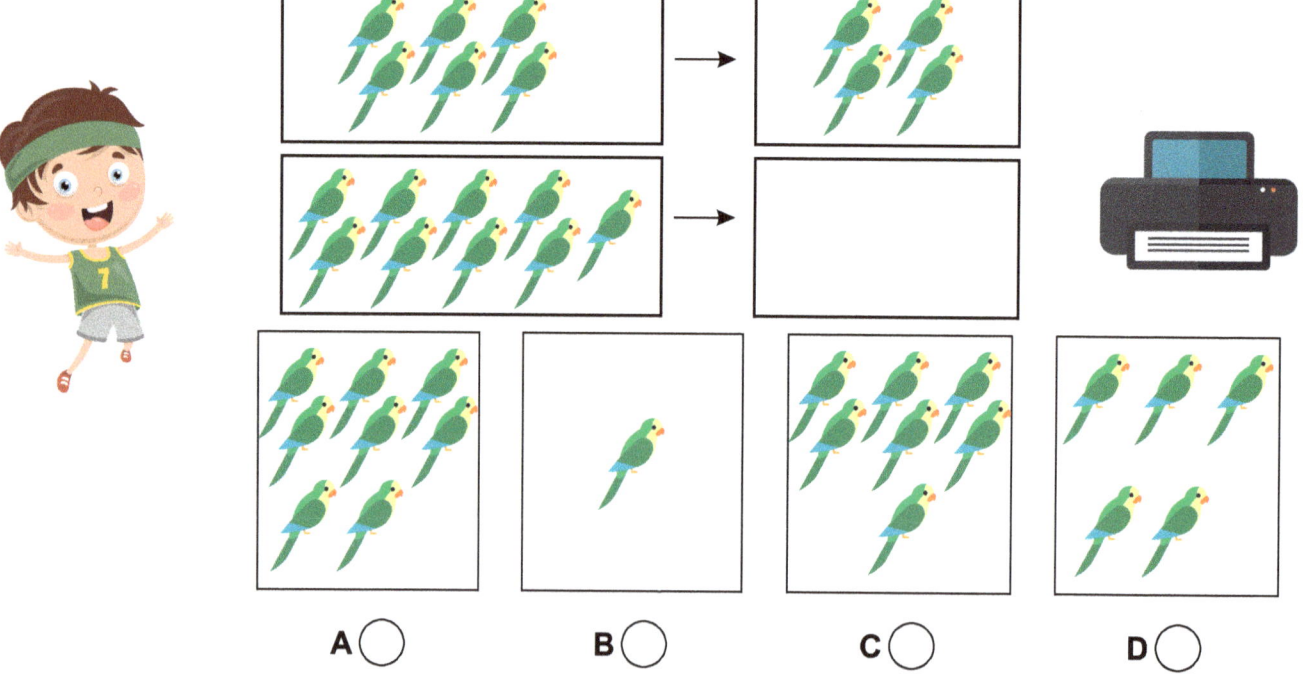

A ◯   B ◯   C ◯   D ◯

www.math-knots.com

Q-9

Look at the question with the CD Player. Two boxes in the first row are related in a certain way which is similar to two boxes in the second row. Alice is trying to fill the bubble under the correct option. Help her to select from options A, B, C, and D.

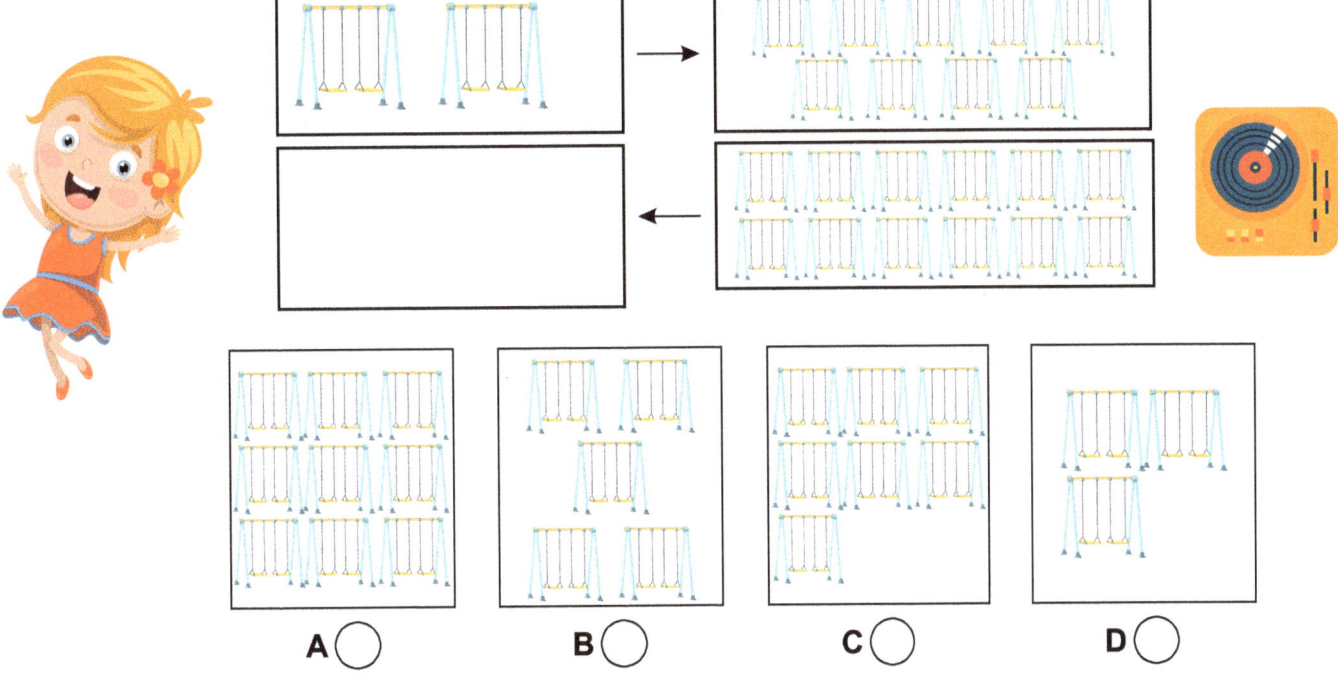

A ◯   B ◯   C ◯   D ◯

Q-10

Look at the question with the Blue Tooth. Two boxes in the first row are related in a certain way which is similar to two boxes in the second row. Lucas is trying to fill the bubble under the correct option. Help him to select from options A, B, C, and D.

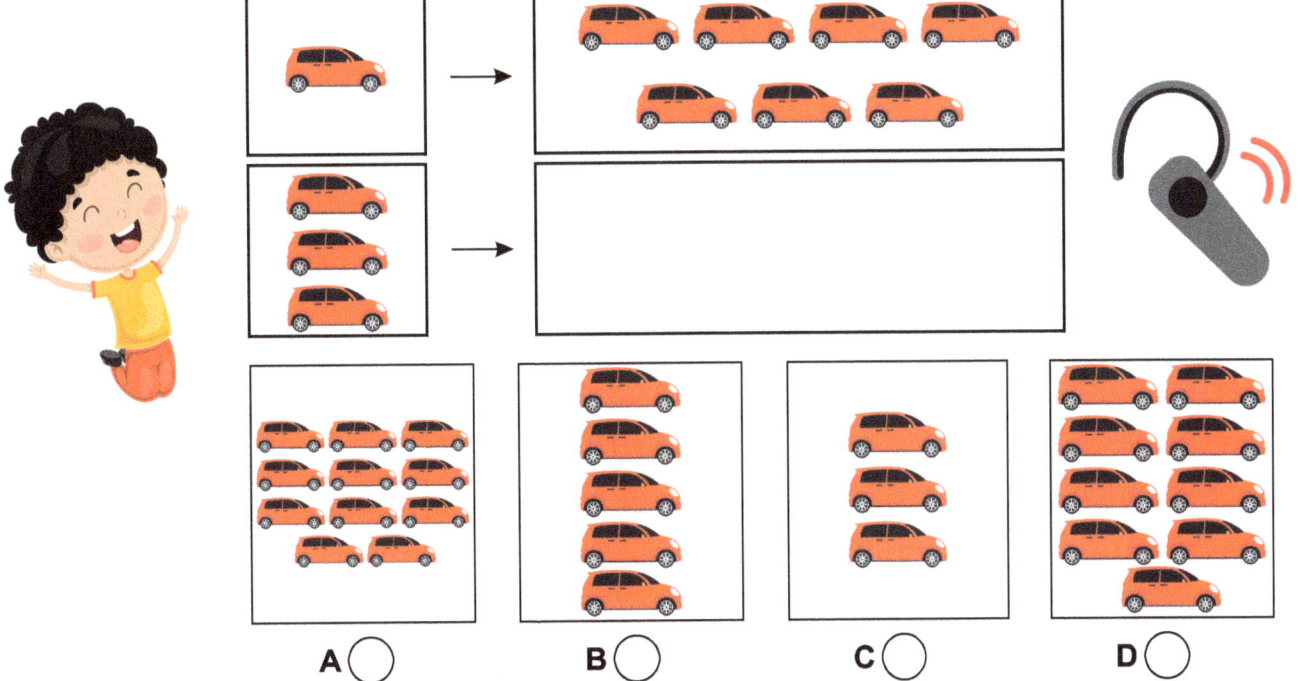

A ◯   B ◯   C ◯   D ◯

www.math-knots.com

Q-11

Look at the question with the Floppy Disk. Two boxes in the first row are related in a certain way which is similar to two boxes in the second row. Ella is trying to fill the bubble under the correct option. Help her to select from options A, B, C, and D.

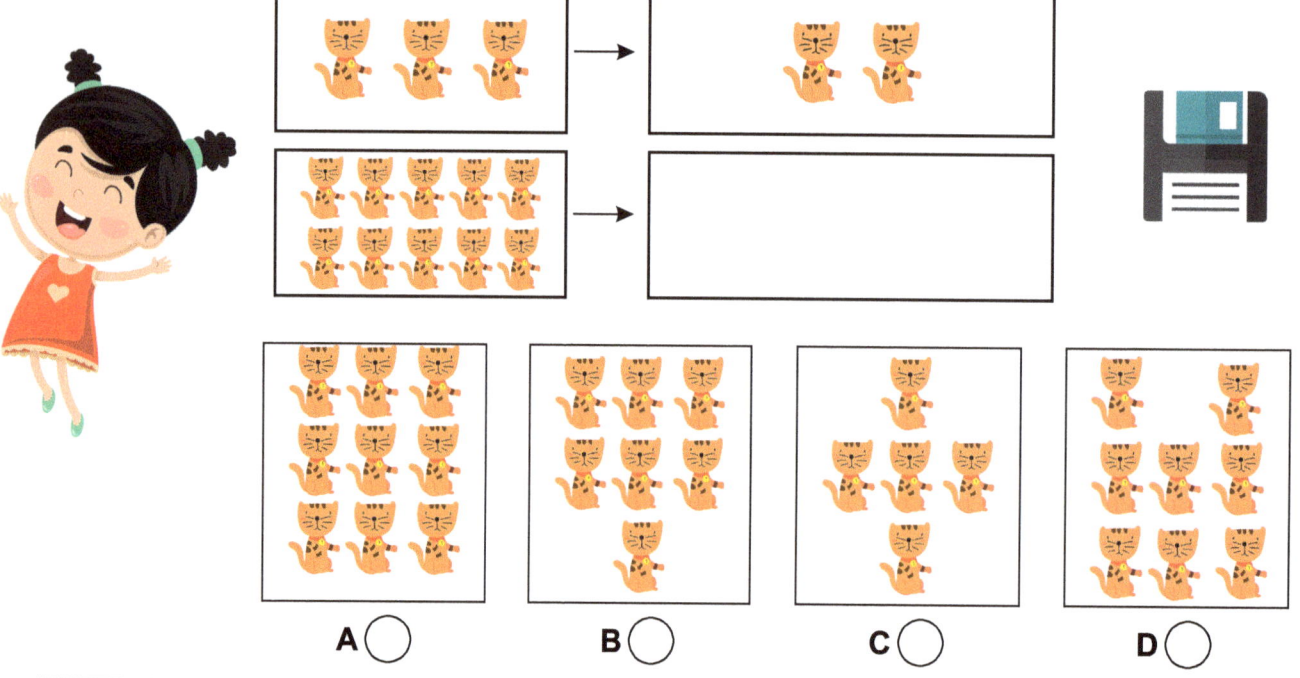

A ◯   B ◯   C ◯   D ◯

Q-12

Look at the question with the Microchip. Two boxes in the first row are related in a certain way which is similar to two boxes in the second row. Samuel is trying to fill the bubble under the correct option. Help him to select from options A, B, C, and D.

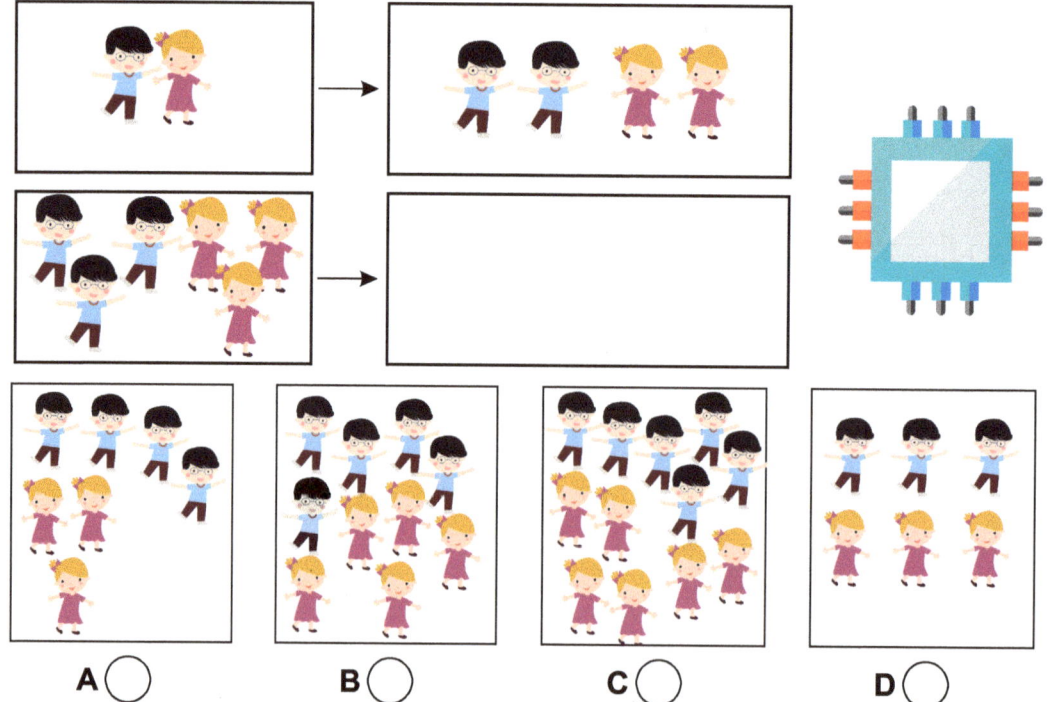

A ◯   B ◯   C ◯   D ◯

www.math-knots.com

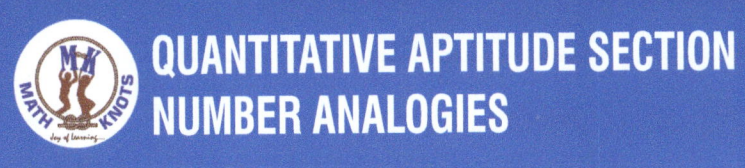

Q-13

Look at the question with the Web Camera. Two boxes in the first row are related in a certain way which is similar to two boxes in the second row. Bella is trying to fill the bubble under the correct option. Help her to select from options A, B, C, and D.

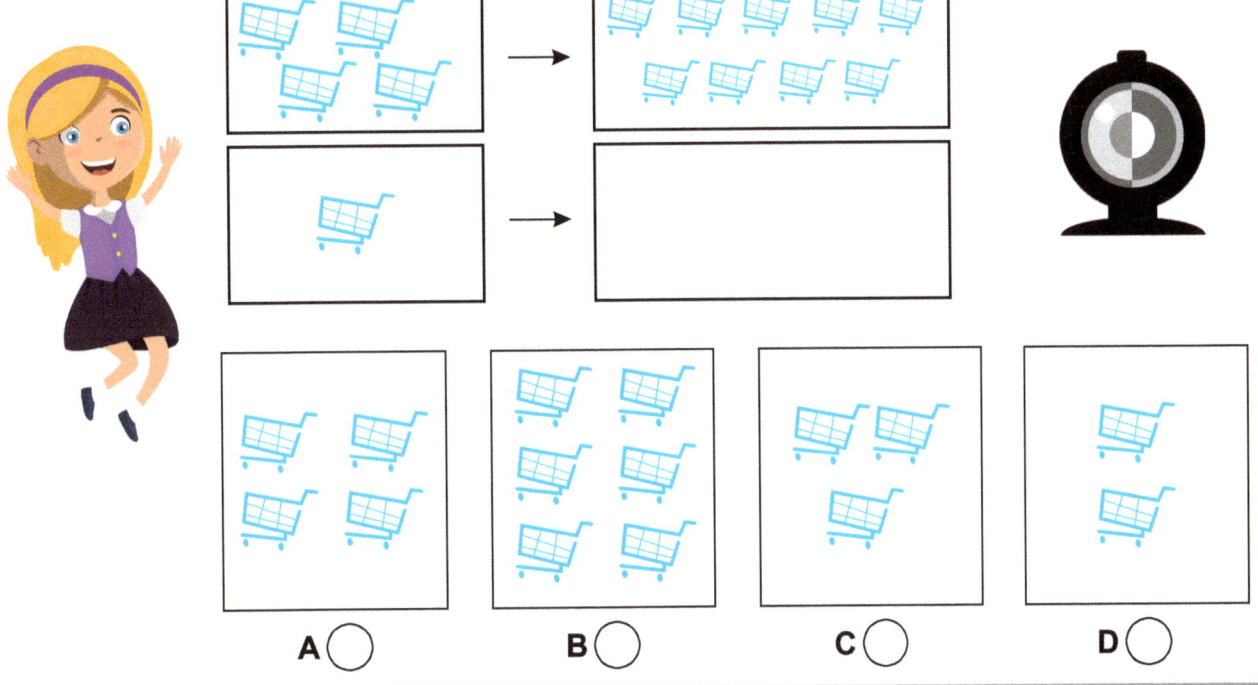

A ◯ B ◯ C ◯ D ◯

Q-14

Look at the question with the Jack Connector. Two boxes in the first row are related in a certain way which is similar to two boxes in the second row. Skylar is trying to fill the bubble under the correct option. Help her to select from options A, B, C, and D.

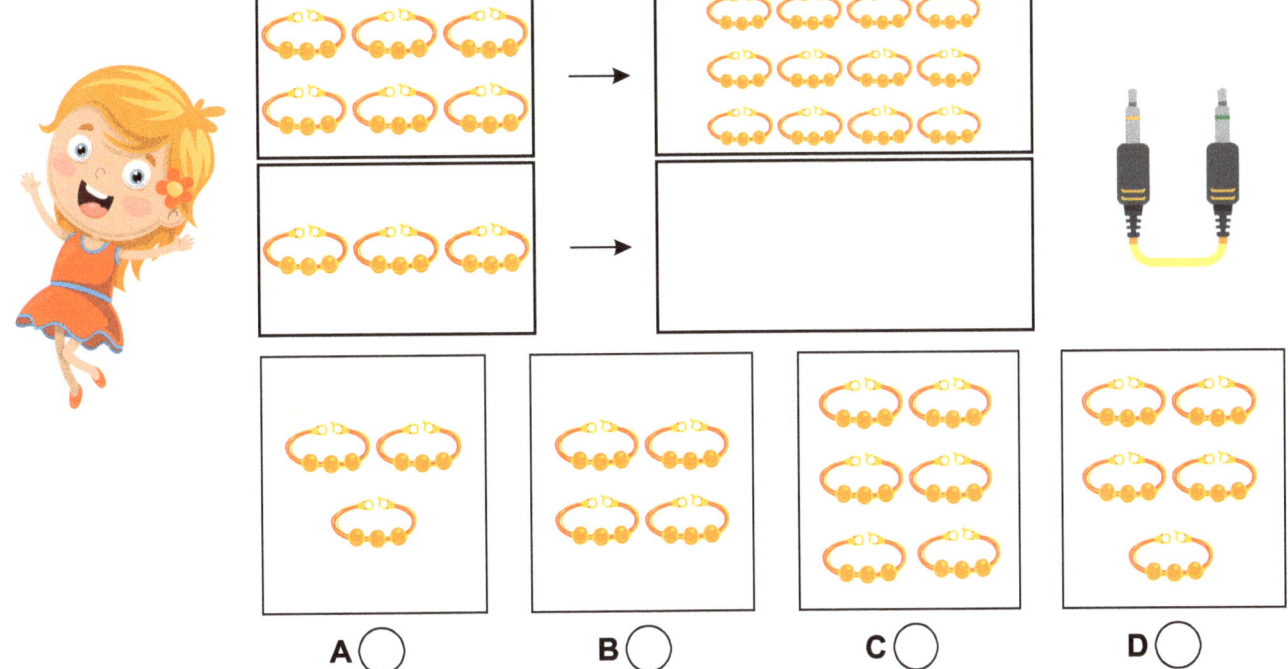

A ◯ B ◯ C ◯ D ◯

Q-15

Look at the question with the tablet HDMI Cable. Two boxes in the first row are related in a certain way which is similar to two boxes in the second row. Hannah is trying to fill the bubble under the correct option. Help her to select from options A, B, C, and D.

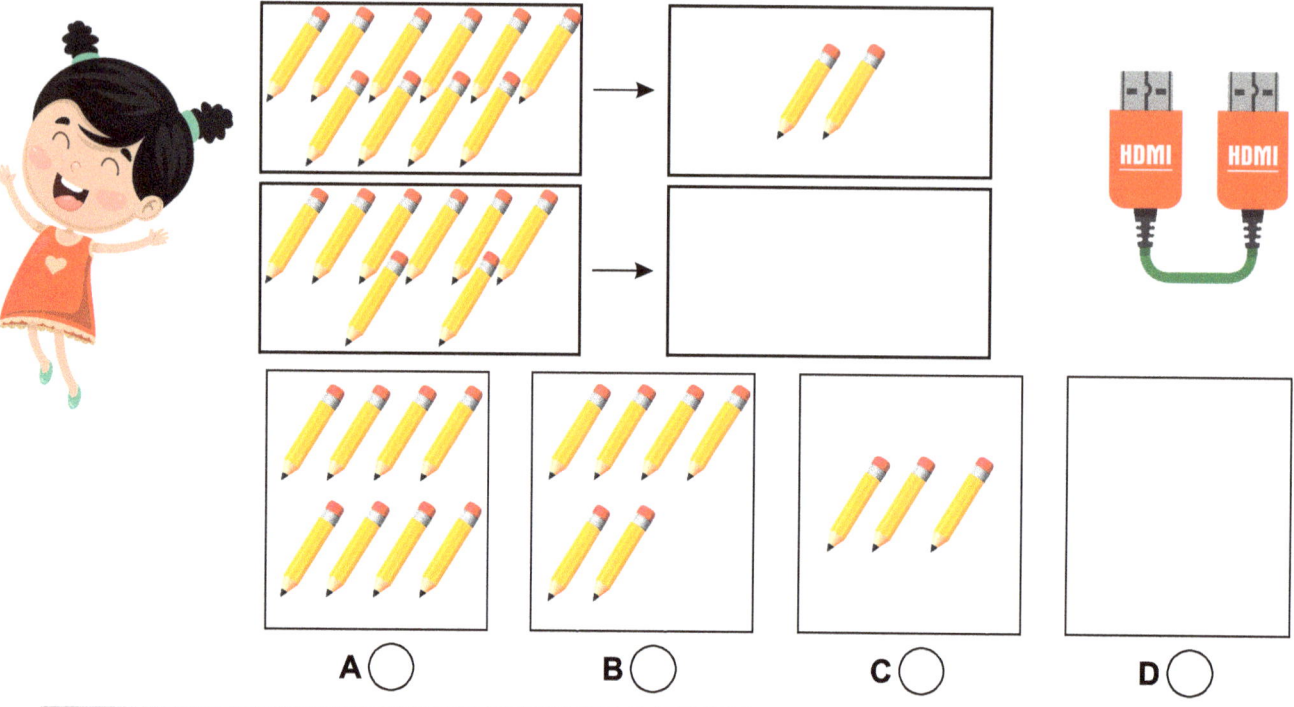

A ◯   B ◯   C ◯   D ◯

Q-16

Look at the question with the usb Flashdrive. Two boxes in the first row are related in a certain way which is similar to two boxes in the second row. Mathew is trying to fill the bubble under the correct option. Help him to select from options A, B, C, and D.

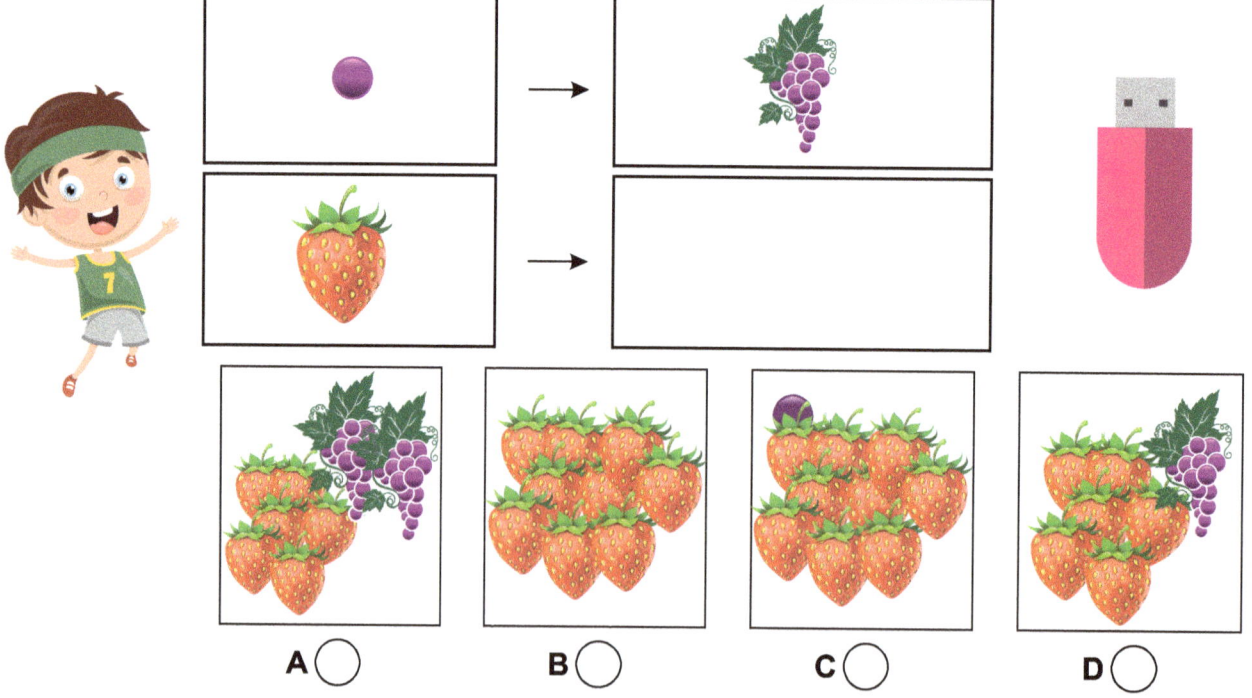

A ◯   B ◯   C ◯   D ◯

www.math-knots.com

Q-17

Look at the question with the Tablet PC. Two boxes in the first row are related in a certain way which is similar to two boxes in the second row. Joseph is trying to fill the bubble under the correct option. Help him to select from options A, B, C, and D.

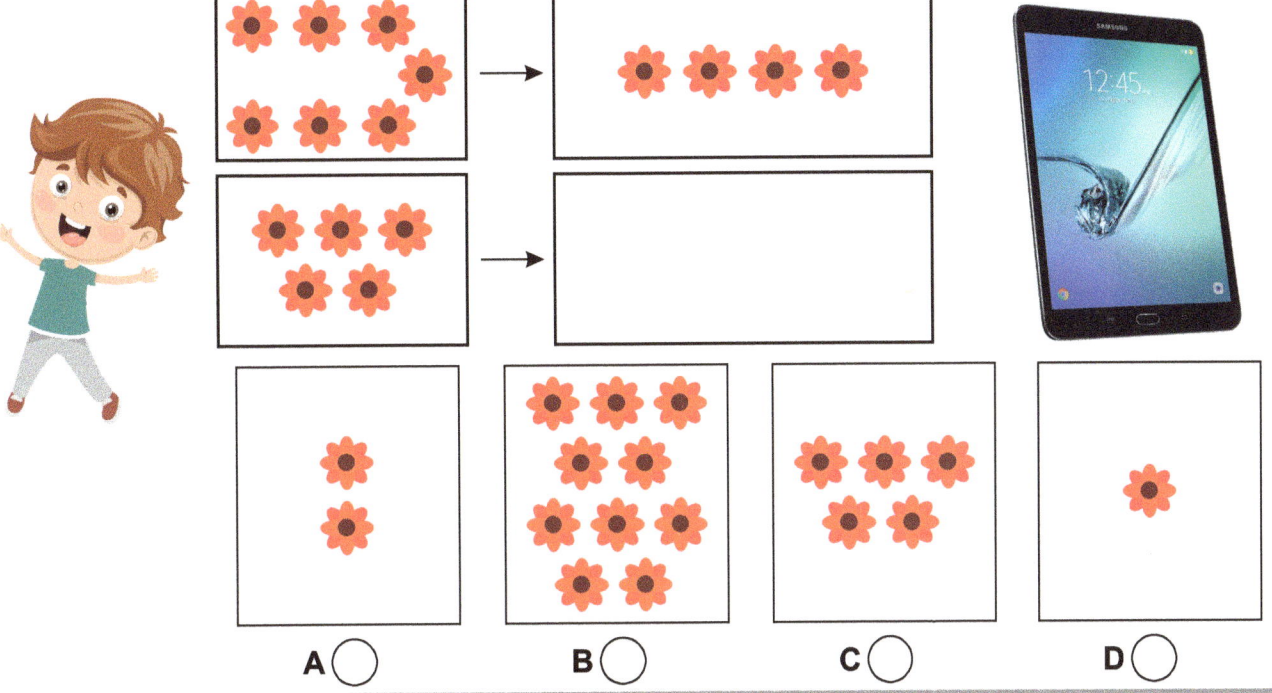

A ◯   B ◯   C ◯   D ◯

Q-18

Look at the question with the Mp3 Player. Two boxes in the first row are related in a certain way which is similar to two boxes in the second row. Chloe is trying to fill the bubble under the correct option. Help her to select from options A, B, C, and D.

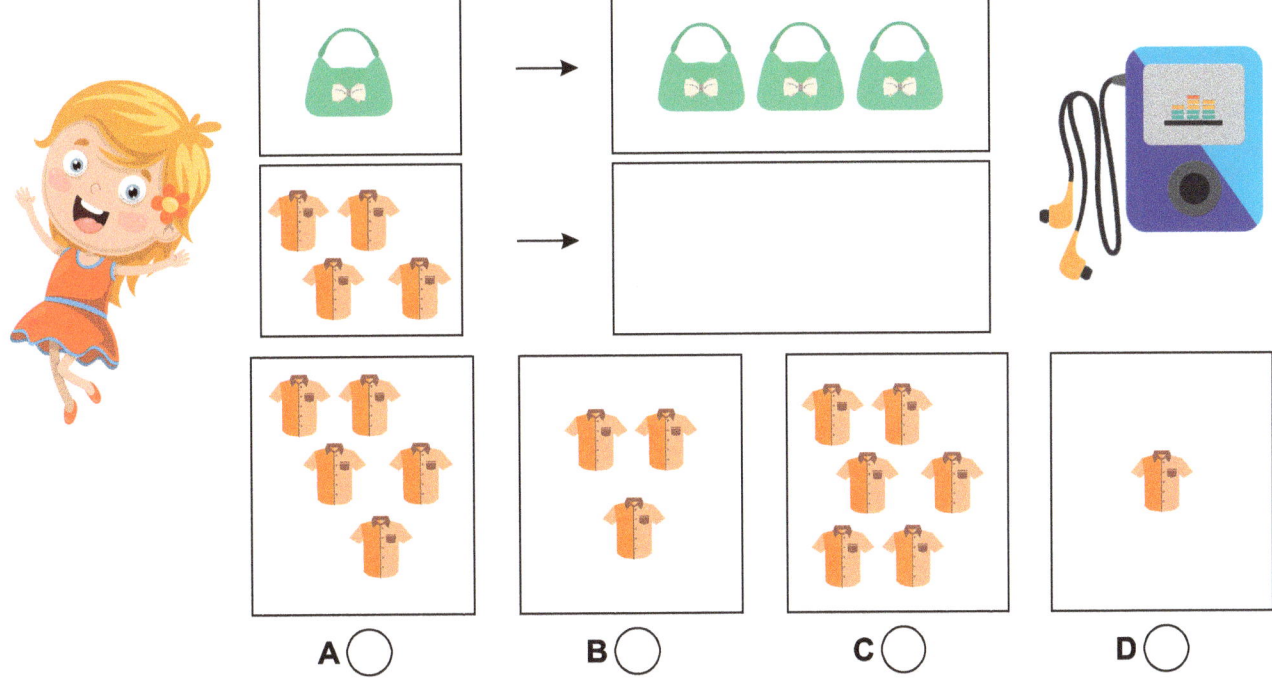

A ◯   B ◯   C ◯   D ◯

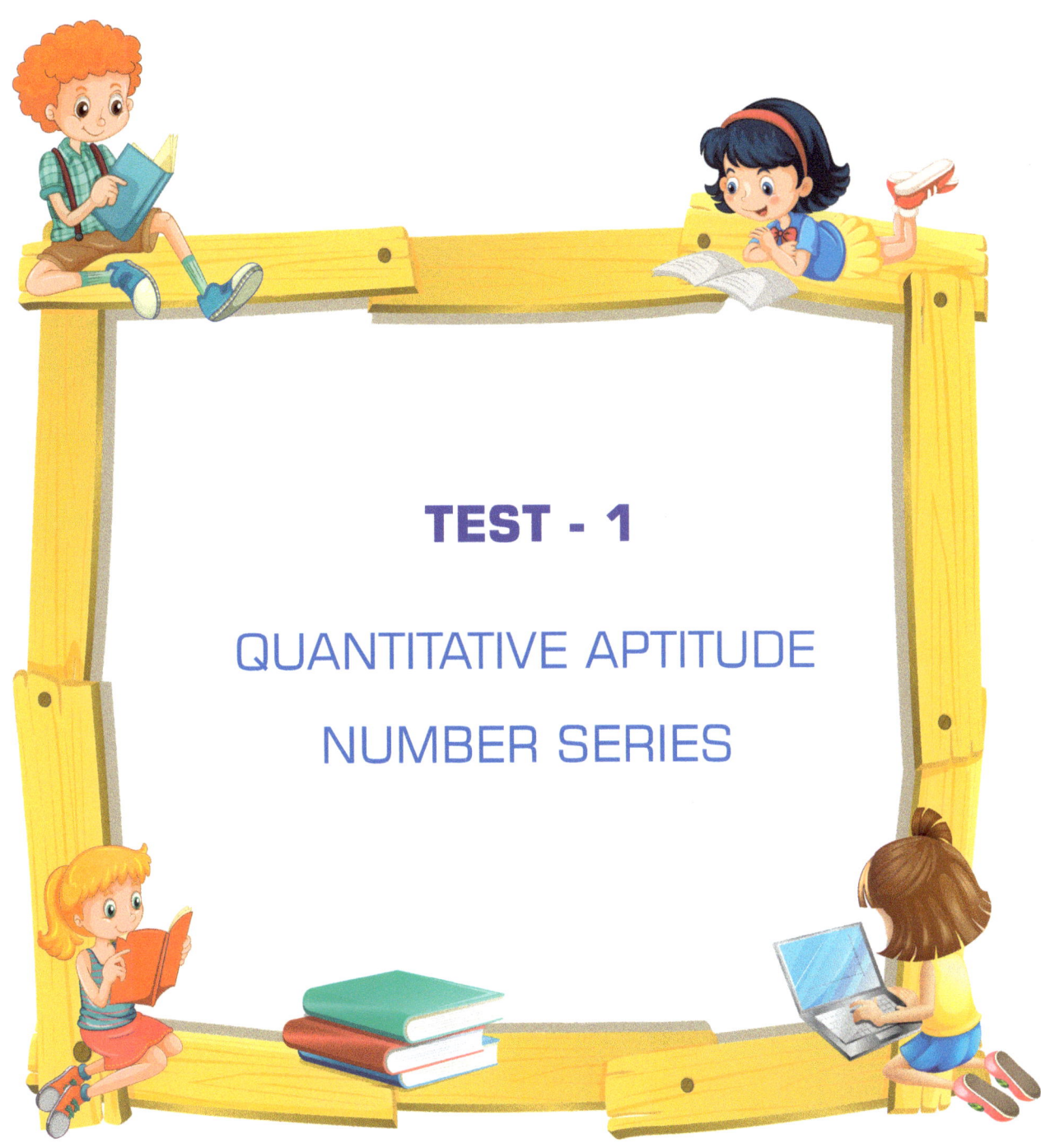

TEST - 1

QUANTITATIVE APTITUDE

NUMBER SERIES

Lets Start the Test...

www.math-knots.com

Sample

Look at the question with the Triangle. Cathy is making a pattern with her hexagon shaped beads. Can you help her to identify what goes in the empty string from the given four options A, B, C, and D.

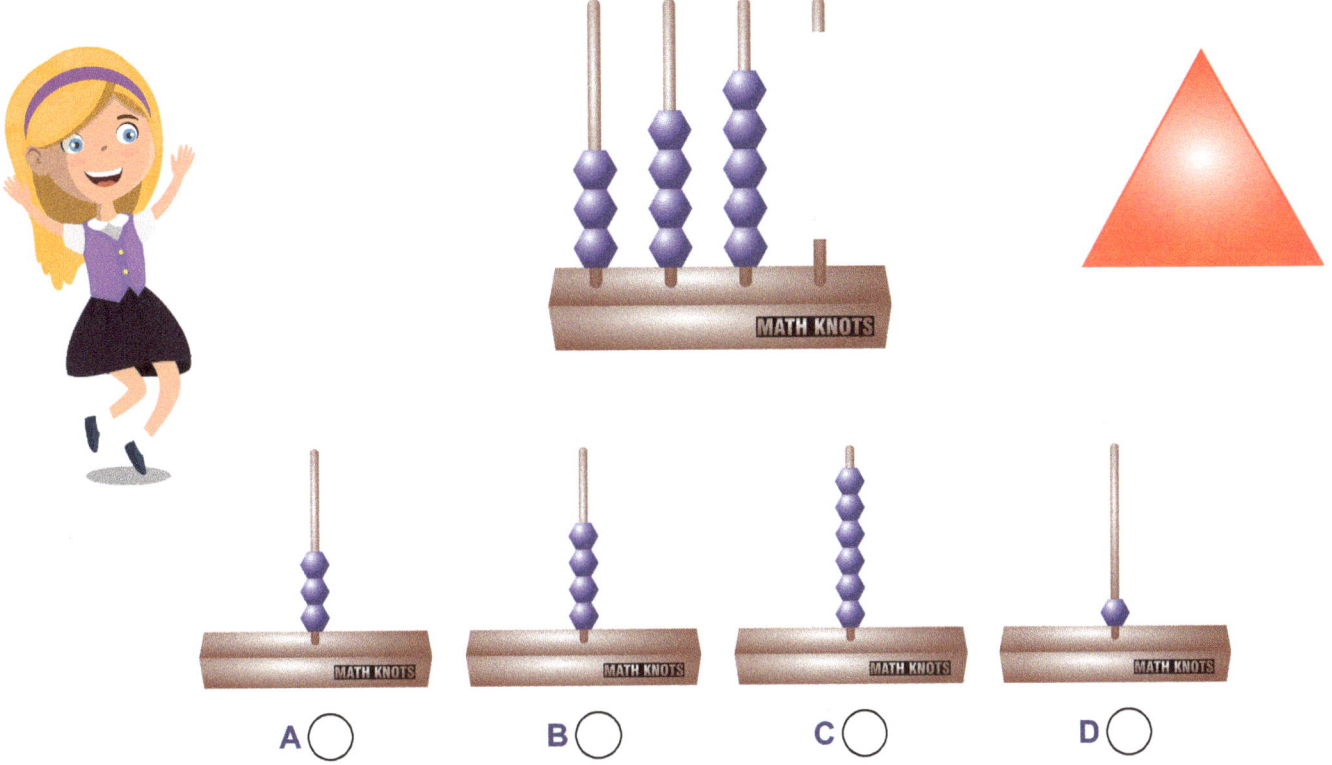

Solution : C

3, 4, 5.....

The beads are increasing by 1. So next string should have six beads. Option C is the correct choice. The patterns can increase or decrease by a certain number of beads. Students are supposed to identify the correct pattern and answer the correct choice.

www.math-knots.com

Q-1 Look at the question with the Truck. Joseph is making a pattern with his hexagon shaped beads. Can you help him to identify what goes in the empty string from the given four options A, B, C, and D.

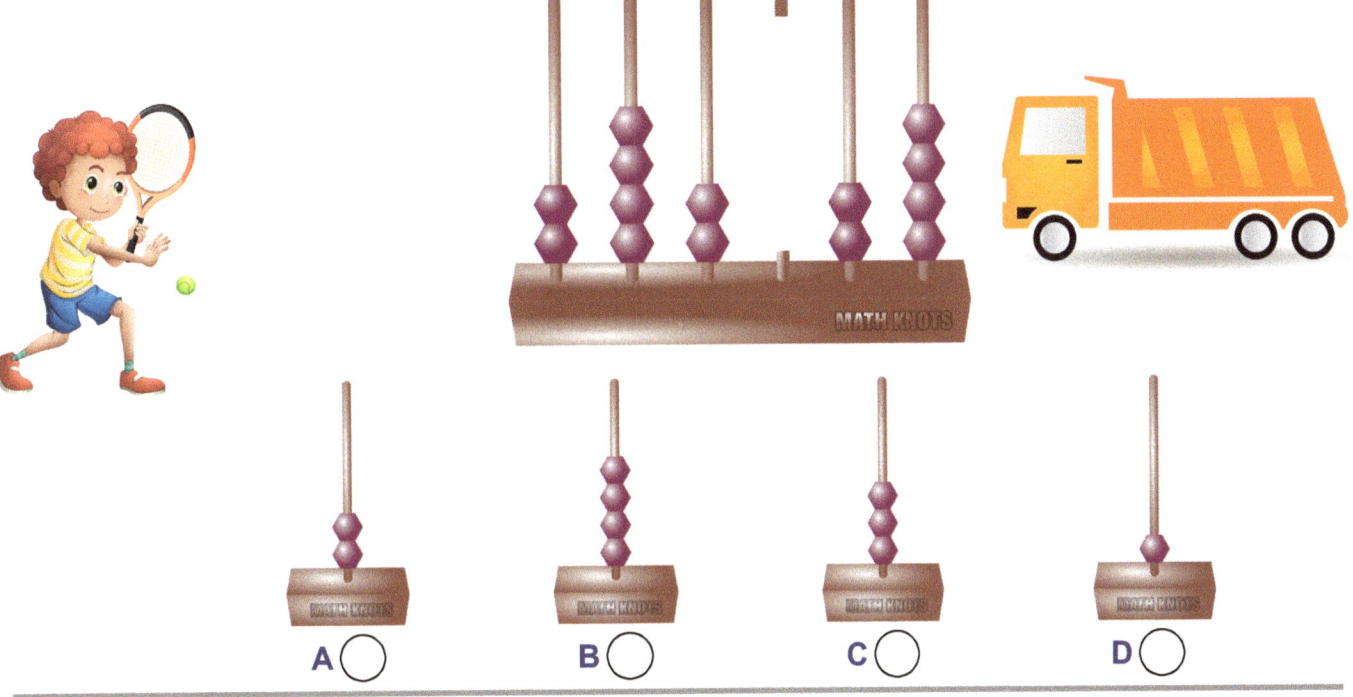

A ◯   B ◯   C ◯   D ◯

Q-2 Look at the question with the look at Bike, Jane is making a pattern with her hexagon shaped beads. Can you help her to identify what goes in the empty string from the given four options A, B, C, and D.

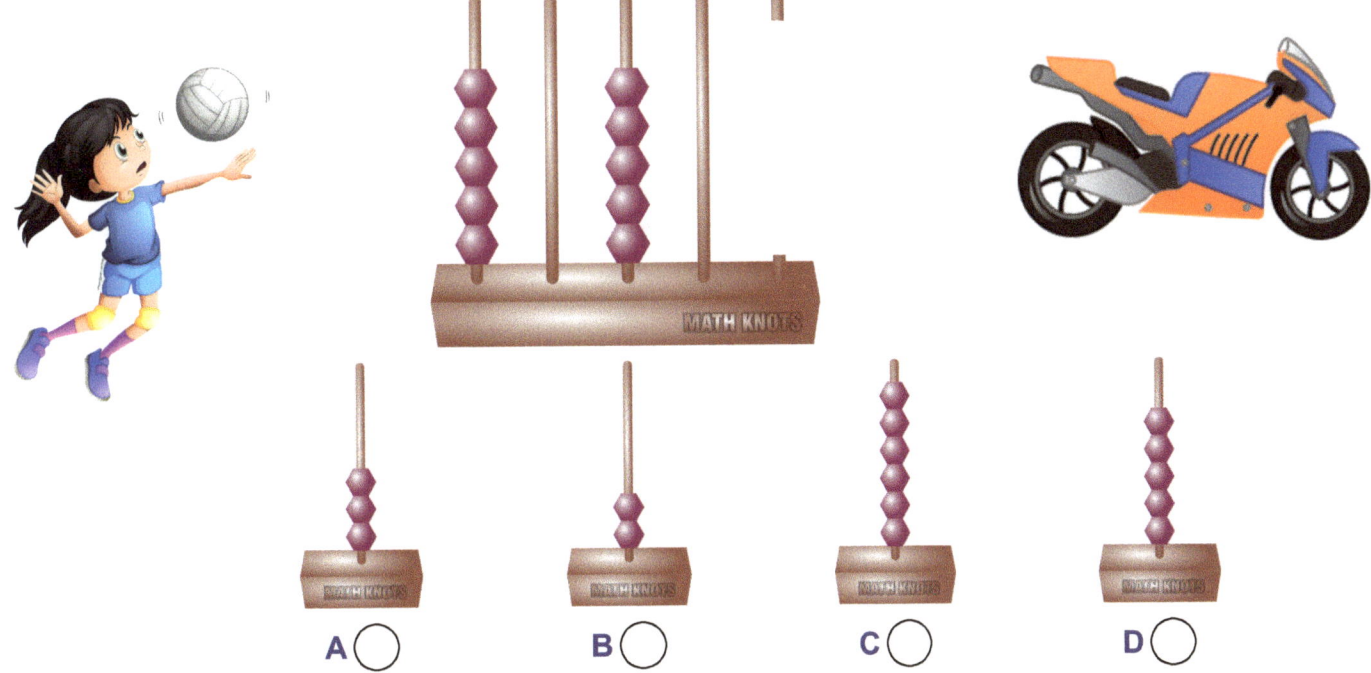

A ◯   B ◯   C ◯   D ◯

www.math-knots.com

Q-3

Look at the question with the Tanker. Logan is making a pattern with his hexagon shaped beads. Can you help him to identify what goes in the empty string from the given four options A, B, C, and D.

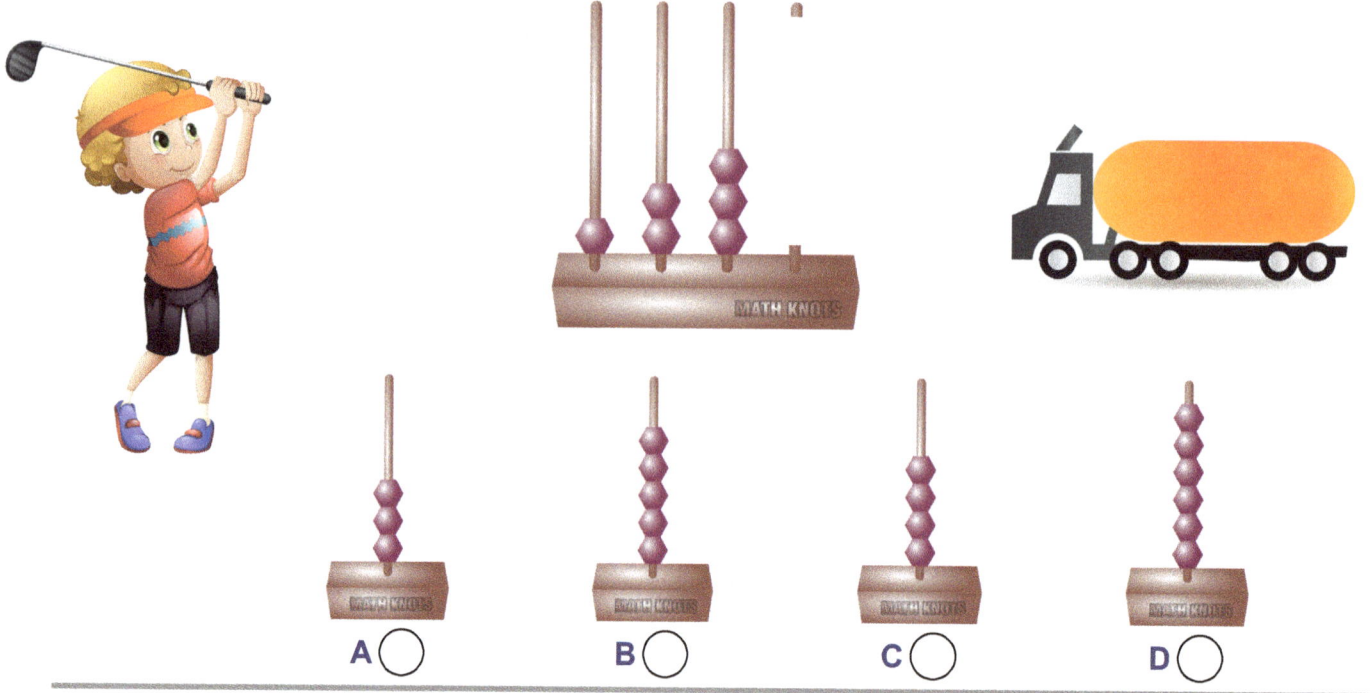

A ◯   B ◯   C ◯   D ◯

Q-4

Look at the question with the Crane, Ava is making a pattern with her hexagon shaped beads. Can you help her to identify what goes in the empty string from the given four options A, B, C, and D.

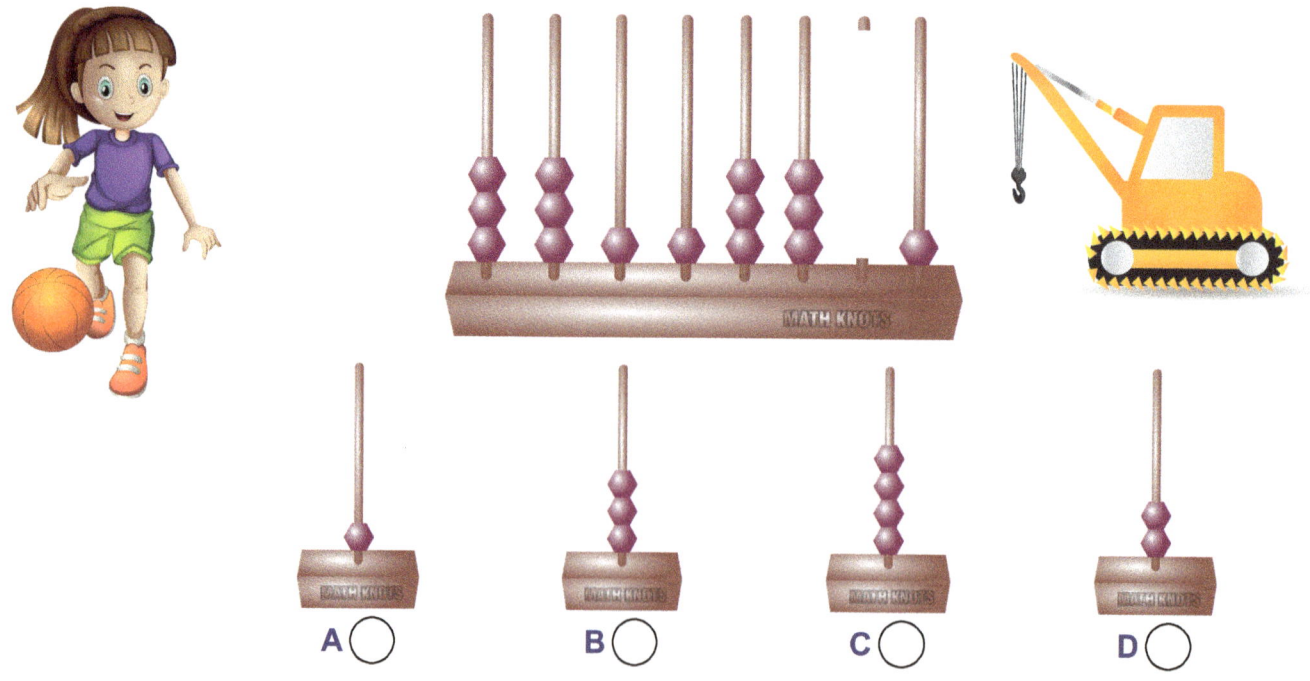

A ◯   B ◯   C ◯   D ◯

www.math-knots.com

Q-5

Look at the question with the Van. Robert is making a pattern with his hexagon shaped beads. Can you help him to identify what goes in the empty string from the given four options A, B, C, and D.

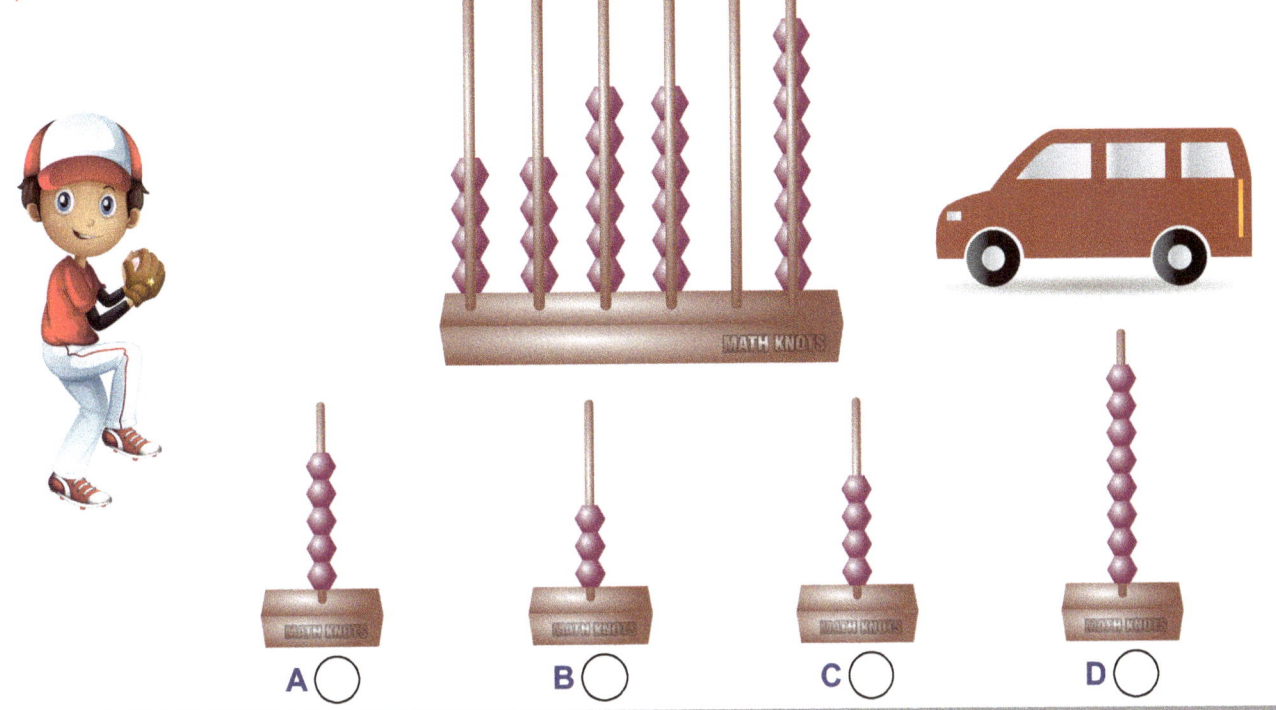

A ◯ B ◯ C ◯ D ◯

Q-6

Look at the question with the Helicopter, Emma is making a pattern with her hexagon shaped beads. Can you help her to identify what goes in the empty string from the given four options A, B, C, and D.

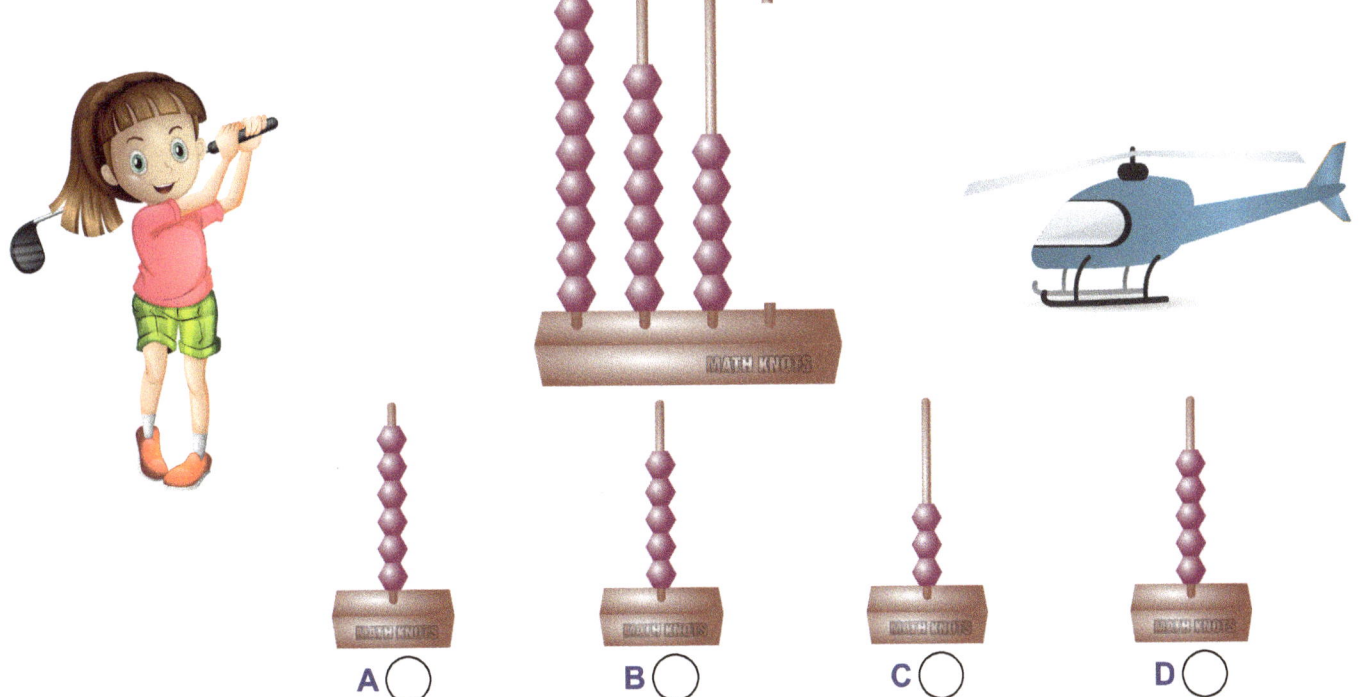

A ◯ B ◯ C ◯ D ◯

Q-7 Look at the question with the Flight. Harry is making a pattern with his hexagon shaped beads. Can you help him to identify what goes in the empty string from the given four options A,B,C, and D.

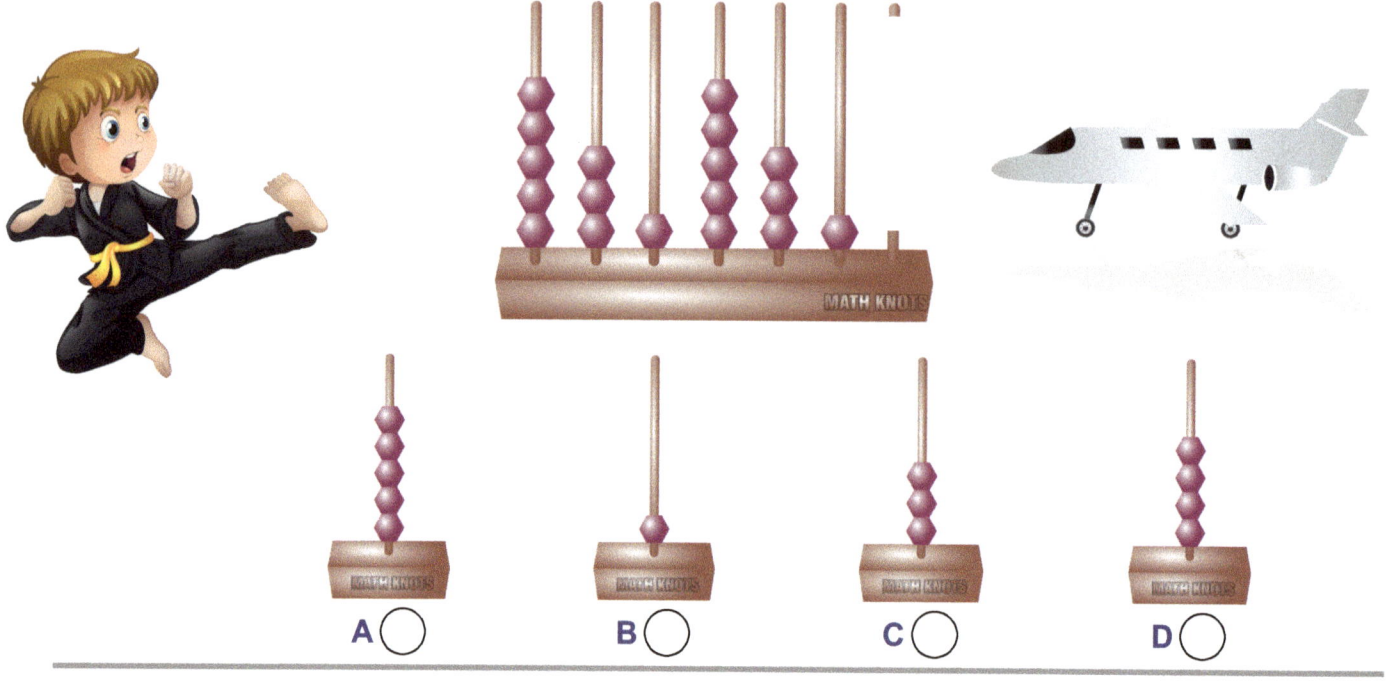

A ◯   B ◯   C ◯   D ◯

Q-8 Look at the question with the Ship, Margaret is making a pattern with her hexagon shaped beads. Can you help her to identify what goes in the empty string from the given four options A,B,C, and D.

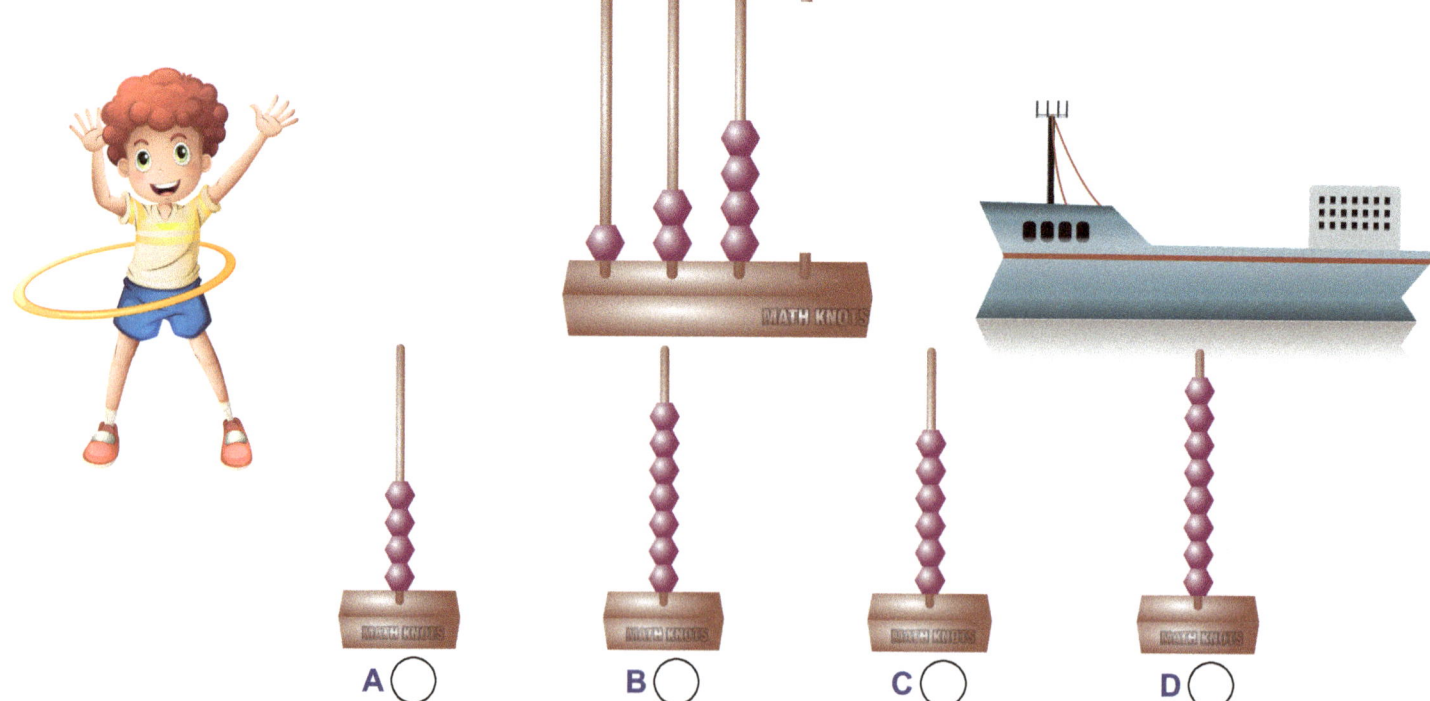

A ◯   B ◯   C ◯   D ◯

www.math-knots.com

Q-9

Look at the question with the Bullet Train. Elizabeth is making a pattern with her hexagon shaped beads. Can you help her to identify what goes in the empty string from the given four options A, B, C, and D.

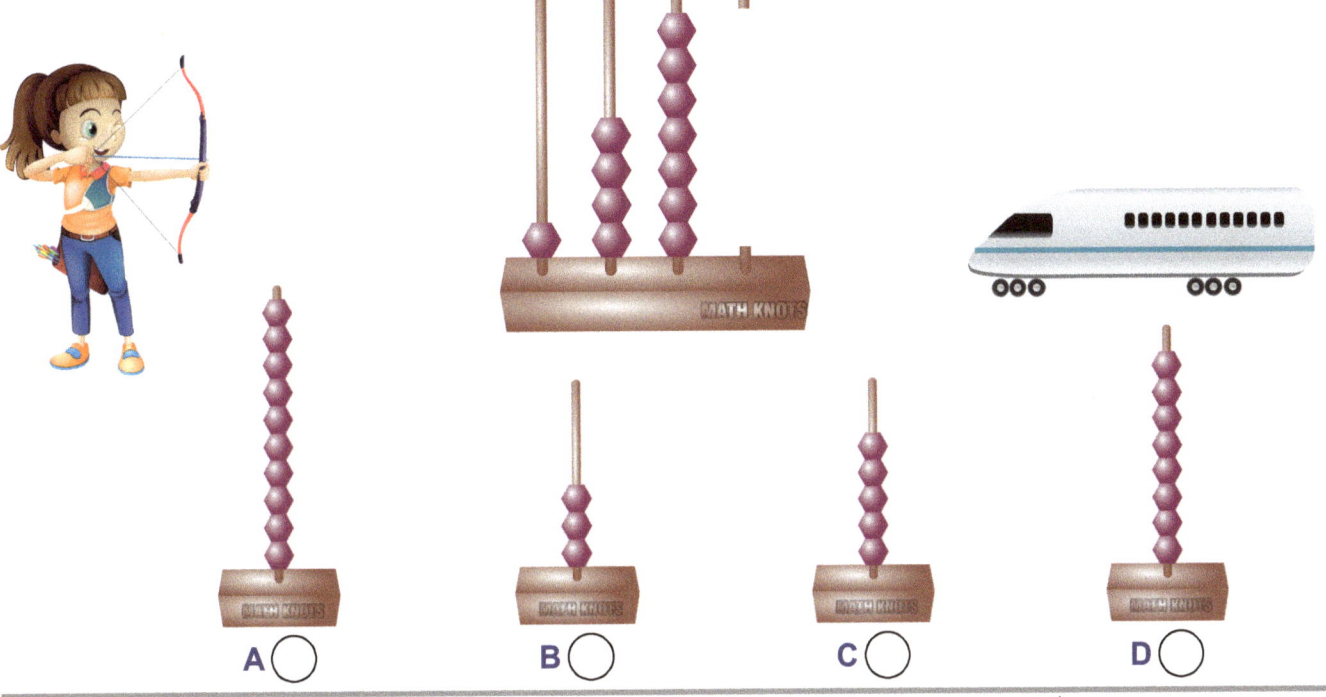

A ◯   B ◯   C ◯   D ◯

Q-10

Look at the question with the Truck. Skylar is making a pattern with her hexagon shaped beads. Can you help her to identify what goes in the empty string from the given four options A, B, C, and D.

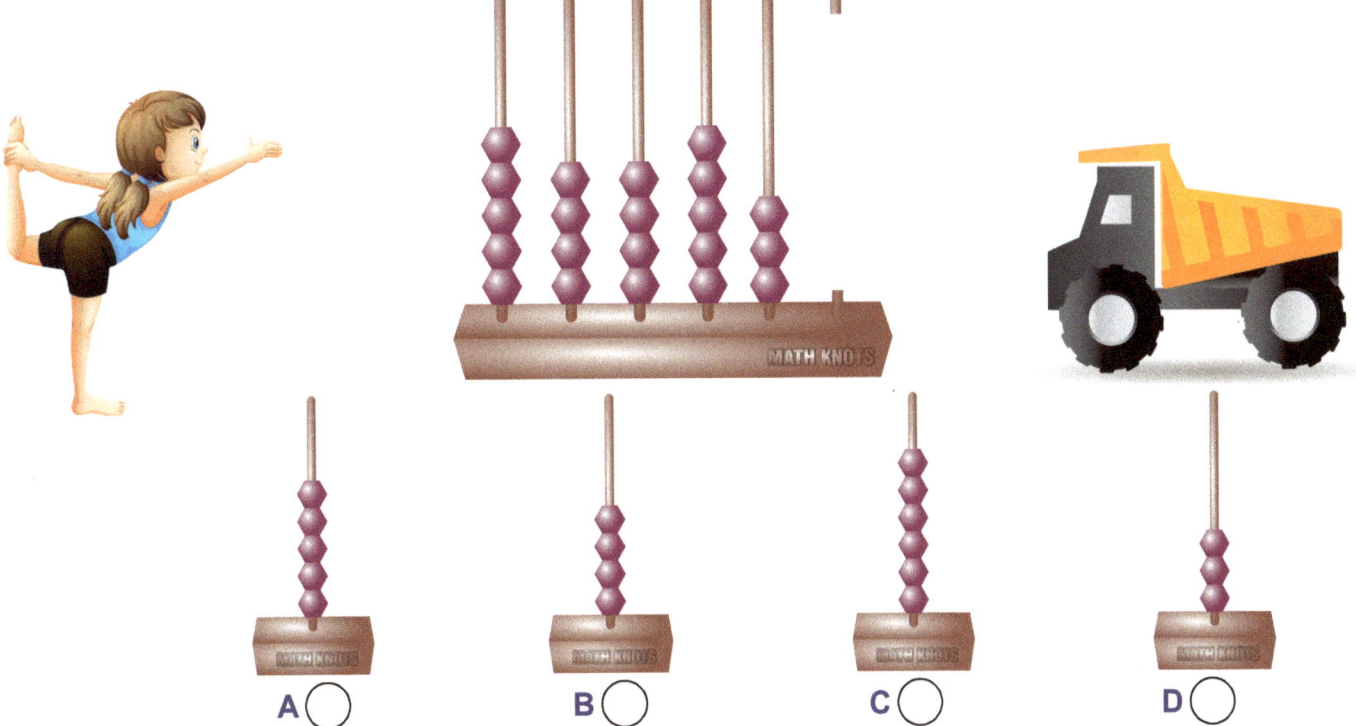

A ◯   B ◯   C ◯   D ◯

www.math-knots.com

Q-11

Look at the question with the Scooter. Brooklyn is making a pattern with his hexagon shaped beads. Can you help him to identify what goes in the empty string from the given four options A, B, C, and D.

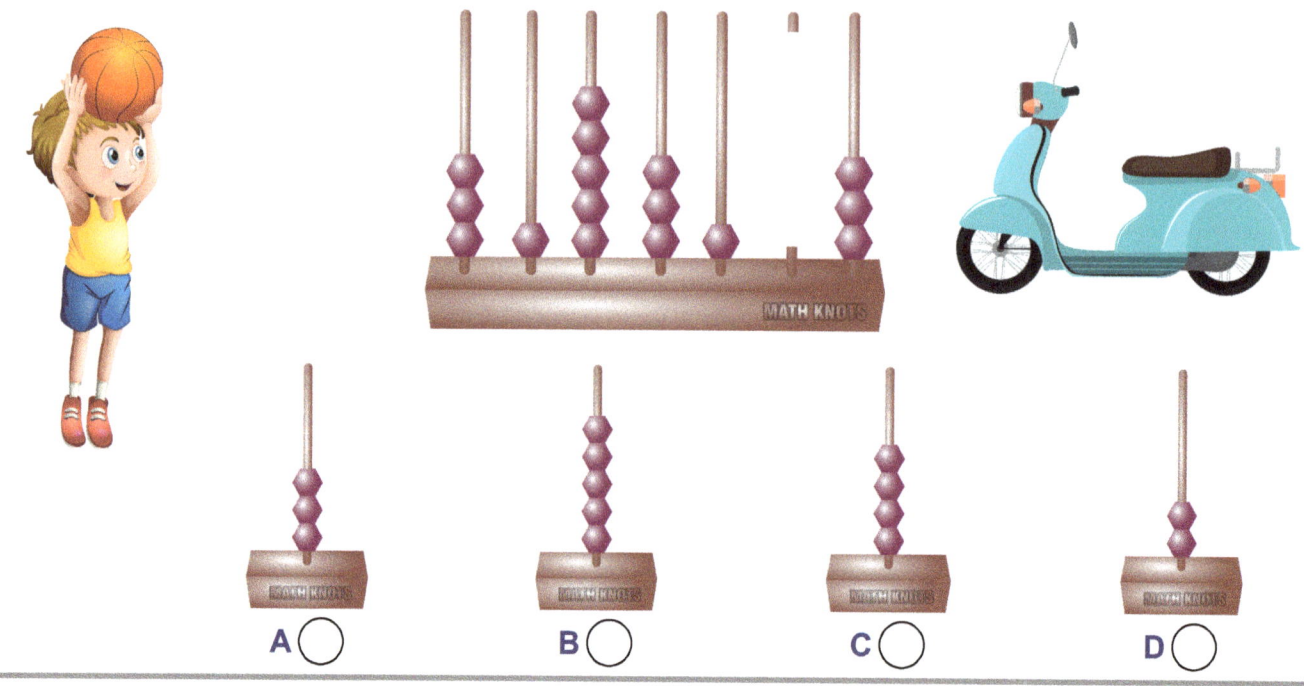

A ◯   B ◯   C ◯   D ◯

Q-12

Look at the question with the Van. Caroline is making a pattern with her hexagon shaped beads. Can you help her to identify what goes in the empty string from the given four options A, B, C, and D.

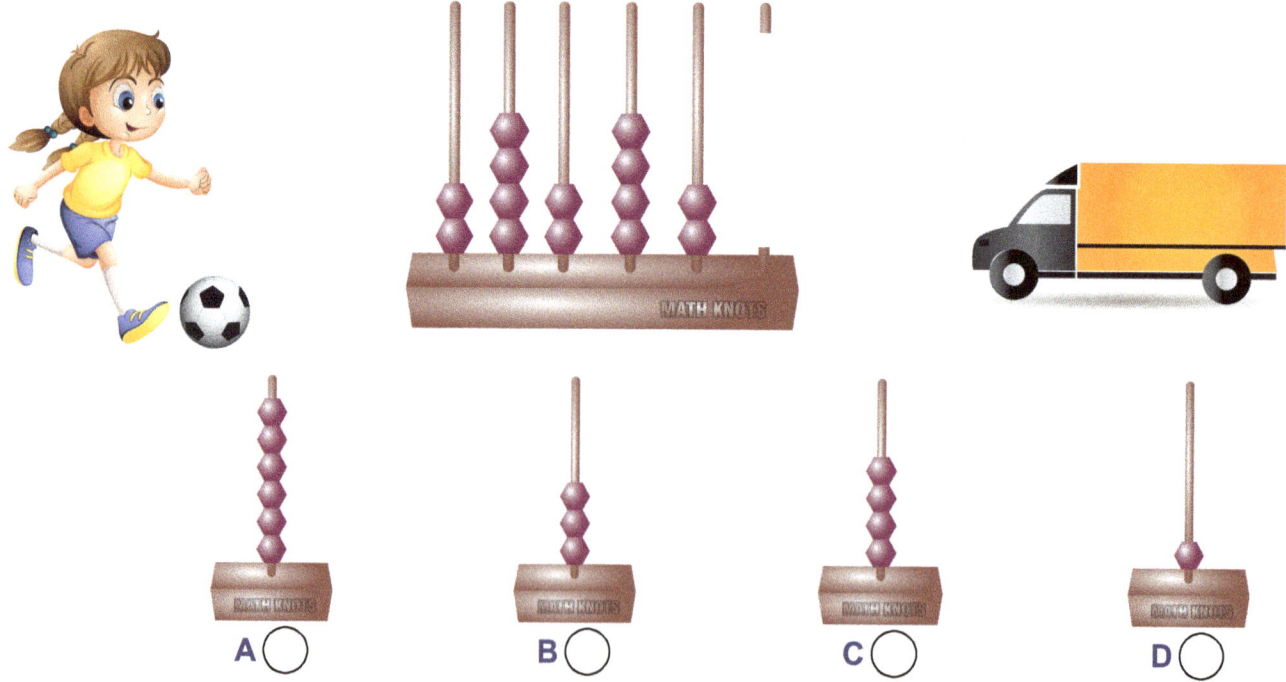

A ◯   B ◯   C ◯   D ◯

www.math-knots.com

Q-13 Look at the question with the Concrete Mixing Truck. Amy is making a pattern with her hexagon shaped beads. Can you help her to identify what goes in the empty string from the given four options A,B,C, and D.

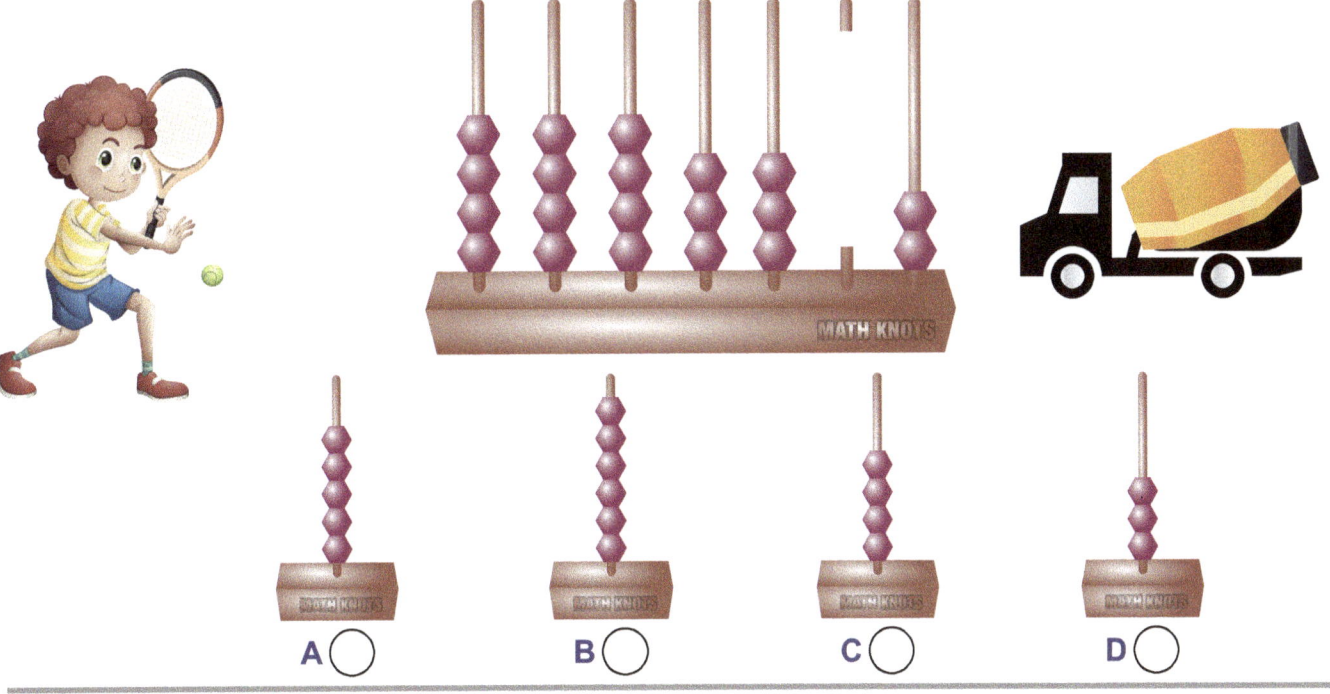

A ◯   B ◯   C ◯   D ◯

Q-14 Look at the question with the Loader Truck. Andy is making a pattern with his hexagon shaped beads. Can you help him to identify what goes in the empty string from the given four options A,B,C, and D.

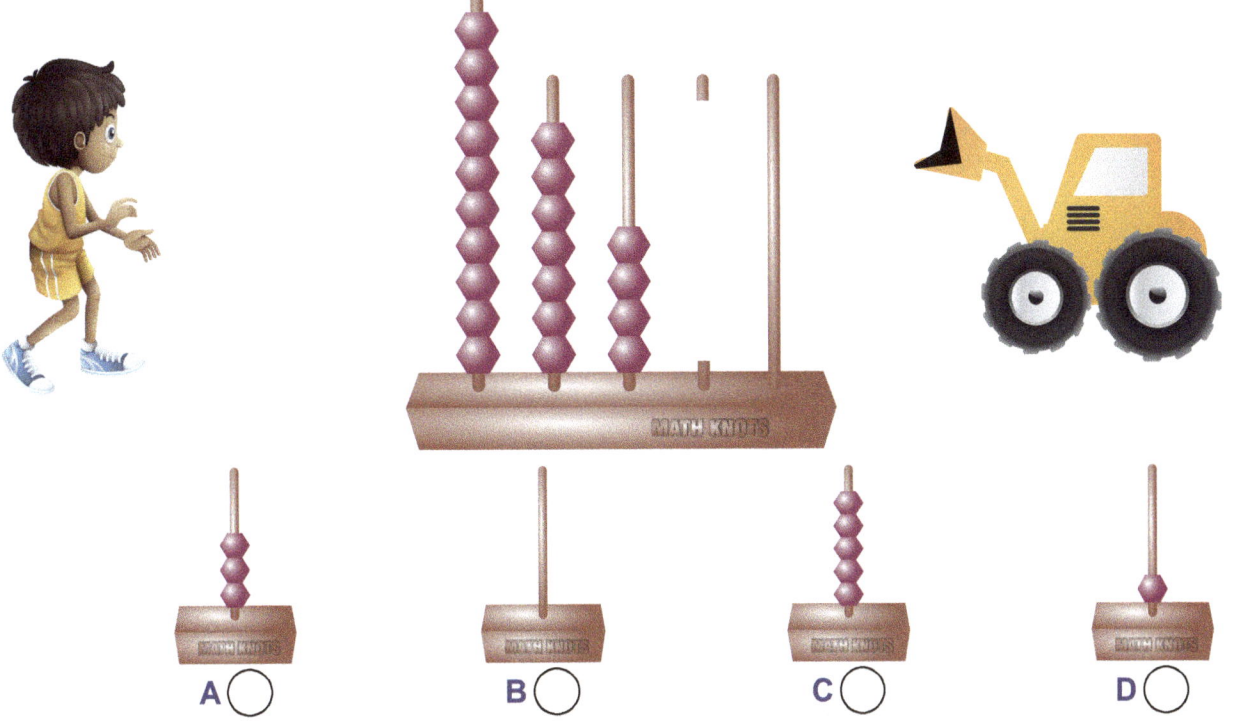

A ◯   B ◯   C ◯   D ◯

Q-15 Look at the question with the Car. Chloe is making a pattern with her hexagon shaped beads. Can you help her to identify what goes in the empty string from the given four options A,B,C, and D.

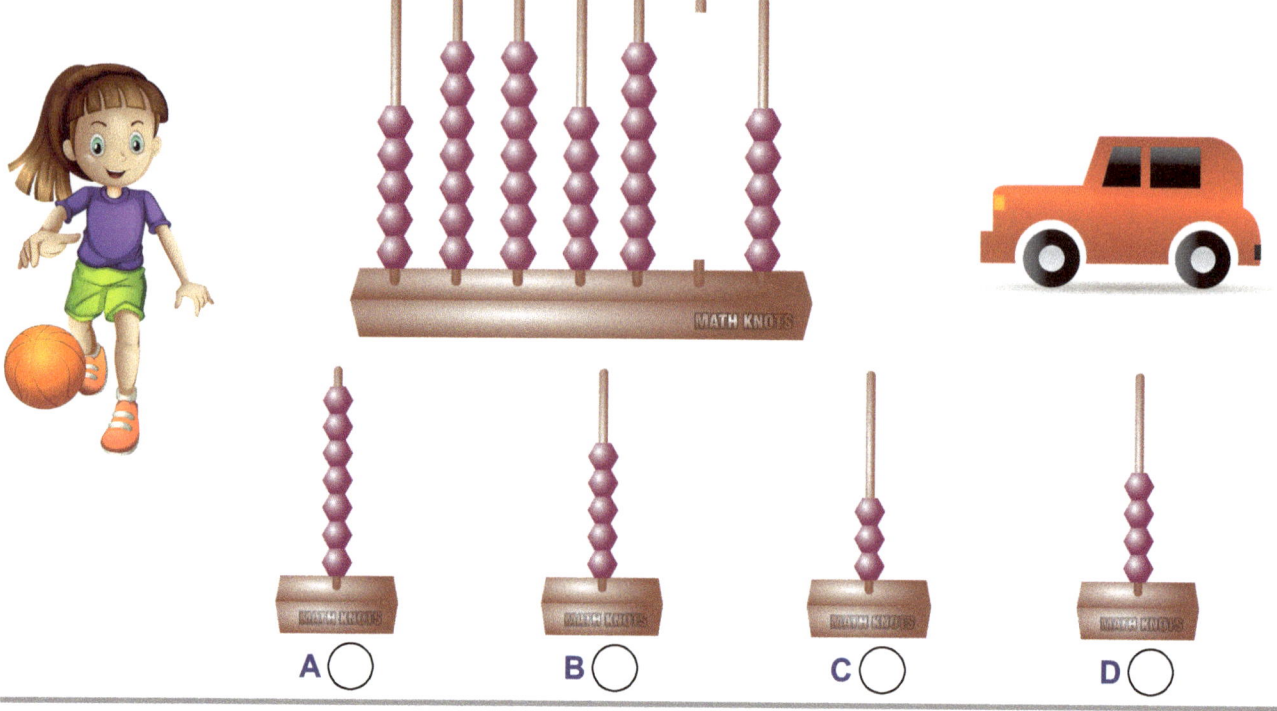

A ○ B ○ C ○ D ○

Q-16 Look at the question with the Bicycle. Mary is making a pattern with her hexagon shaped beads. Can you help her to identify what goes in the empty string from the given four options A,B,C, and D.

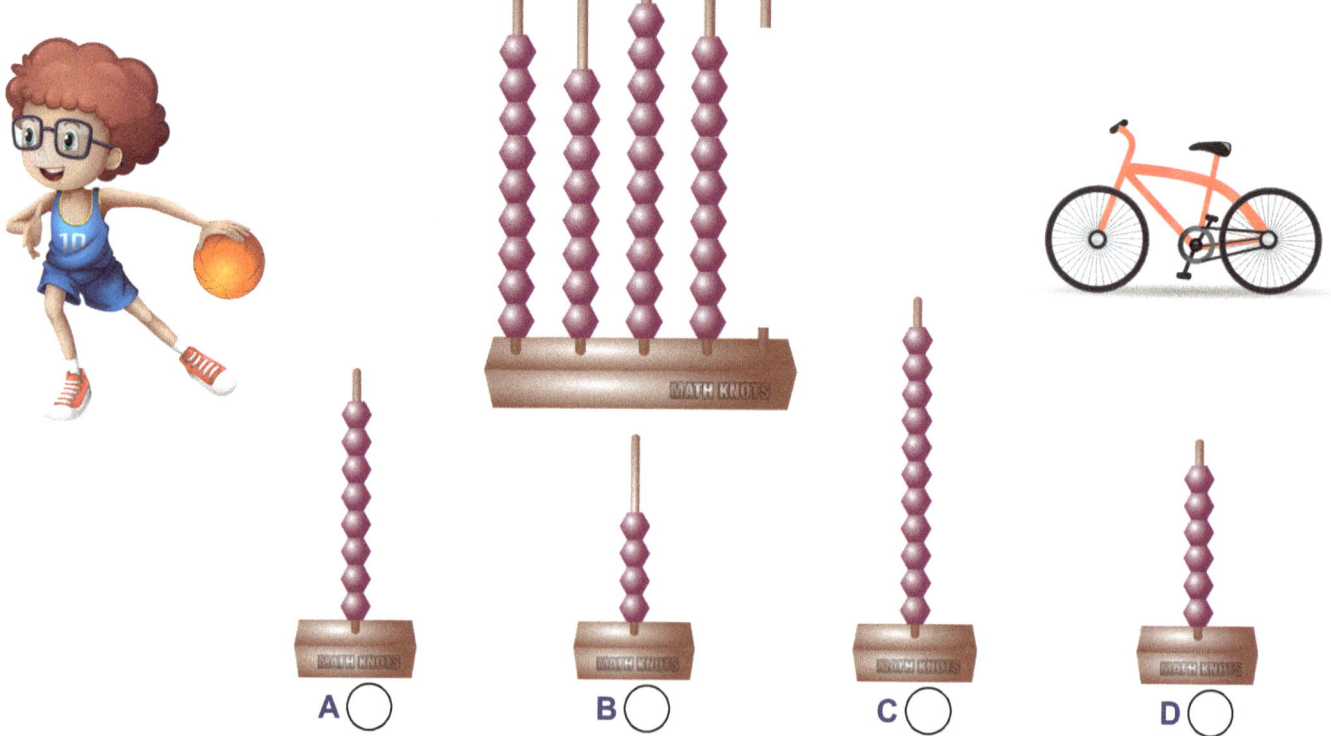

A ○ B ○ C ○ D ○

www.math-knots.com

Q-17 Look at the question with the Flight. Pamela is making a pattern with her hexagon shaped beads. Can you help her to identify what goes in the empty string from the given four options A, B, C, and D.

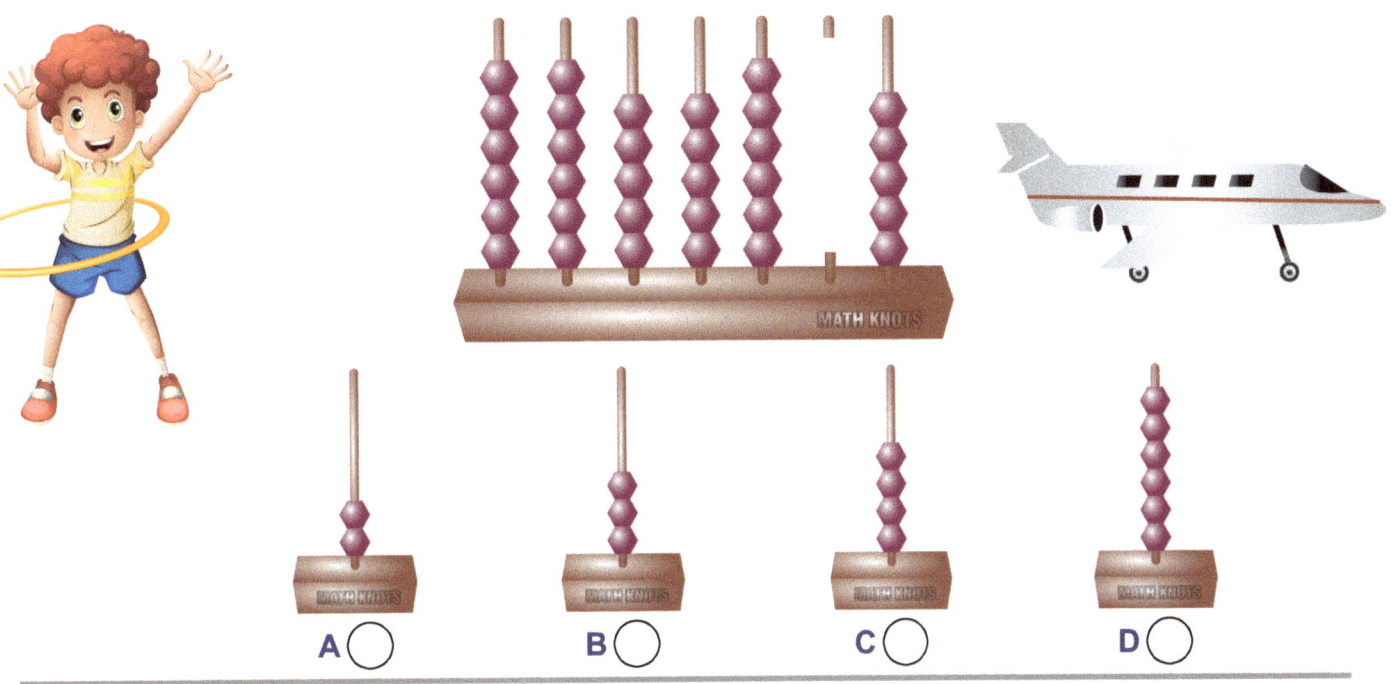

A ◯   B ◯   C ◯   D ◯

Q-18 Look at the question with the Bike. Ethan is making a pattern with her hexagon shaped beads. Can you help him to identify what goes in the empty string from the given four options A, B, C, and D.

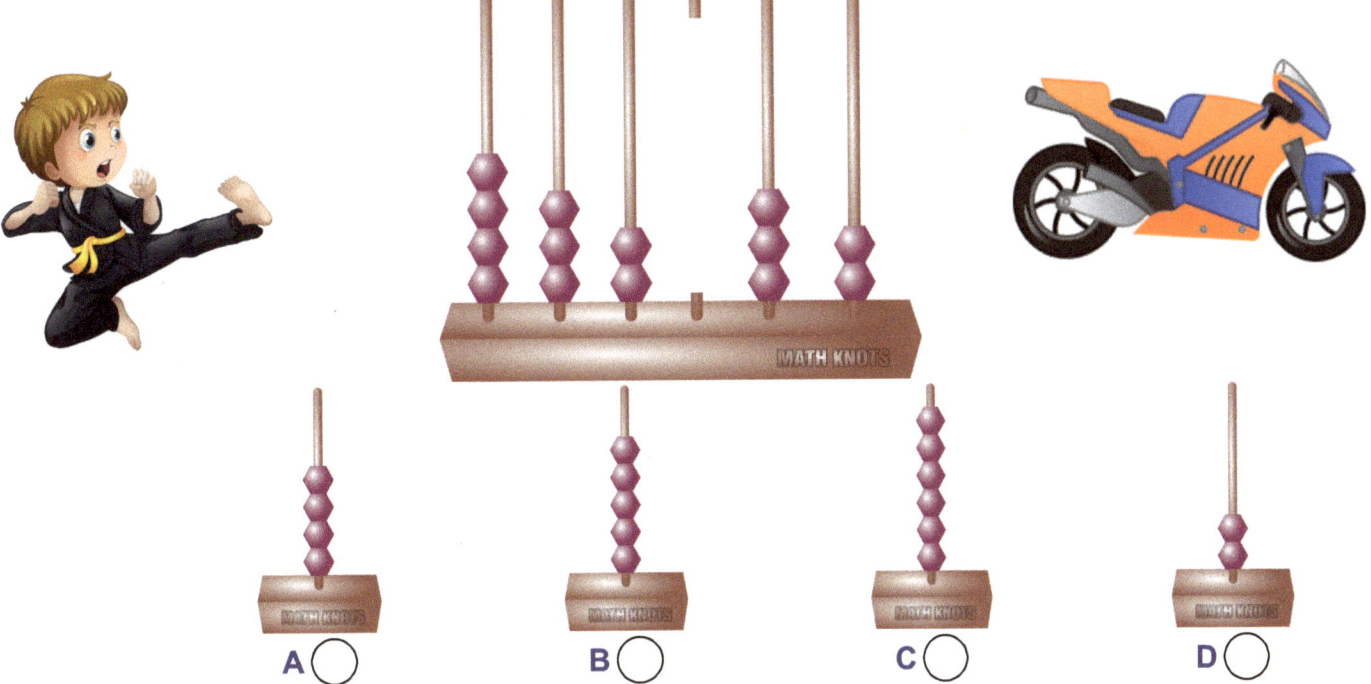

A ◯   B ◯   C ◯   D ◯

TEST - 1

QUANTITATIVE APTITUDE

NUMBER PUZZLES

Lets Start the Test...

Sample Look at the question and put your finger on the Guitar. Ryan is wondering what is the missing number under the question mark ? Help him to find the missing number under the question mark and fill in the bubble.

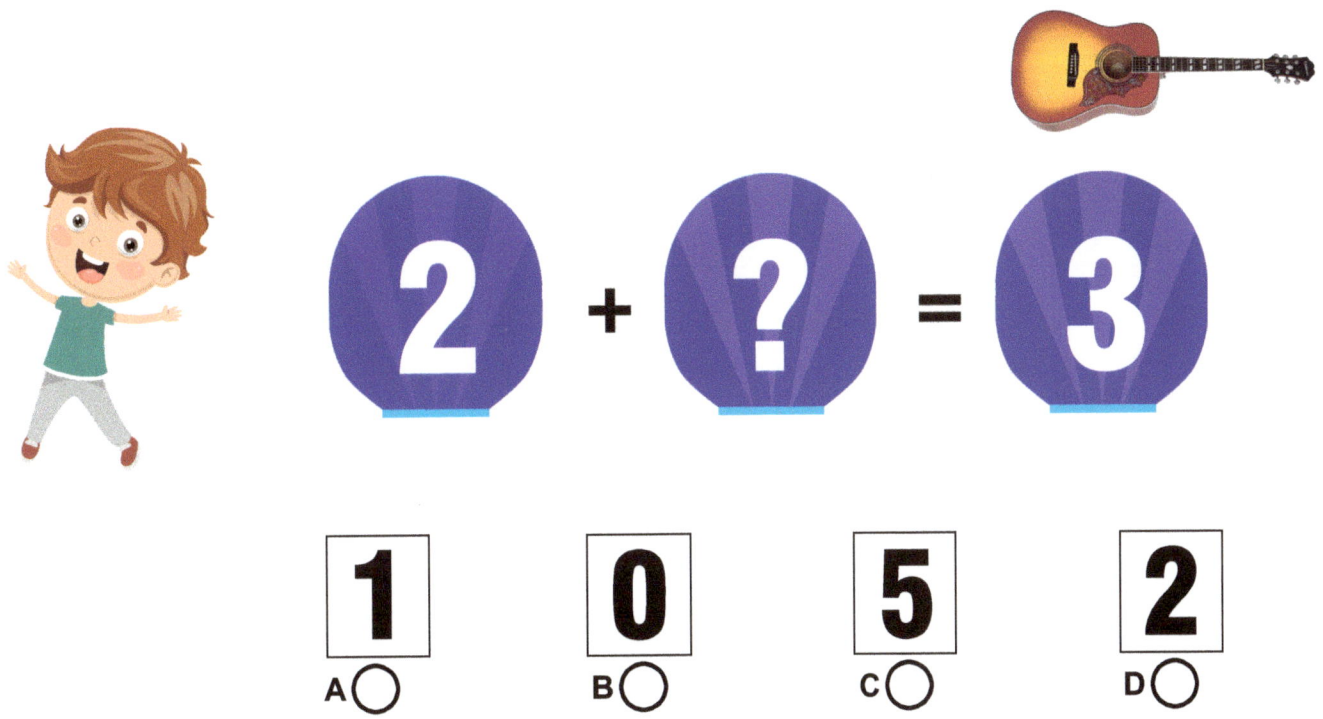

2 + ? = 3

1	0	5	2
A○	B○	C○	D○

Solution : A

How much should be added to 2 to make it 3

3 - 2 = 1

Meaning if we add 1 to 2 we get a total of three

www.math-knots.com

www.math-knots.com

Q-1

Look at the question and put your finger on the Sheep. Kevin is wondering what is the missing number under the question mark ? Help him to find the missing number under the question mark and fill in the bubble.

$$4 + ? = 8$$

A	B	C	D
4	0	2	8
A○	B○	C○	D○

Q-2

Look at the question and put your finger on the Turtle. Lilly is wondering what is the missing number under the question mark ? Help her to find the missing number under the question mark and fill in the bubble.

$$16 + ? = 22$$

A	B	C	D
5	7	0	6
A○	B○	C○	D○

www.math-knots.com

Q-3

Look at the question and put your finger on the Parrot. Riky is wondering what is the missing number under the question mark ? Help him to find the missing number under the question mark and fill in the bubble.

18	19	17	32
A○	B○	C○	D○

Q-4

Look at the question and put your finger on the Vampires Bat. Luke is wondering what is the missing number under the question mark ? Help him to find the missing number under the question mark and fill in the bubble.

15	11	8	7
A○	B○	C○	D○

www.math-knots.com

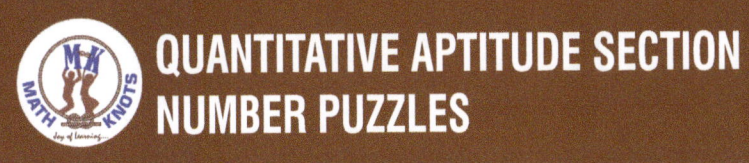
Q-5

Look at the question and put your finger on the Walrus. Bella is wondering what is the missing number under the question mark ? Help her to find the missing number under the question mark and fill in the bubble.

16	**22**	**14**	**15**
A ○	B ○	C ○	D ○

Q-6

Look at the question and put your finger on the Fish. Emma is wondering what is the missing number under the question mark ? Help her to find the missing number under the question mark and fill in the bubble.

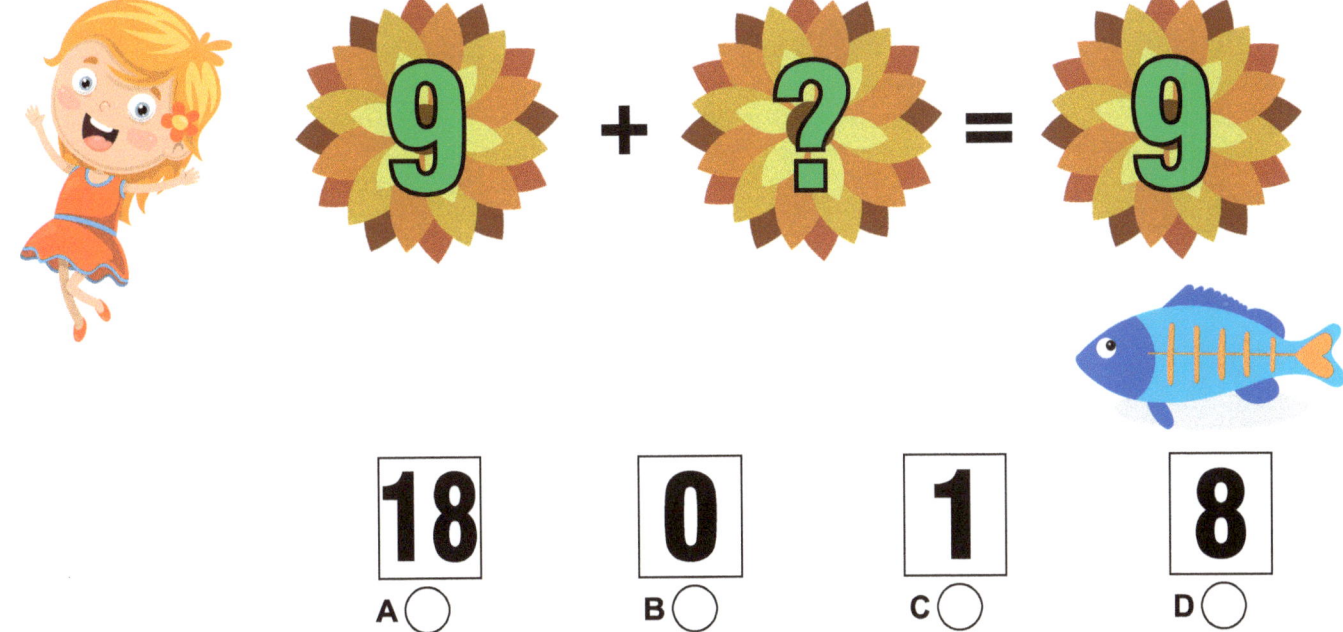

18	**0**	**1**	**8**
A ○	B ○	C ○	D ○

www.math-knots.com

Q-7 Look at the question and put your finger on the Yak. Sarah is wondering what is the missing number under the question mark ? Help her to find the missing number under the question mark and fill in the bubble.

| A ⭘ 10 | B ⭘ 9 | C ⭘ 15 | D ⭘ 14 |

Q-8 Look at the question and put your finger on the Zebra. Carter is wondering what is the missing number under the question mark ? Help him to find the missing number under the question mark and fill in the bubble.

| A ⭘ 0 | B ⭘ 3 | C ⭘ 9 | D ⭘ 6 |

www.math-knots.com

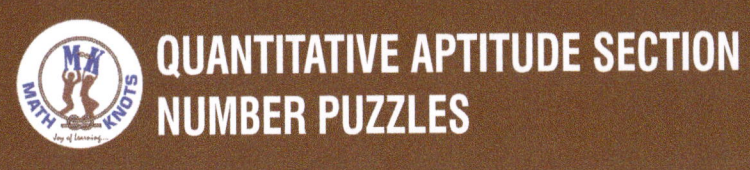
Q-9

Look at the question and put your finger on the Peacock. Zoe is wondering what is the missing number under the question mark ? Help her to find the missing number under the question mark and fill in the bubble.

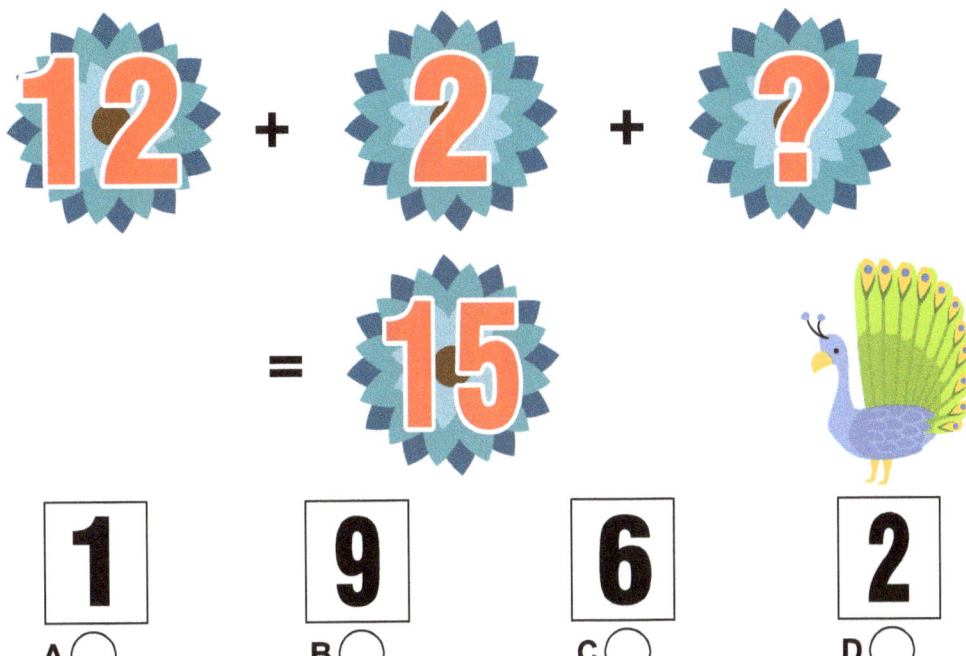

$$12 + 2 + ? $$
$$= 15$$

A	B	C	D
1	9	6	2

Q-10

Look at the question and put your finger on the Bird. Joshua is wondering what is the missing number under the question mark ? Help him to find the missing number under the question mark and fill in the bubble.

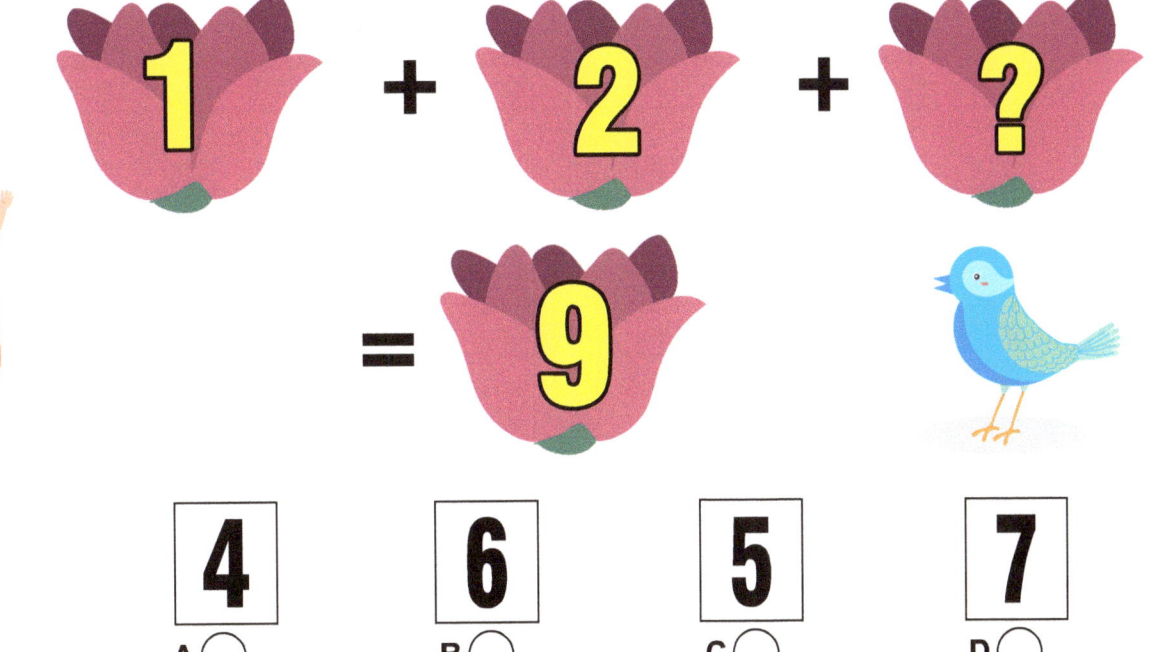

$$1 + 2 + ?$$
$$= 9$$

A	B	C	D
4	6	5	7

www.math-knots.com

Q-11 Look at the question and put your finger on the Cow. Julia is wondering what is the missing number under the question mark ? Help her to find the missing number under the question mark and fill in the bubble.

$$12 + ? + 12 = 36$$

| A ○ 14 | B ○ 12 | C ○ 10 | D ○ 11 |

Q-12 Look at the question and put your finger on the Dolphin. Aaron is wondering what is the missing number under the question mark ? Help him to find the missing number under the question mark and fill in the bubble.

$$13 + 14 + ? = 42$$

| A ○ 19 | B ○ 12 | C ○ 15 | D ○ 17 |

www.math-knots.com

Q-13 Look at the question and put your finger on the Elephant. Henry is wondering what is the missing number under the question mark ? Help him to find the missing number under the question mark and fill in the bubble.

$$25 + ? + 25 = 50$$

- A ○ **0**
- B ○ **10**
- C ○ **25**
- D ○ **20**

Q-14 Look at the question and put your finger on the Fox. Stella is wondering what is the missing number under the question mark ? Help her to find the missing number under the question mark and fill in the bubble.

$$9 + 16 + ? = 35$$

- A ○ **8**
- B ○ **12**
- C ○ **10**
- D ○ **11**

Q-15

Look at the question and put your finger on the Giraffe. Ruby is wondering what is the missing number under the question mark ? Help her to find the missing number under the question mark and fill in the bubble.

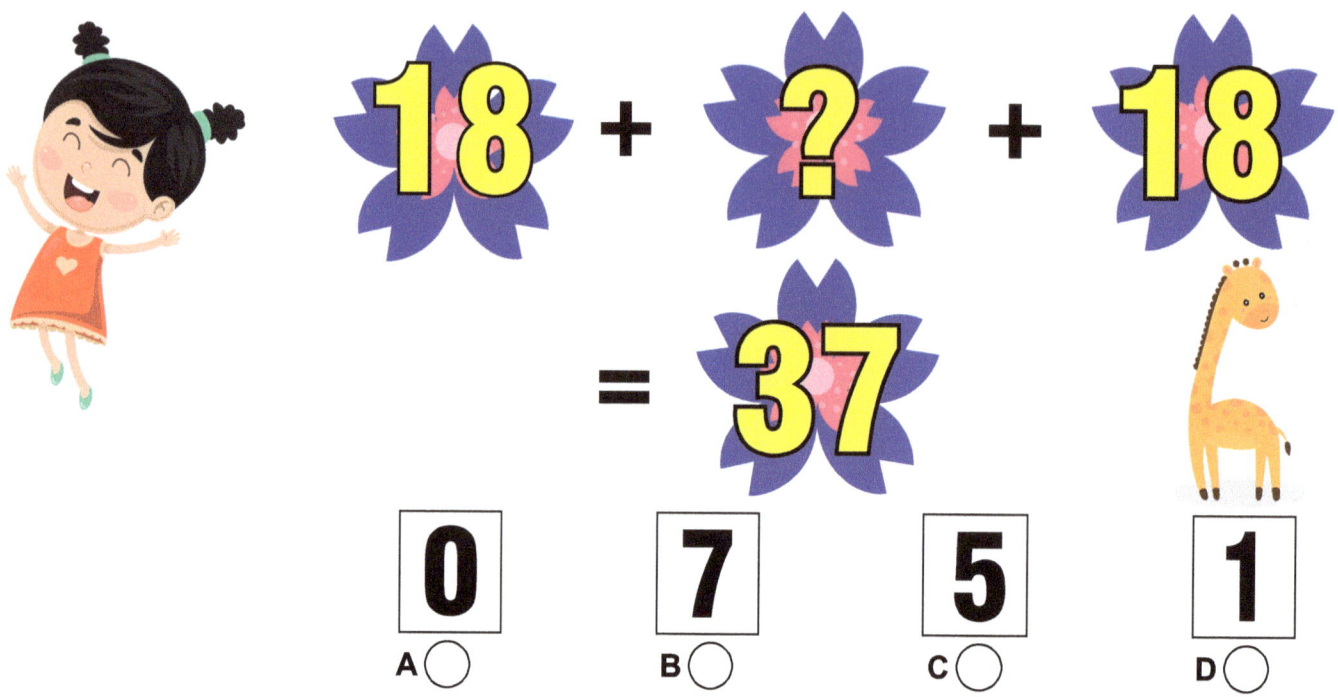

$$18 + ? + 18 = 37$$

A	B	C	D
0	7	5	1

Q-16

Look at the question and put your finger on the Hegehog. Diana is wondering what is the missing number under the question mark ? Help her to find the missing number under the question mark and fill in the bubble.

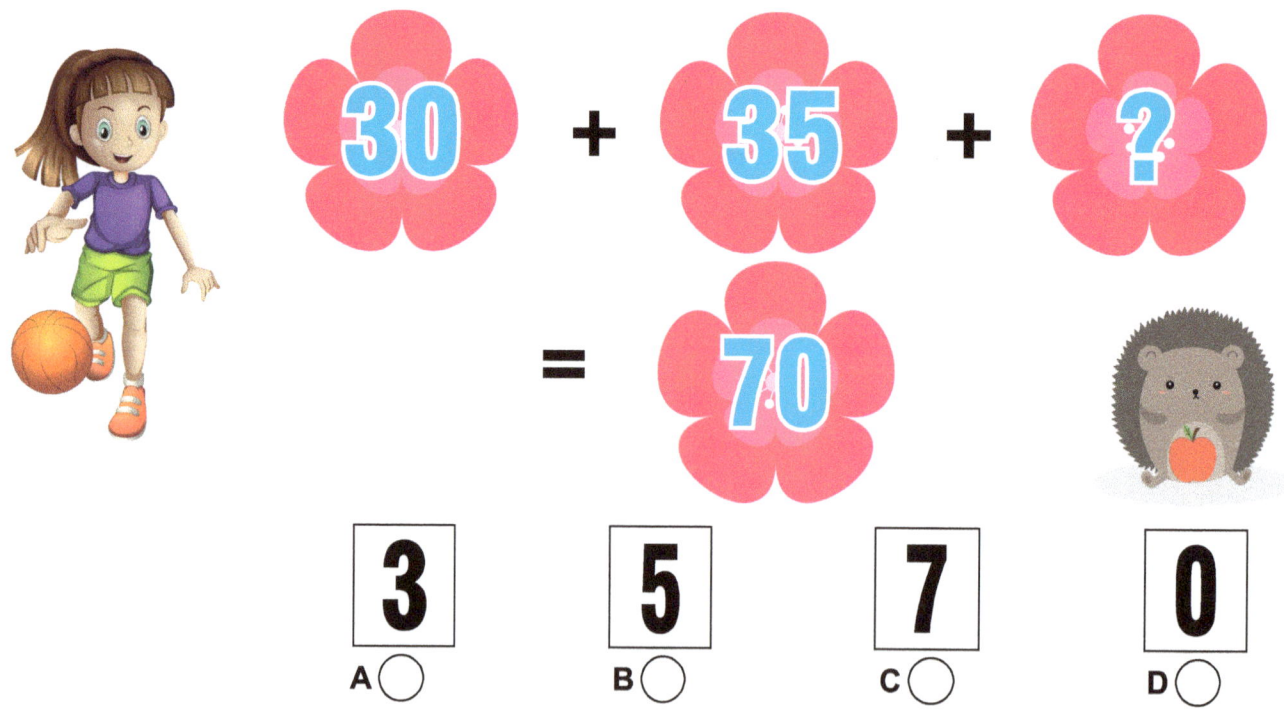

$$30 + 35 + ? = 70$$

A	B	C	D
3	5	7	0

www.math-knots.com

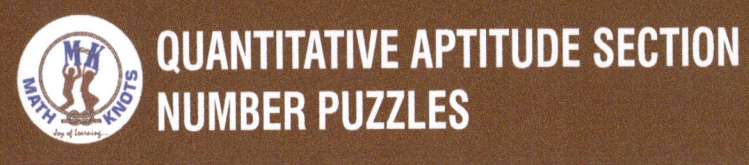
Q-17

Look at the question and put your finger on the Iguana. Nina is wondering what is the missing number under the question mark ? Help her to find the missing number under the question mark and fill in the bubble.

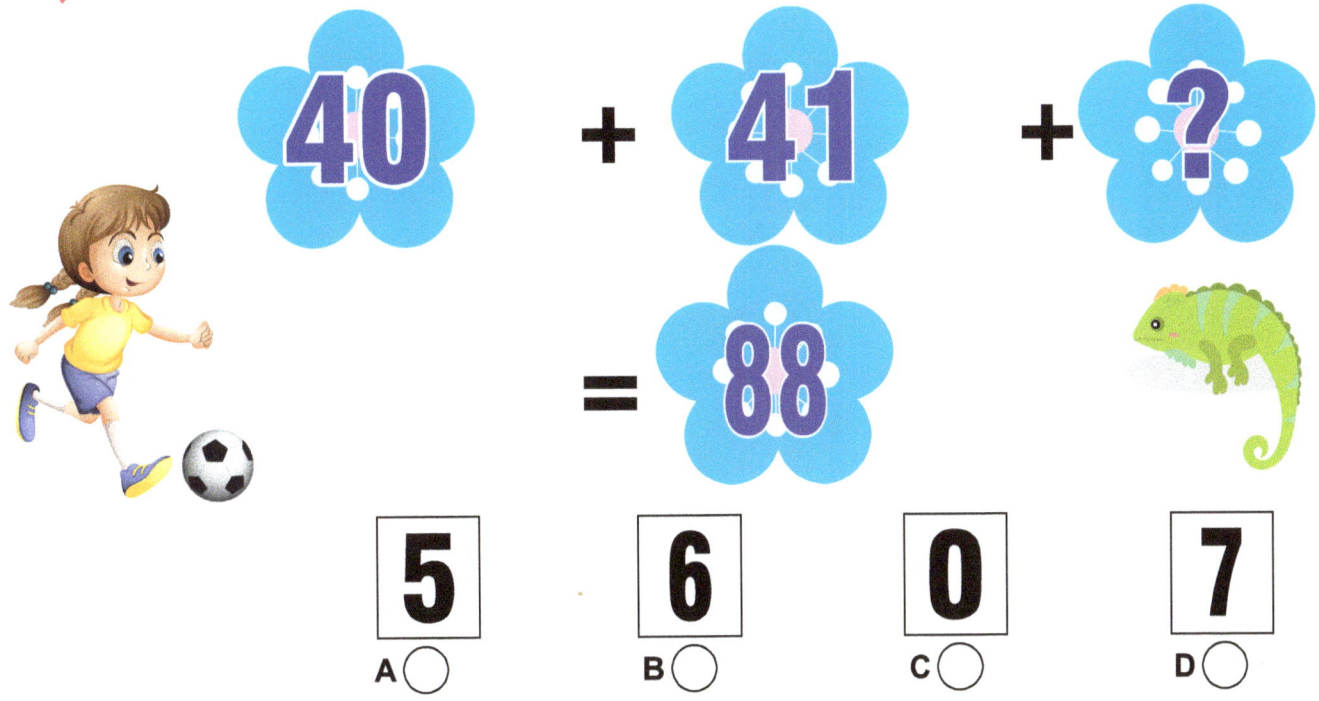

$$40 + 41 + ? = 88$$

A	B	C	D
5	6	0	7

Q-18

Look at the question and put your finger on the Jelly Fish. Lola is wondering what is the missing number under the question mark ? Help her to find the missing number under the question mark and fill in the bubble.

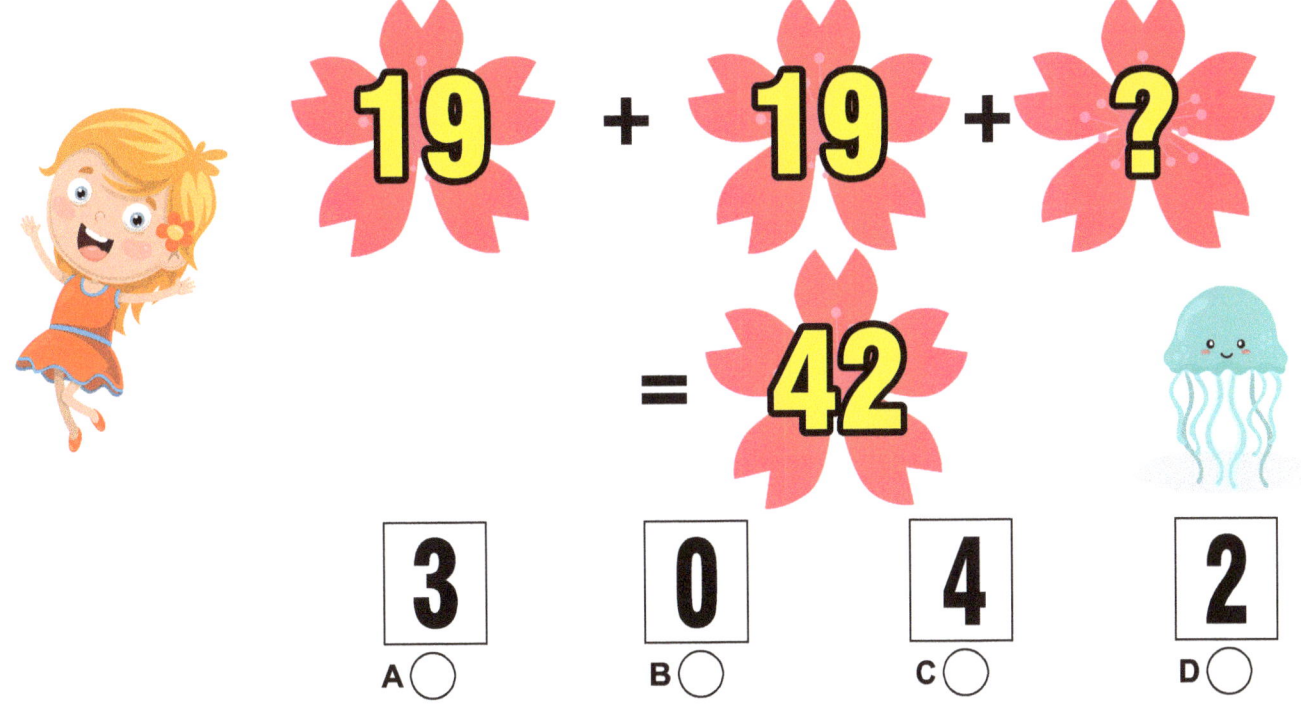

$$19 + 19 + ? = 42$$

A	B	C	D
3	0	4	2

www.math-knots.com

Q-19 Look at the question and put your finger on the Koala Bear. Erick is wondering what is the missing number under the question mark ? Help him to find the missing number under the question mark and fill in the bubble.

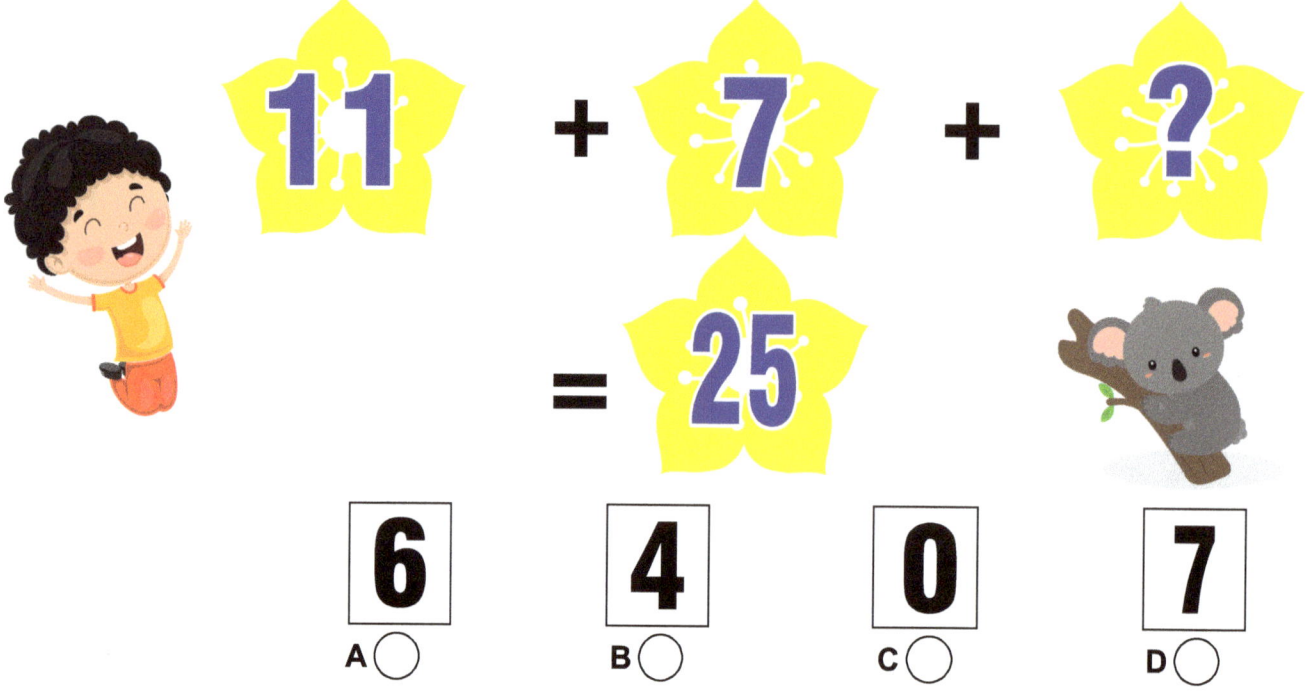

$$11 + 7 + ? = 25$$

A	B	C	D
6	4	0	7
○	○	○	○

Q-20 Look at the question and put your finger on the Lion. Amber is wondering what is the missing number under the question mark ? Help her to find the missing number under the question mark and fill in the bubble.

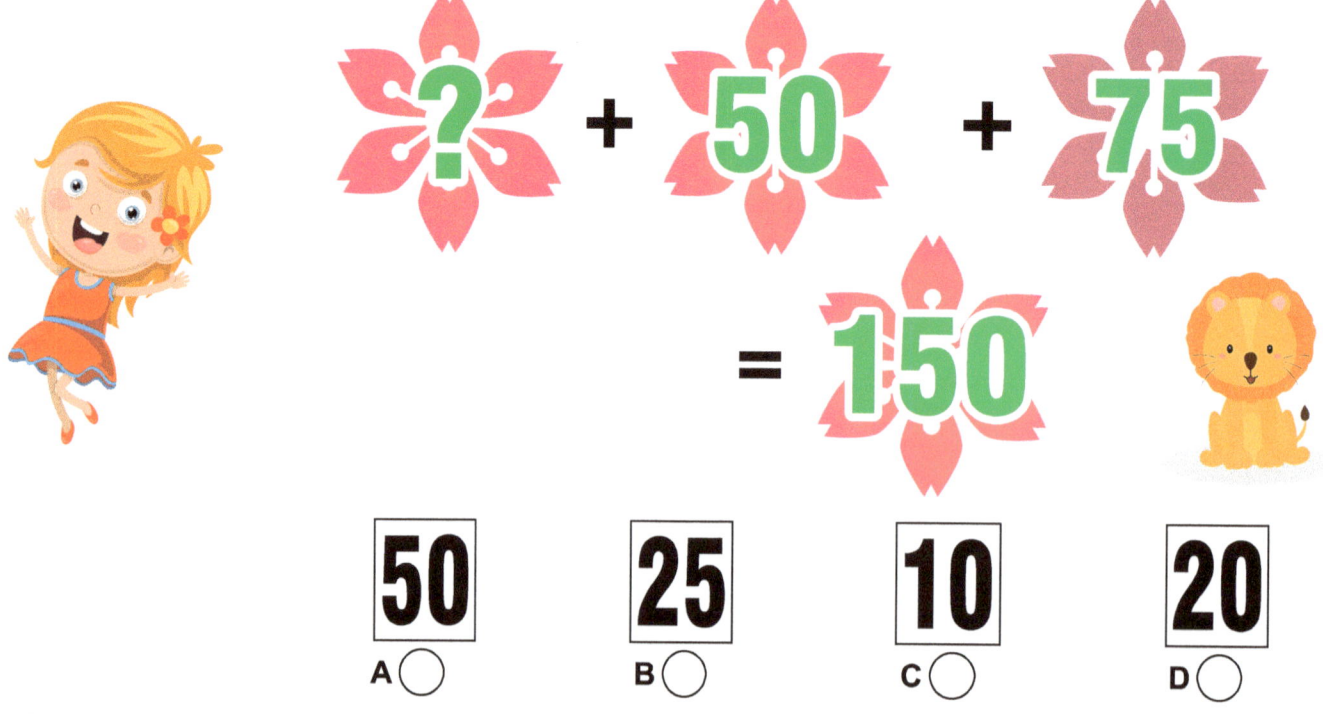

$$? + 50 + 75 = 150$$

A	B	C	D
50	25	10	20
○	○	○	○

www.math-knots.com

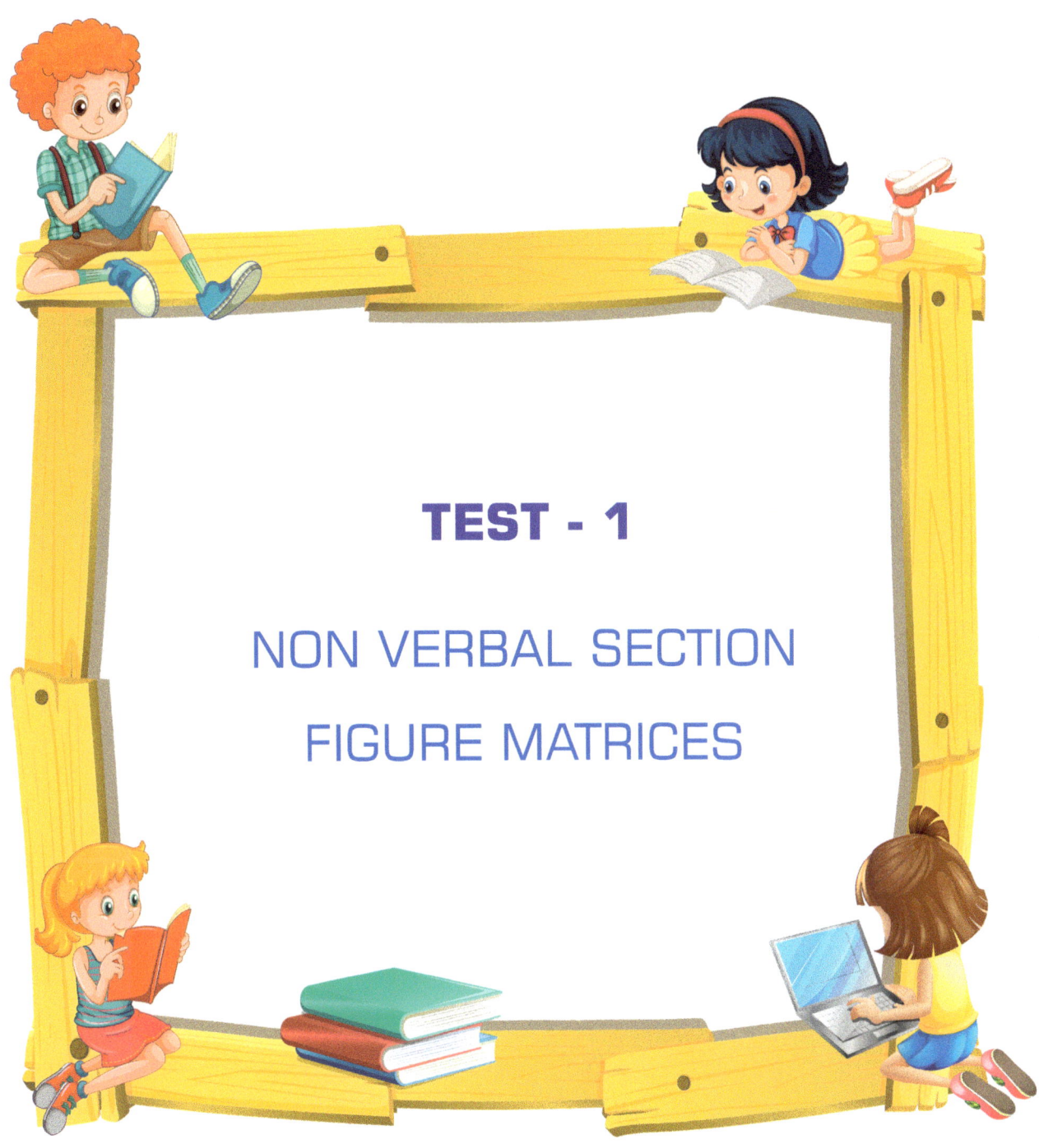

TEST - 1

NON VERBAL SECTION

FIGURE MATRICES

Lets Start the Test...

www.math-knots.com

Sample Look at the question with the Tree. The first three pictures belong to one group in a common way. Help Bob to find out which of the below options belong to the same group. Identify the correct picture and help him to bubble the right choice.

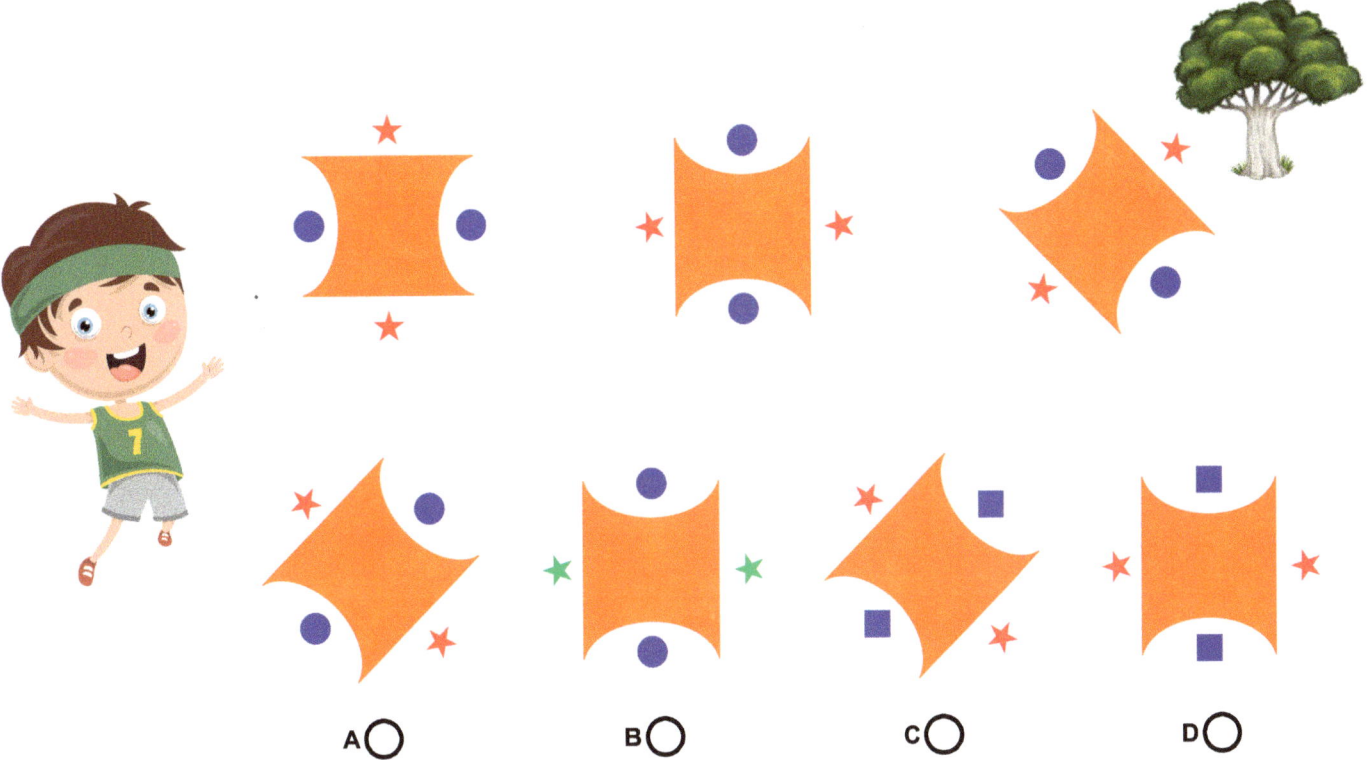

A○   B○   C○   D○

Solution : A

Option A is the only right choice. Option A matches the rest of the figure group in the same way. The other option vary in some way. Pay attention to all options before answering the right choice.

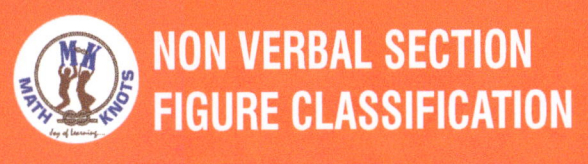

Q-1

Look at the question with the Coconut. The first three pictures belong to one group in a common way. Help Jacob to find out which of the below options belong to the same group. Identify the correct picture and help him to bubble the right choice.

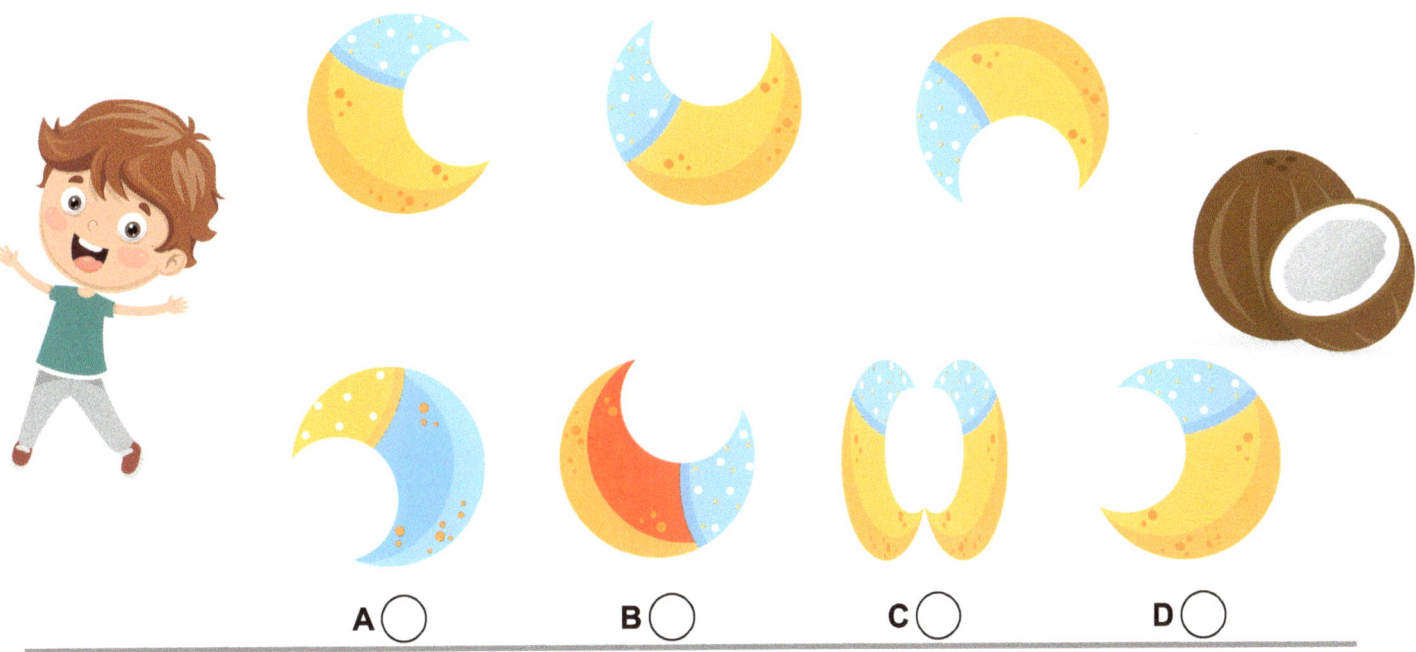

A ◯   B ◯   C ◯   D ◯

Q-2

Look at the question with the Banana. The first three pictures belong to one group in a common way. Help Emma to find out which of the below options belong to the same group. Identify the correct picture and help her to bubble the right choice.

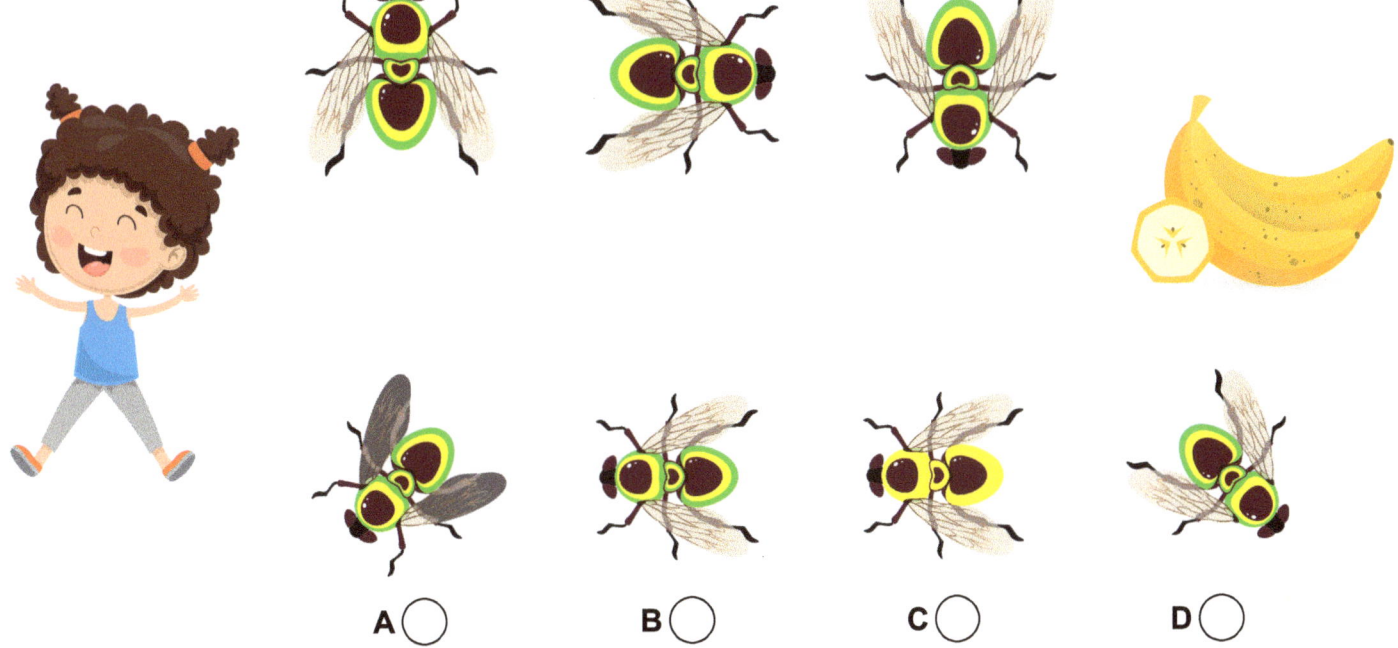

A ◯   B ◯   C ◯   D ◯

www.math-knots.com

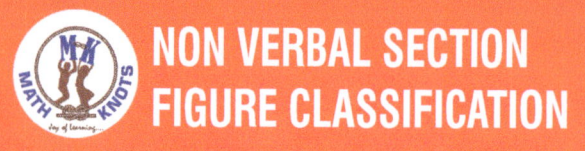
Q-3

Look at the question with the Mangosteen. The first three pictures belong to one group in a common way. Help Michael to find out which of the below options belong to the same group. Identify the correct picture and help him to bubble the right choice.

A ⃝　　B ⃝　　C ⃝　　D ⃝

Q-4

Look at the question with the Apple. The first three pictures belong to one group in a common way. Help Olivia to find out which of the below options belong to the same group. Identify the correct picture and help her to bubble the right choice.

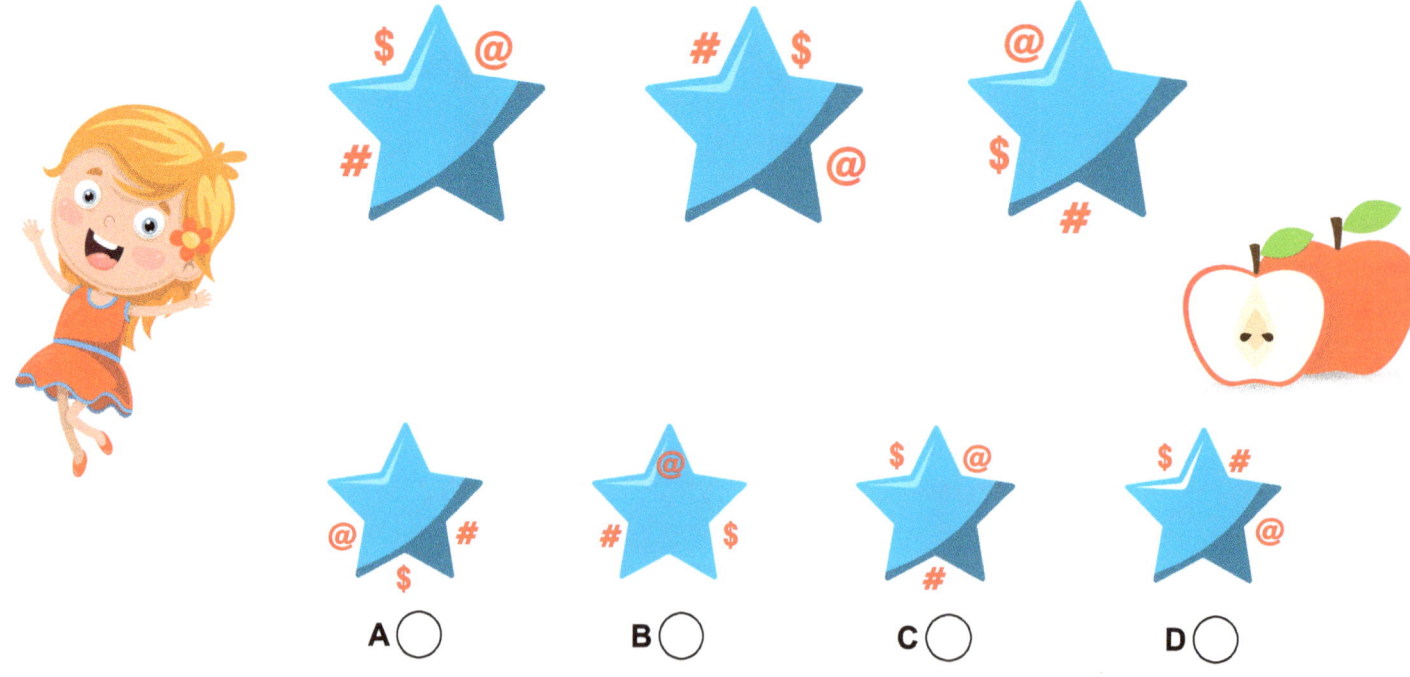

A ⃝　　B ⃝　　C ⃝　　D ⃝

www.math-knots.com

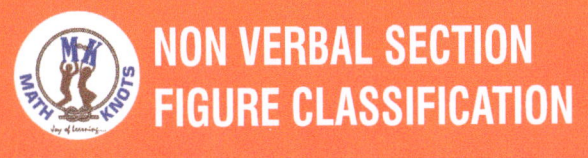
Q-5

Look at the question with the Pear. The first three pictures belong to one group in a common way. Help Matthew to find out which of the below options belong to the same group. Identify the correct picture and help him to bubble the right choice.

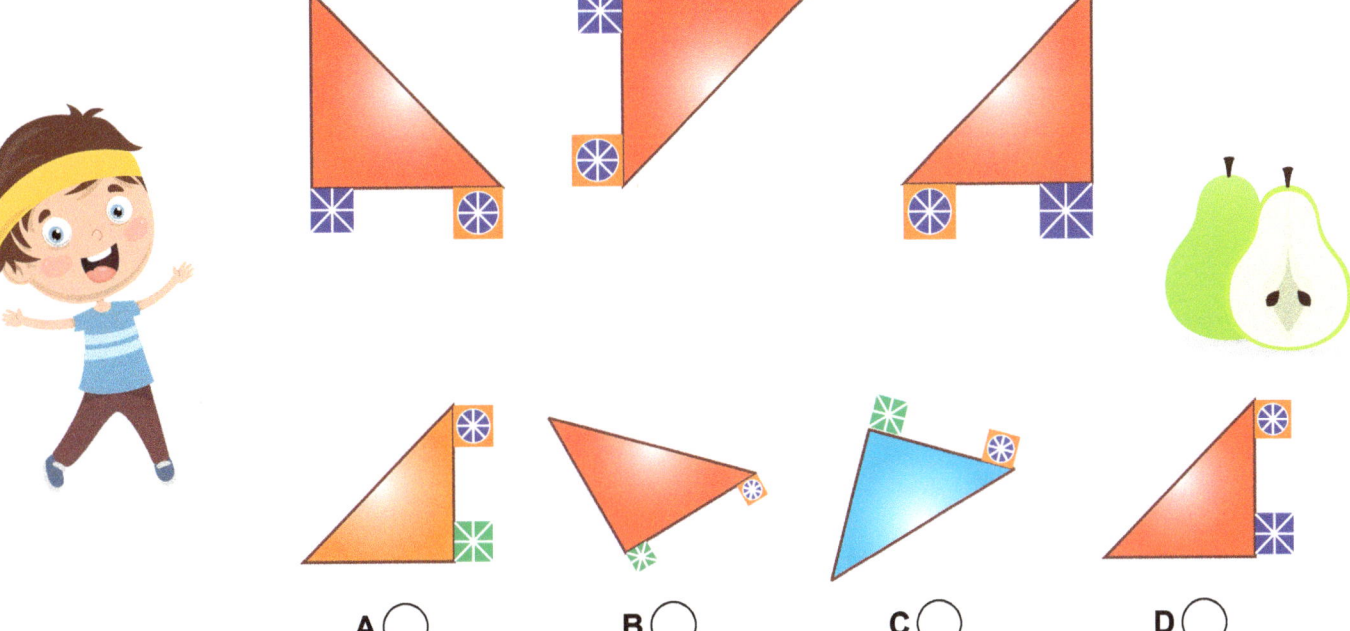

A ◯   B ◯   C ◯   D ◯

Q-6

Look at the question with the Durian. The first three pictures belong to one group in a common way. Help Sophia to find out which of the below options belong to the same group. Identify the correct picture and help her to bubble the right choice.

A ◯   B ◯   C ◯   D ◯

www.math-knots.com

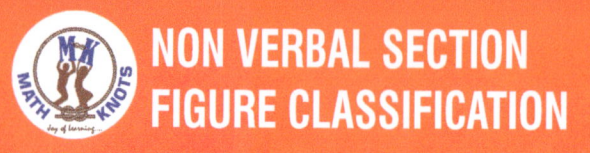

Q-7

Look at the question with the Peach. The first three pictures belong to one group in a common way. Help Ethan to find out which of the below options belong to the same group. Identify the correct picture and help him to bubble the right choice.

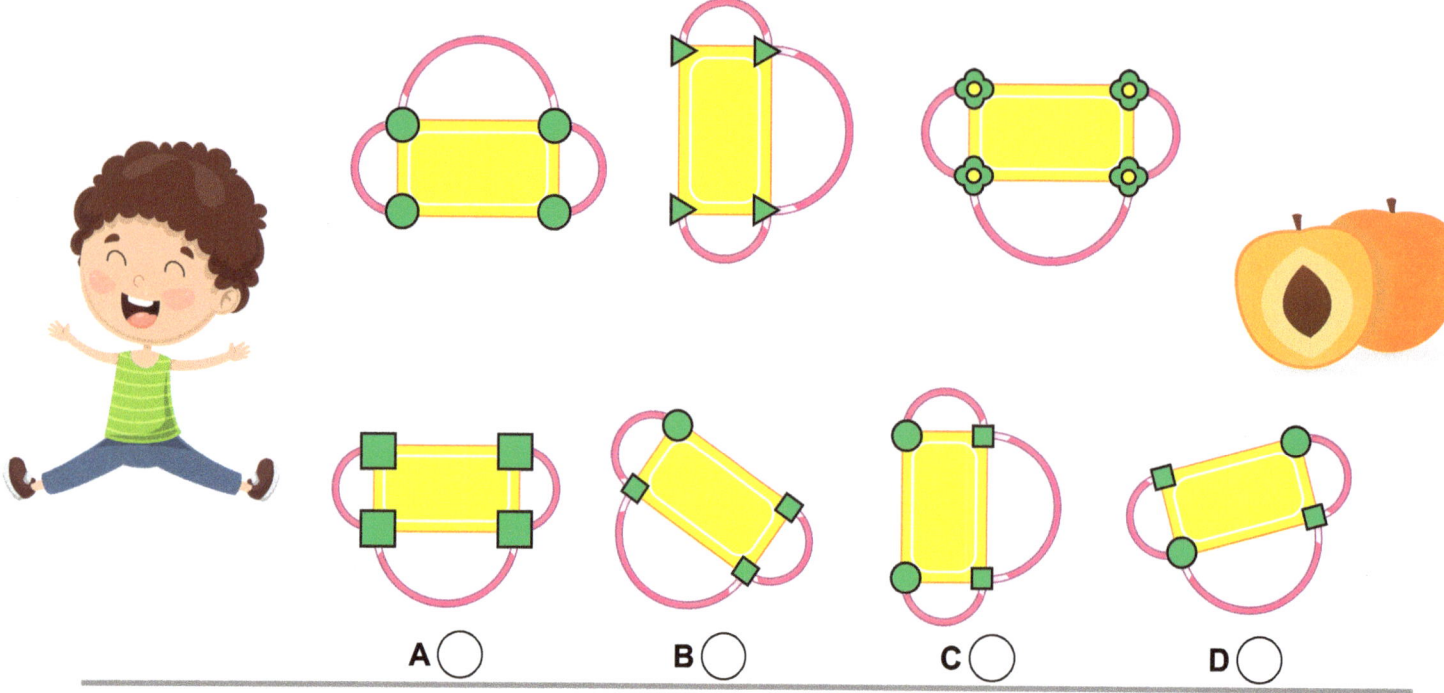

A ◯　　B ◯　　C ◯　　D ◯

Q-8

Look at the question with the Dragon Fruit. The first three pictures belong to one group in a common way. Help Elizabeth to find out which of the below options belong to the same group. Identify the correct picture and help her to bubble the right choice.

A ◯　　B ◯　　C ◯　　D ◯

www.math-knots.com

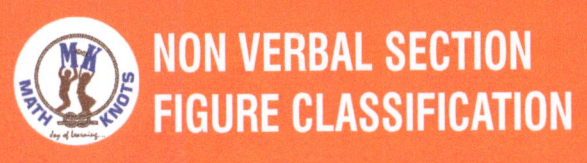

Q-9 Look at the question with the Plum. The first three pictures belong to one group in a common way. Help Andrew to find out which of the below options belong to the same group. Identify the correct picture and help him to bubble the right choice.

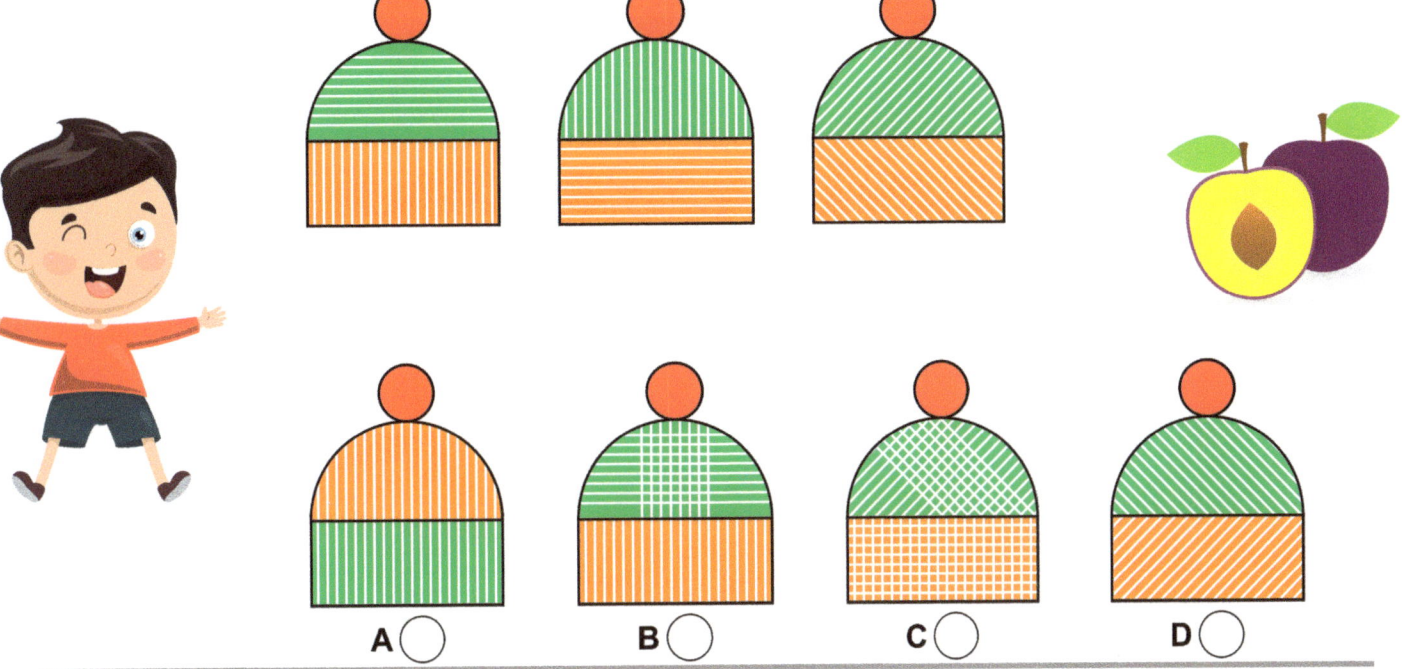

A ○ B ○ C ○ D ○

Q-10 Look at the question with the Papaya. The first three pictures belong to one group in a common way. Help Jessica to find out which of the below options belong to the same group. Identify the correct picture and help her to bubble the right choice.

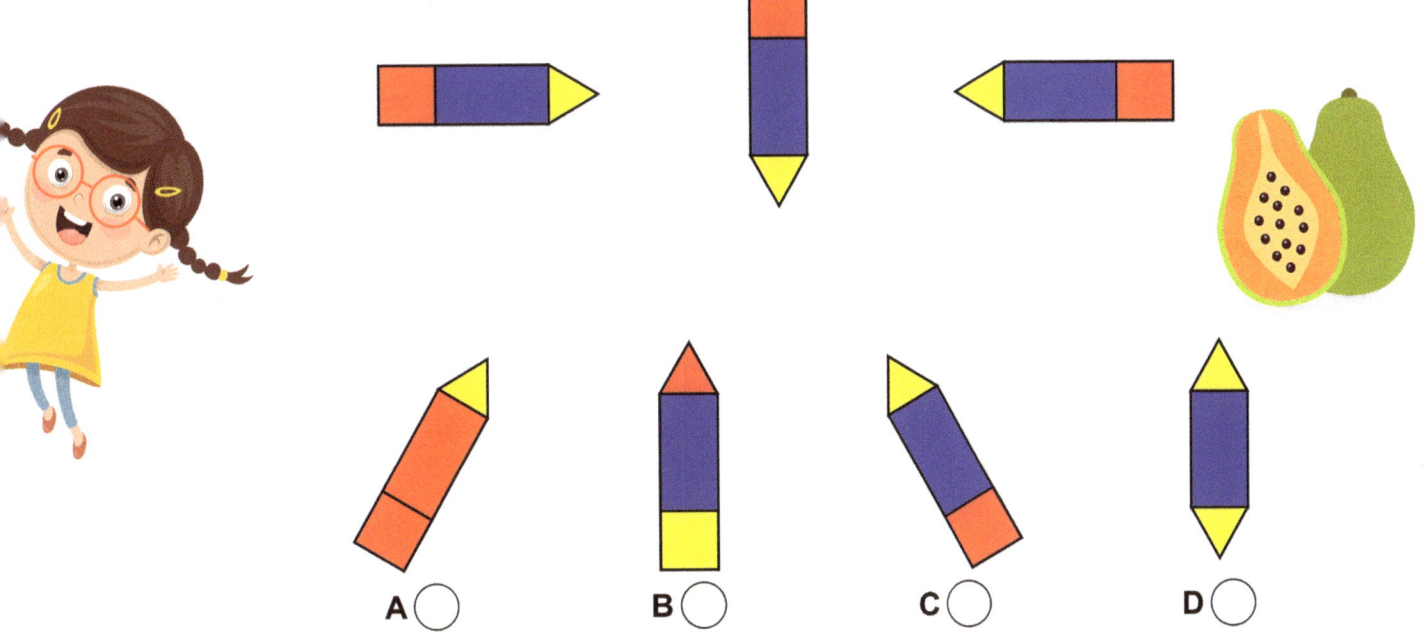

A ○ B ○ C ○ D ○

www.math-knots.com

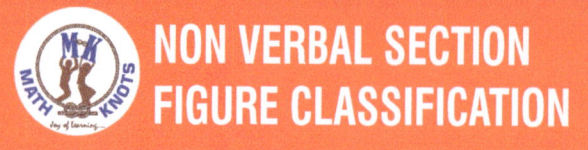

Q-11

Look at the question with the Watermelon. The first three pictures belong to one group in a common way. Help Daniel to find out which of the below options belong to the same group. Identify the correct picture and help him to bubble the right choice.

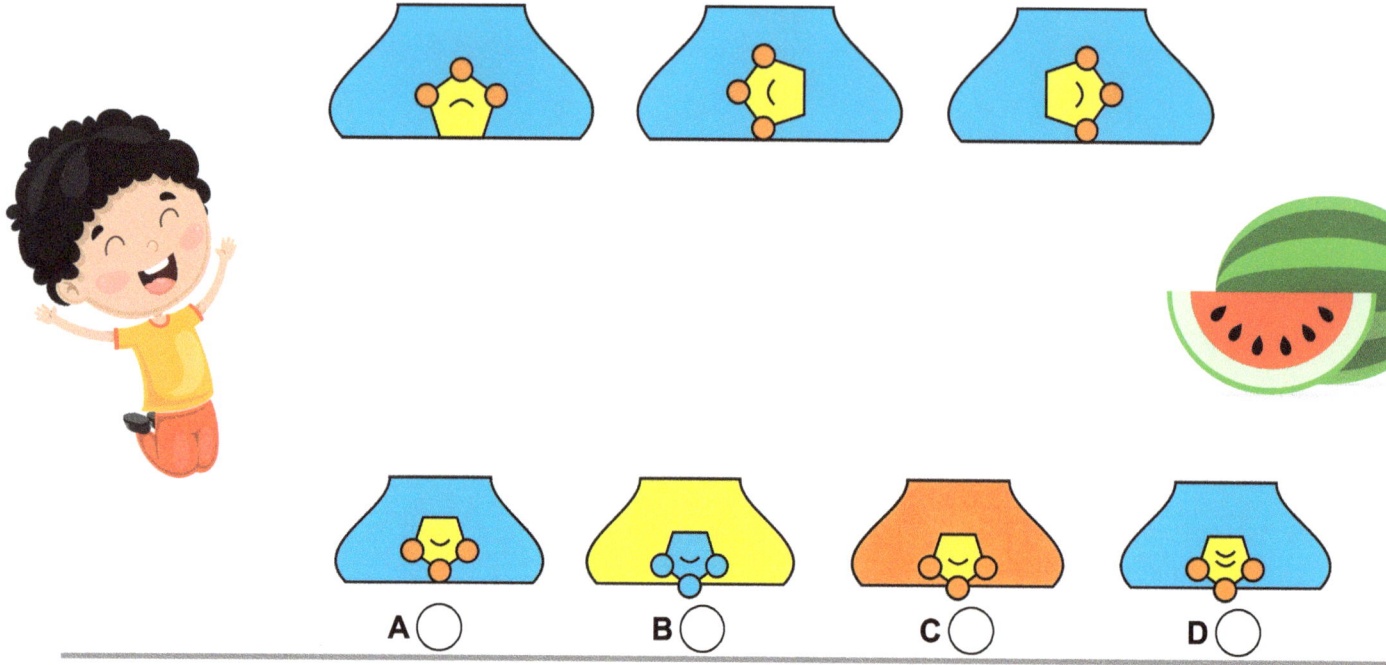

A ◯ B ◯ C ◯ D ◯

Q-12

Look at the question with the Orange. The first three pictures belong to one group in a common way. Help Julia to find out which of the below options belong to the same group. Identify the correct picture and help her to bubble the right choice.

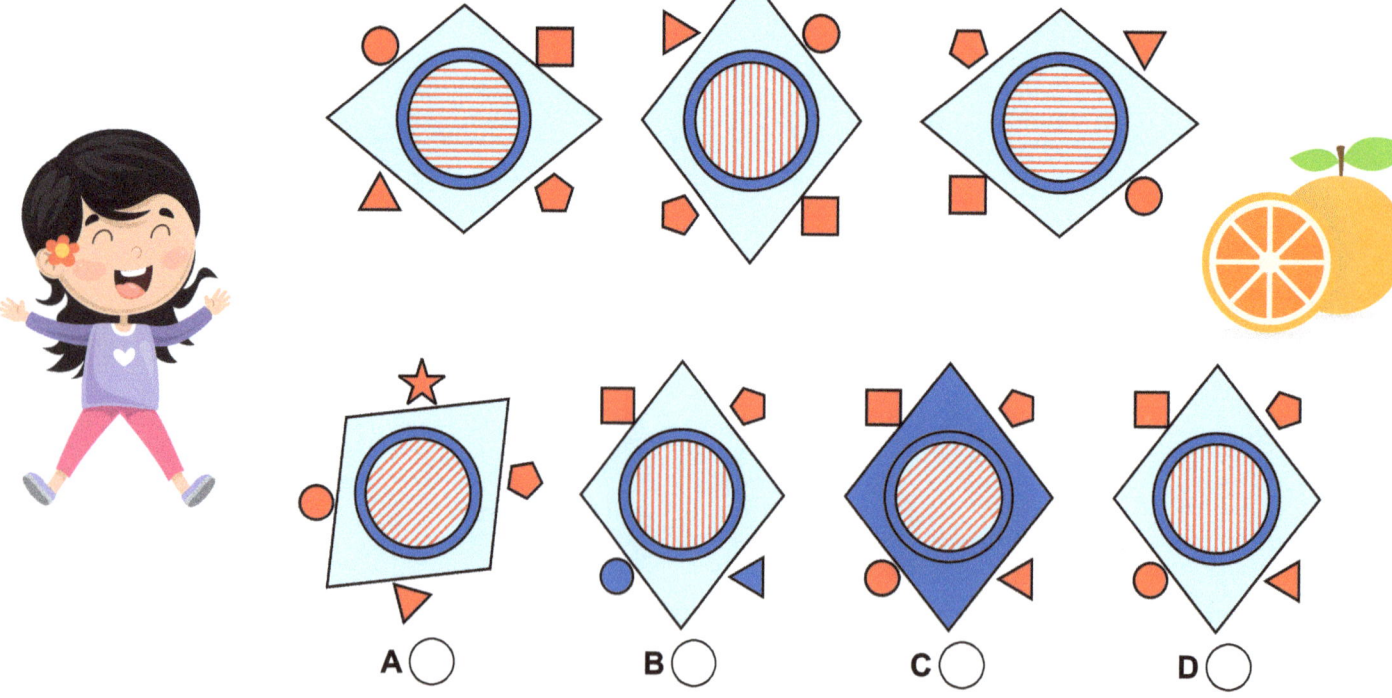

A ◯ B ◯ C ◯ D ◯

www.math-knots.com

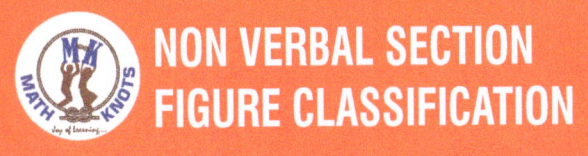
Q-13

Look at the question with the Kiwi. The first three pictures belong to one group in a common way. Help Anthony to find out which of the below options belong to the same group. Identify the correct picture and help him to bubble the right choice.

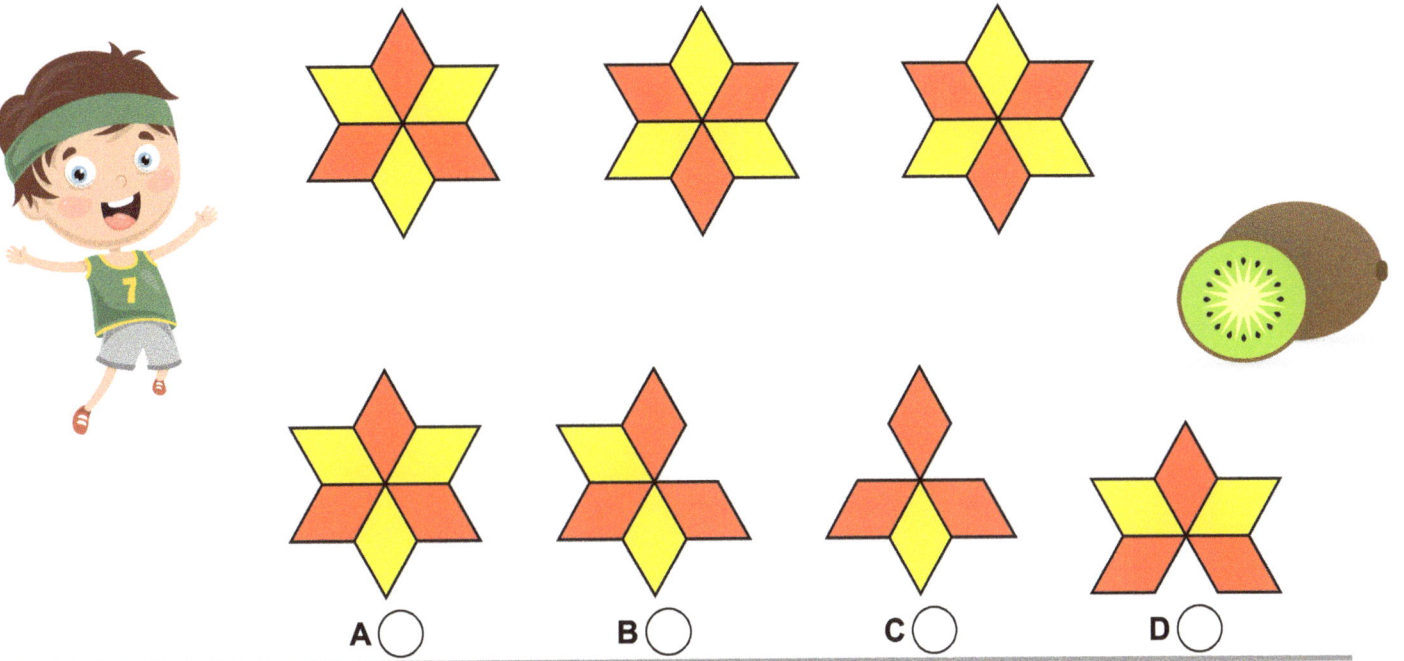

A◯   B◯   C◯   D◯

Q-14

Look at the question with the Lemon. The first three pictures belong to one group in a common way. Help Jenna to find out which of the below options belong to the same group. Identify the correct picture and help her to bubble the right choice.

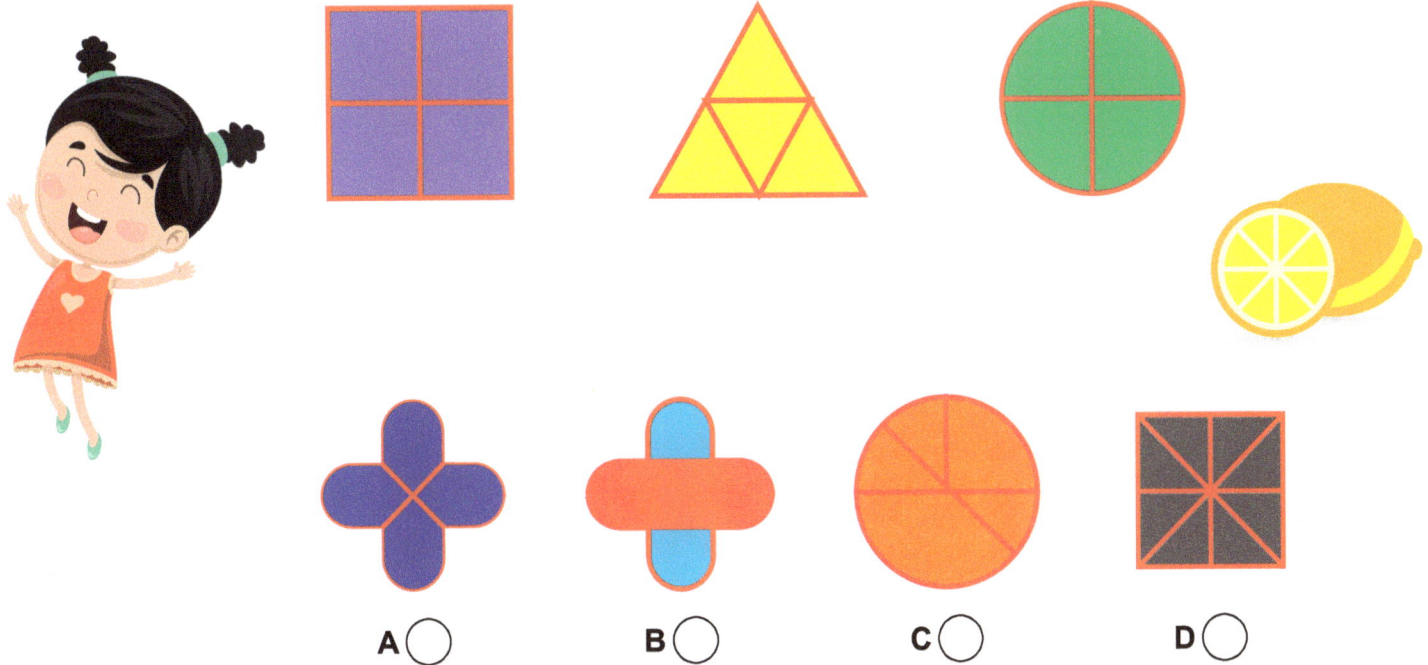

A◯   B◯   C◯   D◯

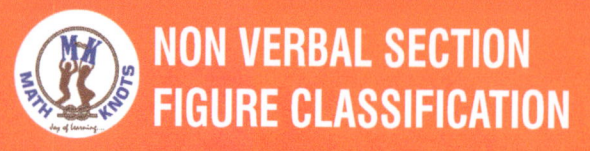
Q-15

Look at the question with the Avocado. The first three pictures belong to one group in a common way. Help William to find out which of the below options belong to the same group. Identify the correct picture and help him to bubble the right choice.

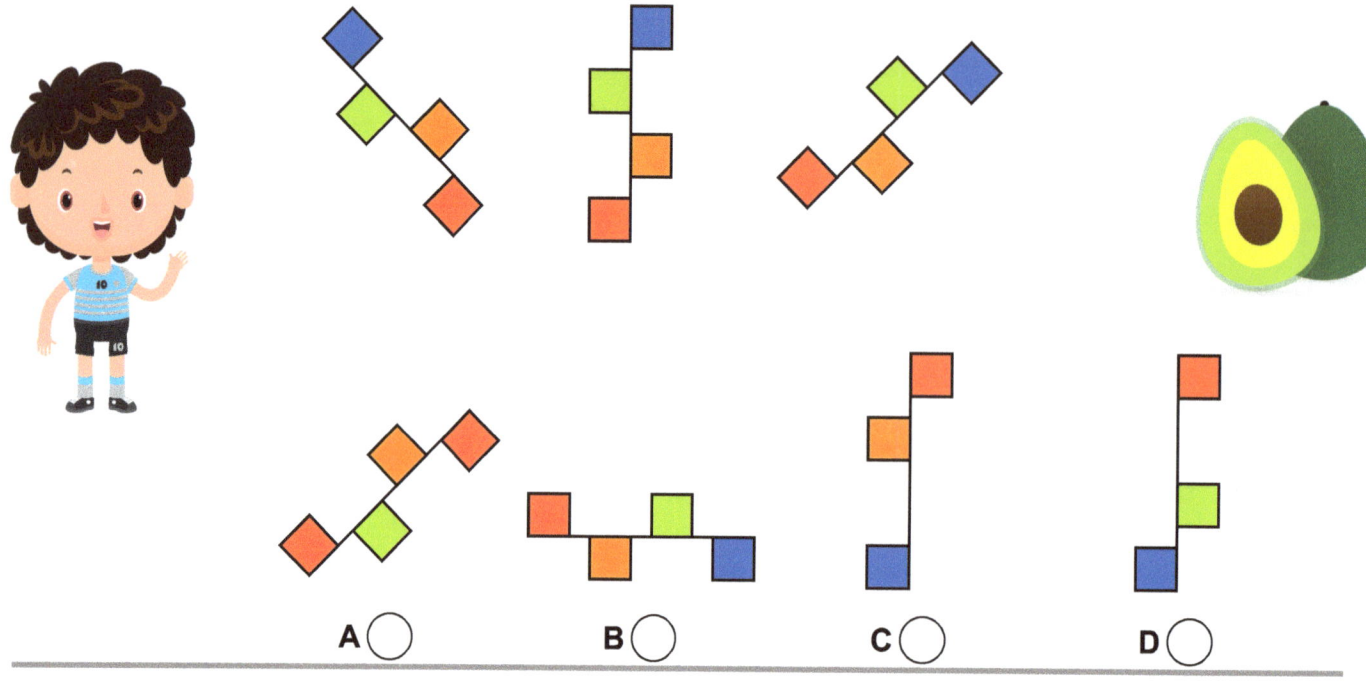

A ◯   **B** ◯   **C** ◯   **D** ◯

Q-16

Look at the question with the Grapes. The first three pictures belong to one group in a common way. Help Mary to find out which of the below options belong to the same group. Identify the correct picture and help her to bubble the right choice.

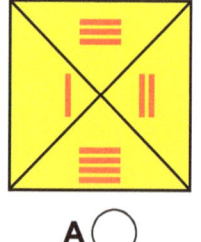
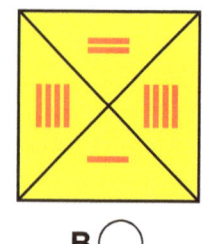
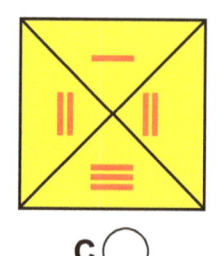

A ◯   **B** ◯   **C** ◯   **D** ◯

www.math-knots.com

Q-17

Look at the question with the Capsicum. The first three pictures belong to one group in a common way. Help David to find out which of the below options belong to the same group. Identify the correct picture and help him to bubble the right choice.

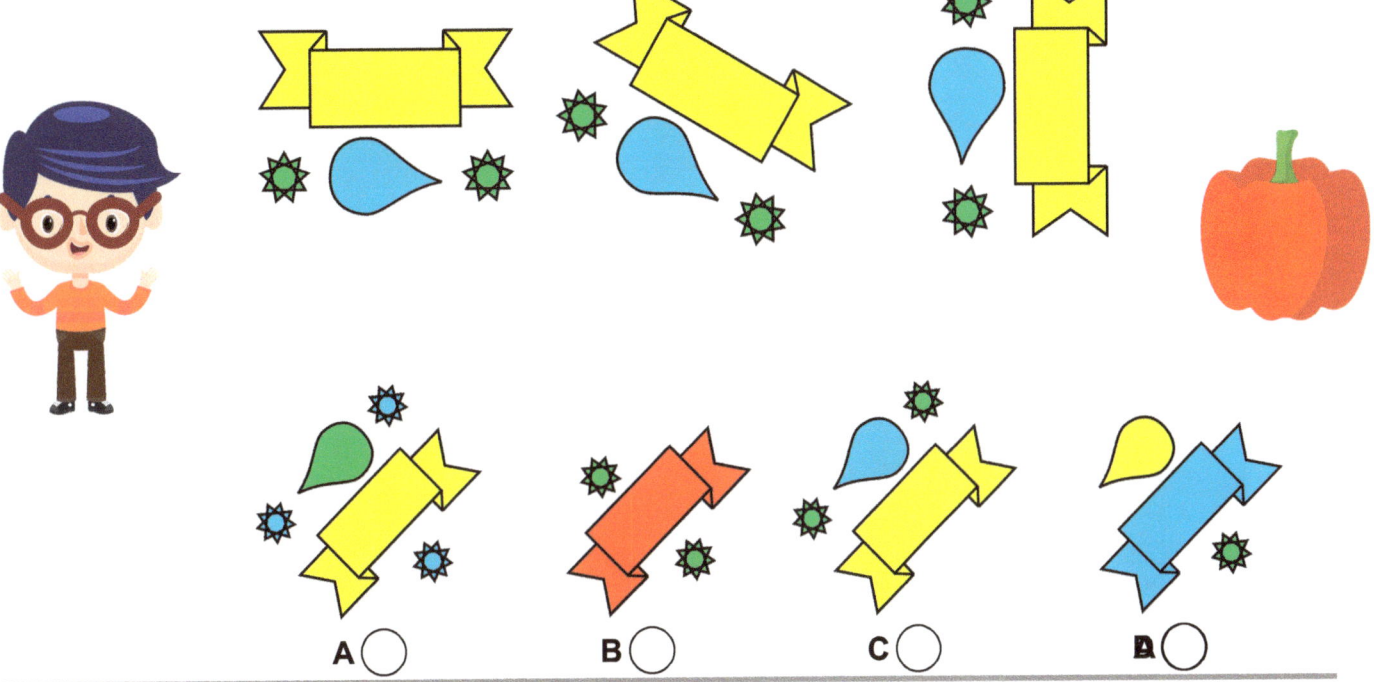

A◯   B◯   C◯   D◯

Q-18

Look at the question with the Cucumber. The first three pictures belong to one group in a common way. Help Amy to find out which of the below options belong to the same group. Identify the correct picture and help her to bubble the right choice.

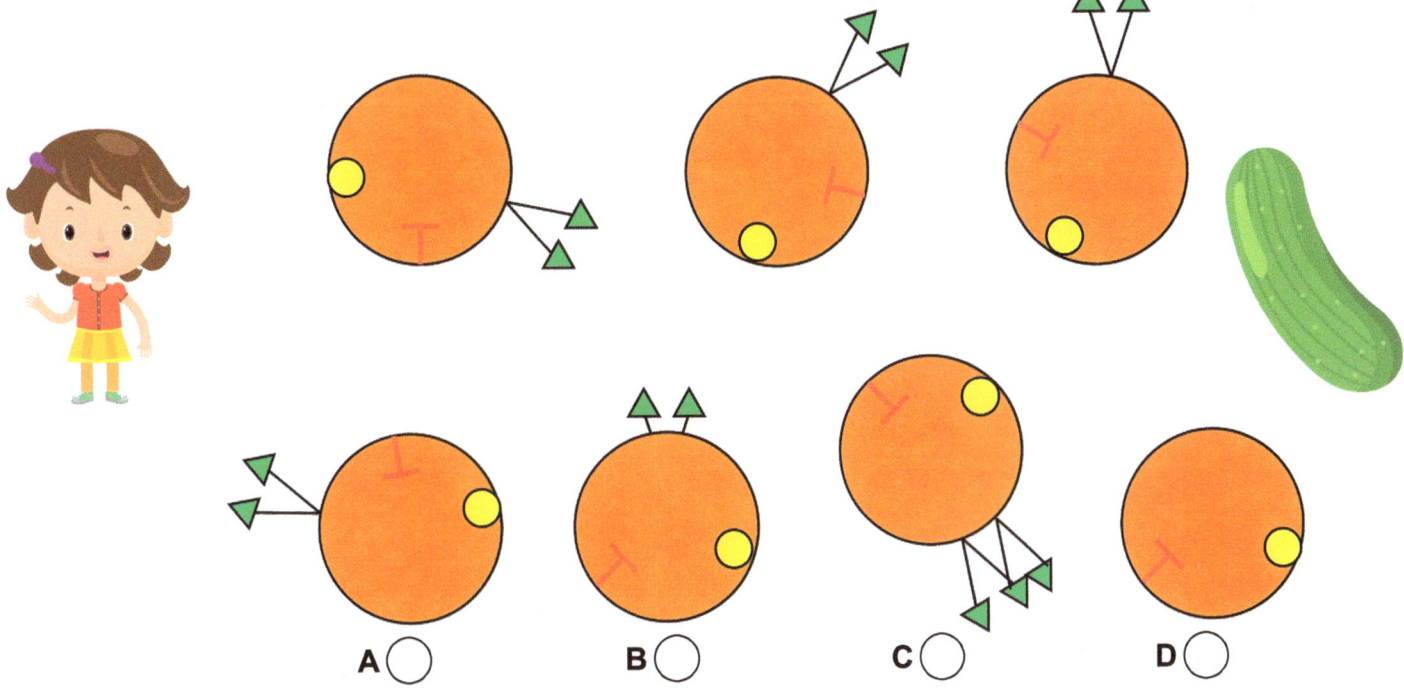

A◯   B◯   C◯   D◯

www.math-knots.com

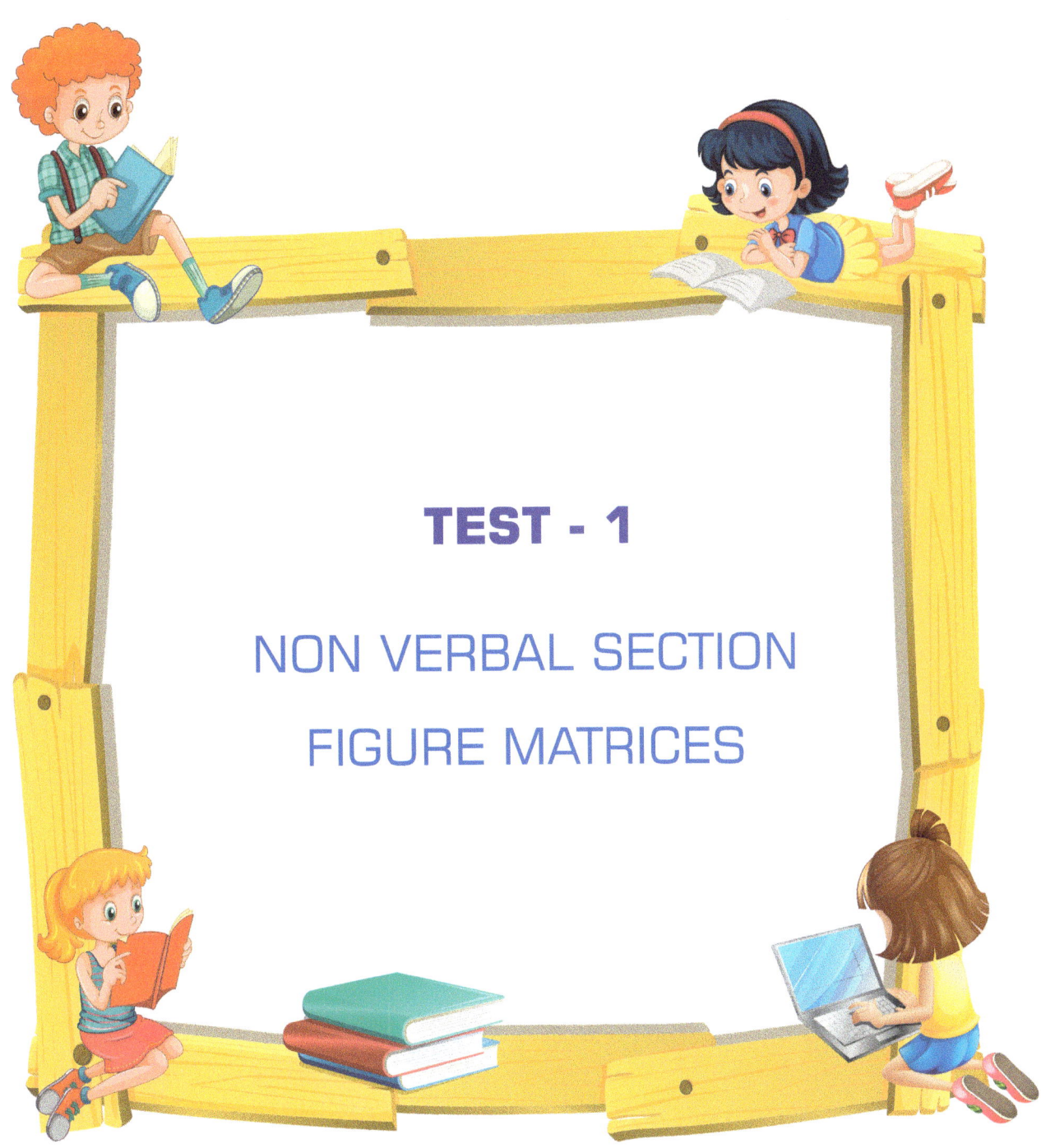

TEST - 1

NON VERBAL SECTION

FIGURE MATRICES

Lets Start the Test...

www.math-knots.com

Sample

Look at the question with the Grapes. The first row has some thing in common as the second row. Can you help Mary to identify what goes in the space of the question mark from the four given options A, B, C, and D. Choose the correct option.

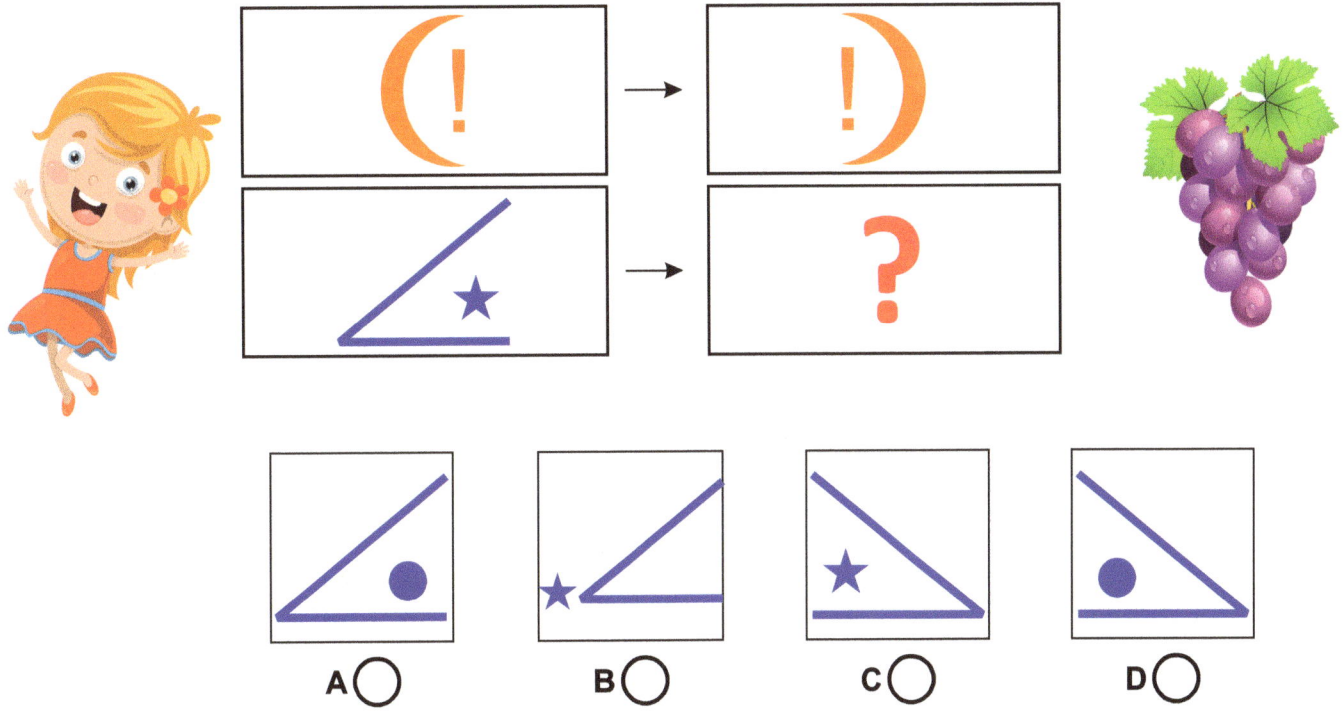

Solution : C

Option C is the right choice.

Two pictures in the first row are related in a certain way and the figures and flipped.

When the picture in the second row is flipped it will be match to option C.

Students need to pay attention. Figures can be turning clock wise into anti clock wise, and other possibilities.

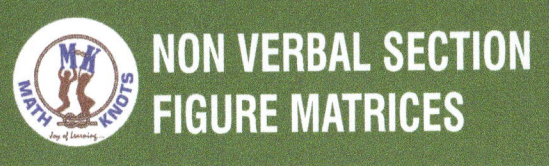

Q-1

Look at the question with the Lion Fish. The first row has some thing in common as the second row. Can you help Sophia to identify what goes in the space of the question mark from the four given options A, B, C, and D. Choose the correct option.

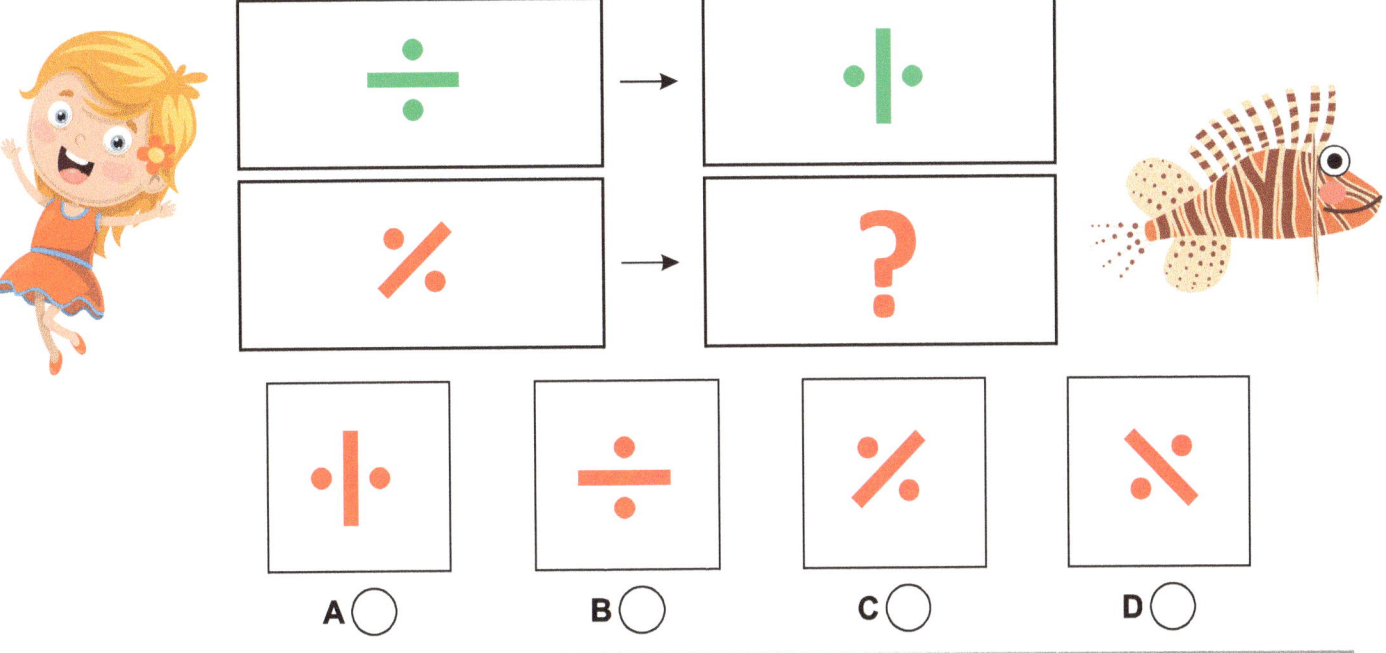

Q-2

Look at the question with the Blow Fish. The first row has some thing in common as the second row. Can you help George to identify what goes in the space of the question mark from the four given options A, B, C, and D. Choose the correct option.

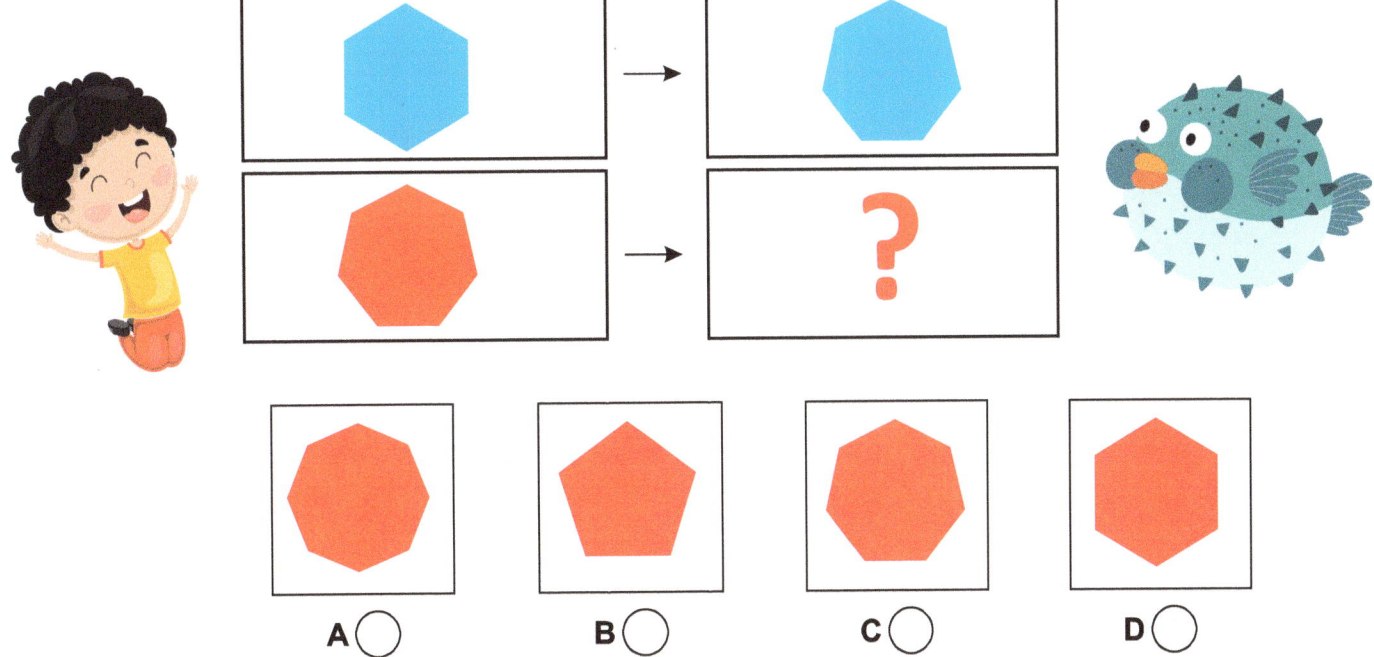

www.math-knots.com

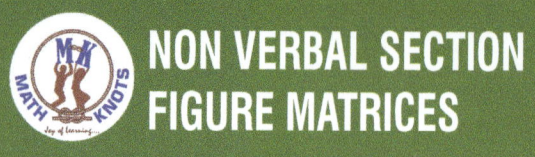

Q-3

Look at the question with the Jackknife Fish. The first row has some thing in common as the second row. Can you help Harry to identify what goes in the space of the question mark from the four given options A, B, C, and D. Choose the correct option.

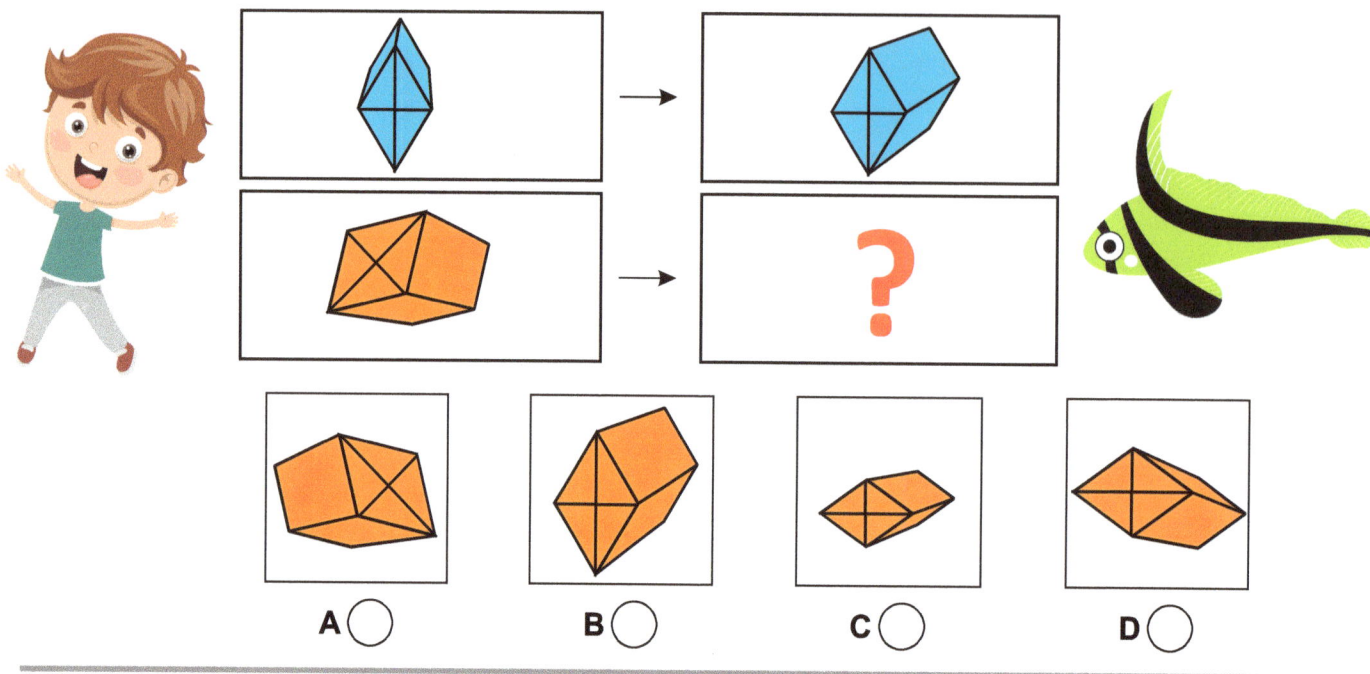

Q-4

Look at the question with the Sponge Fish. The first row has some thing in common as the second row. Can you help Jack to identify what goes in the space of the question mark from the four given options A, B, C, and D. Choose the correct option.

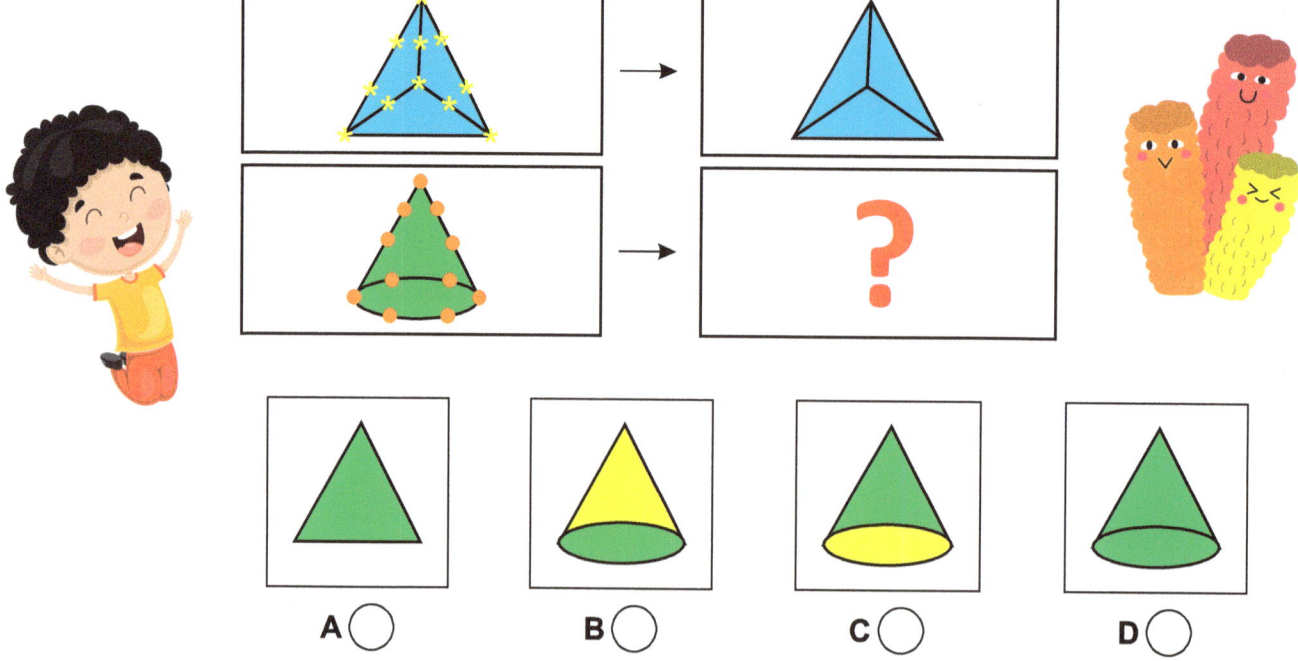

www.math-knots.com

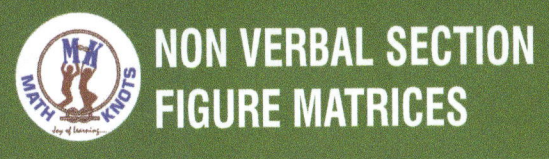

Q-5

Look at the question with the Blob Fish. The first row has some thing in common as the second row. Can you help Emily to identify what goes in the space of the question mark from the four given options A, B, C, and D. Choose the correct option.

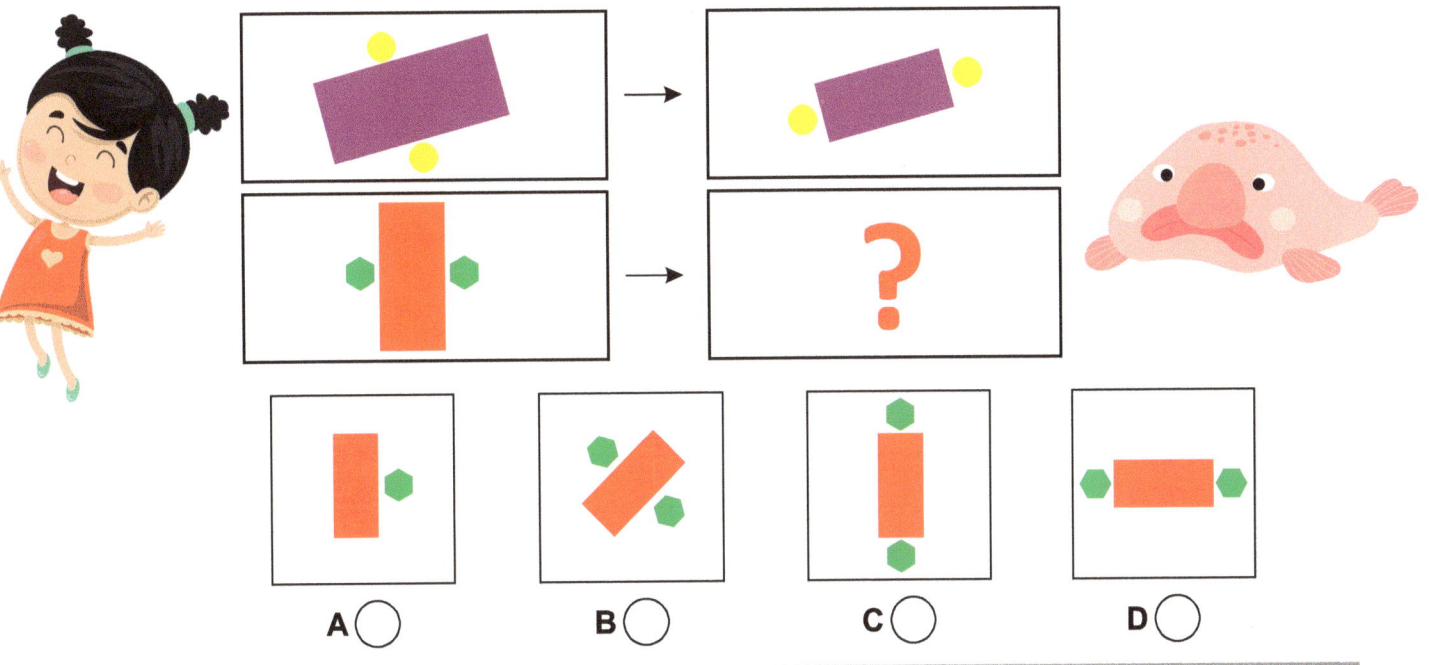

A ○ B ○ C ○ D ○

Q-6

Look at the question with the Hammerhead Shark. The first row has some thing in common as the second row. Can you help Isabella to identify what goes in the space of the question mark from the four given options A, B, C, and D. Choose the correct option.

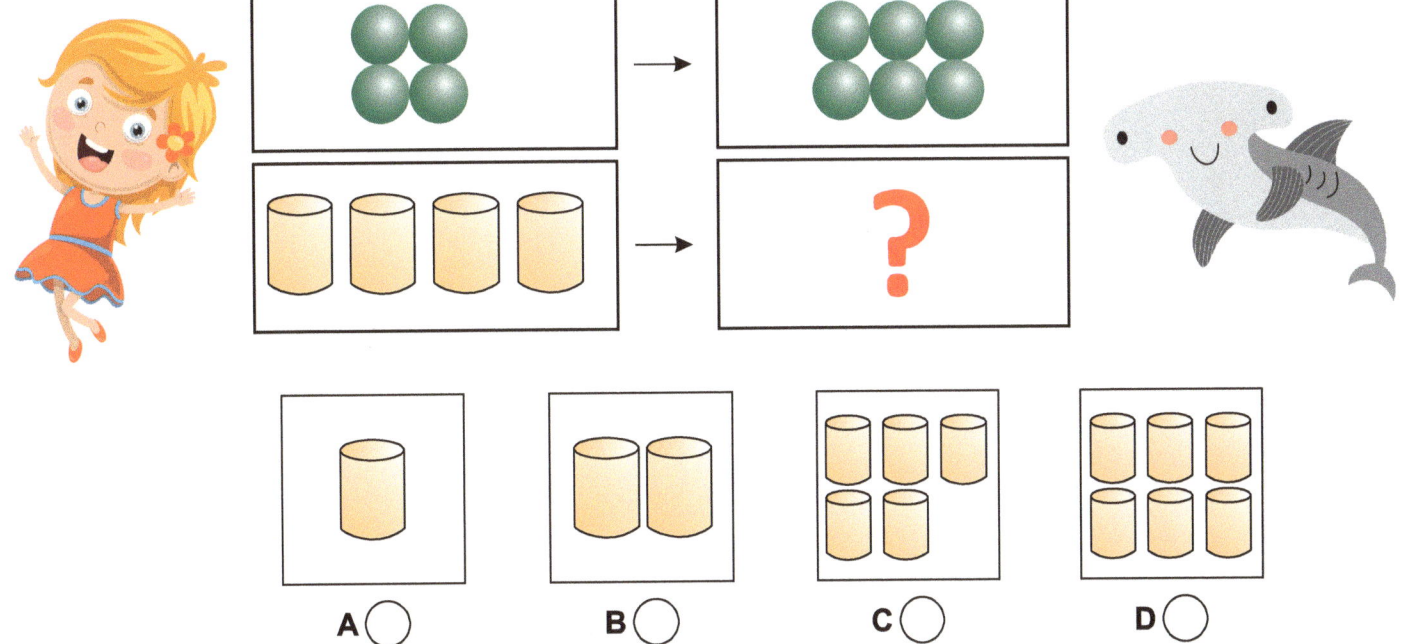

A ○ B ○ C ○ D ○

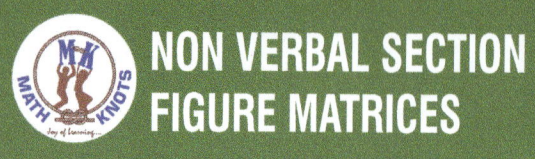

Q-7

Look at the question with the Angel Fish. The first row has some thing in common as the second row. Can you help Leo to identify what goes in the space of the question mark from the four given options A, B, C, and D. Choose the correct option.

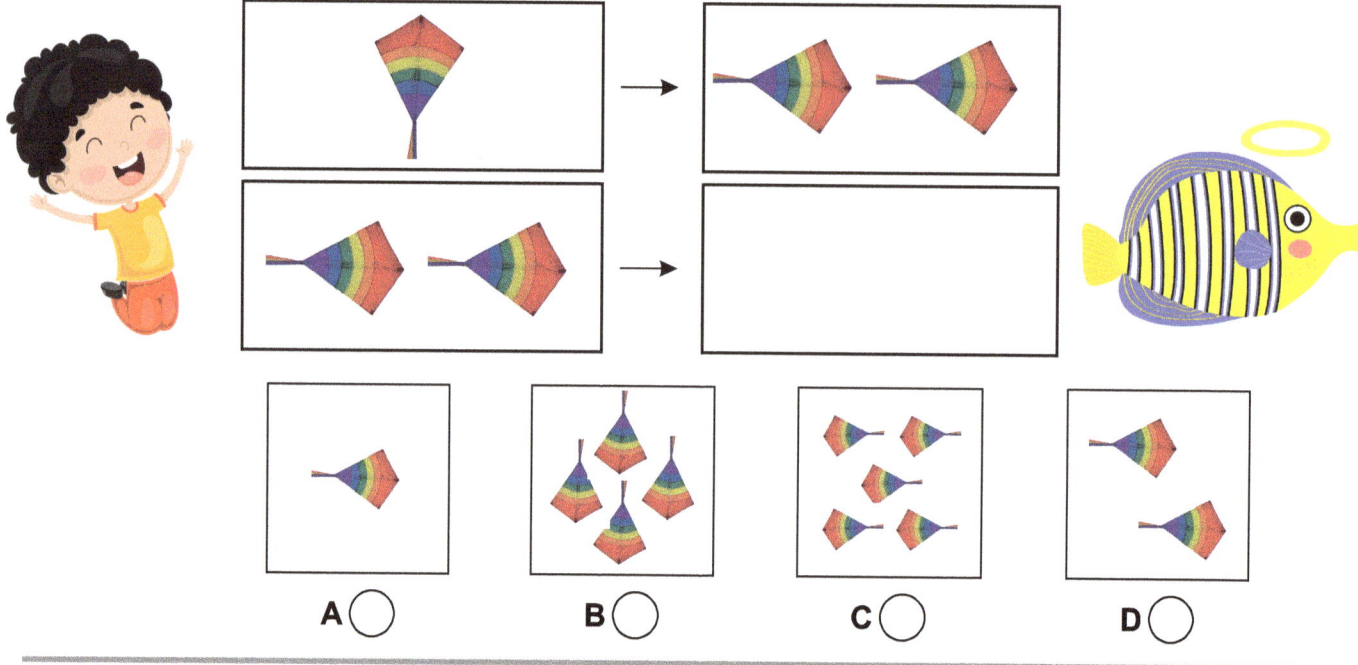

A◯　　B◯　　C◯　　D◯

Q-8

Look at the question with the Red Waratah Anemone Fish. The first row has some thing in common as the second row. Can you help Alice to identify what goes in the space of the question mark from the four given options A, B, C, and D. Choose the correct option.

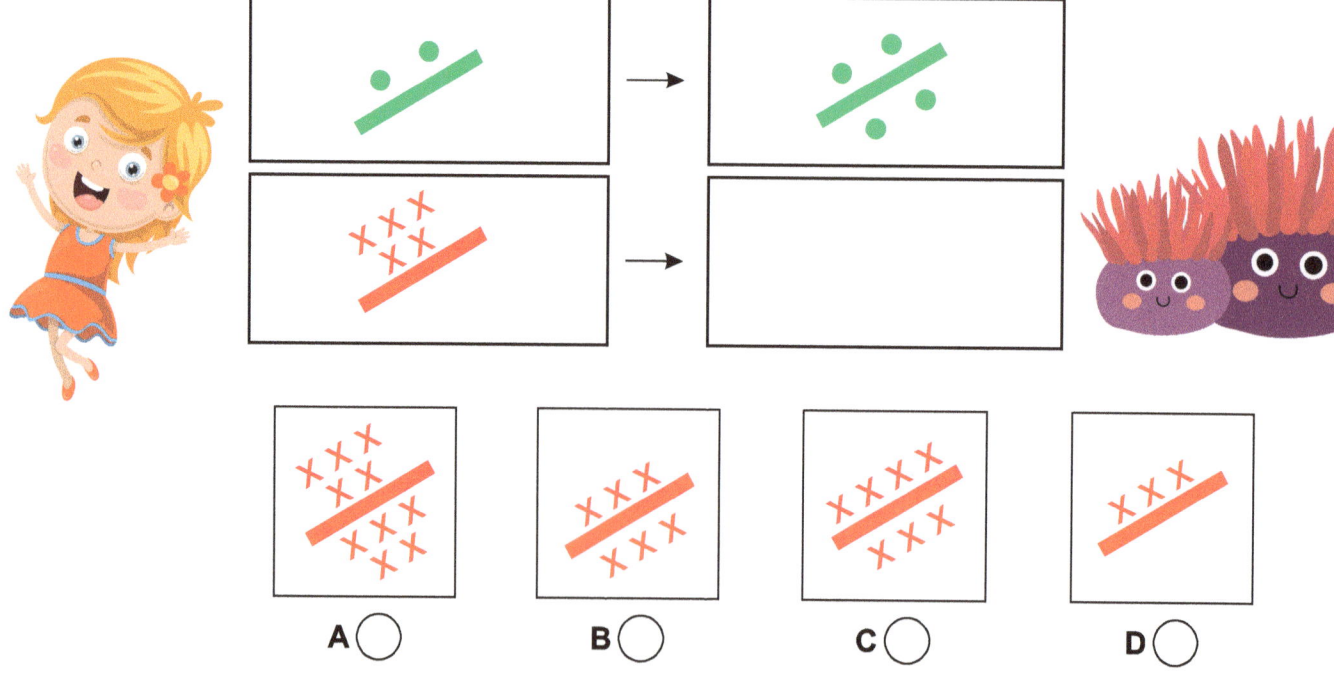

A◯　　B◯　　C◯　　D◯

www.math-knots.com

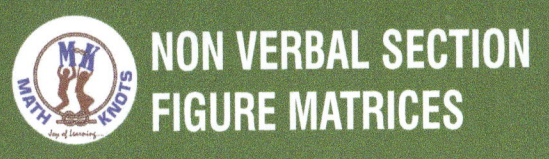
Q-9 Look at the question with the Hermit Crab. The first row has some thing in common as the second row. Can you help James to identify what goes in the space of the question mark from the four given options A, B, C, and D. Choose the correct option.

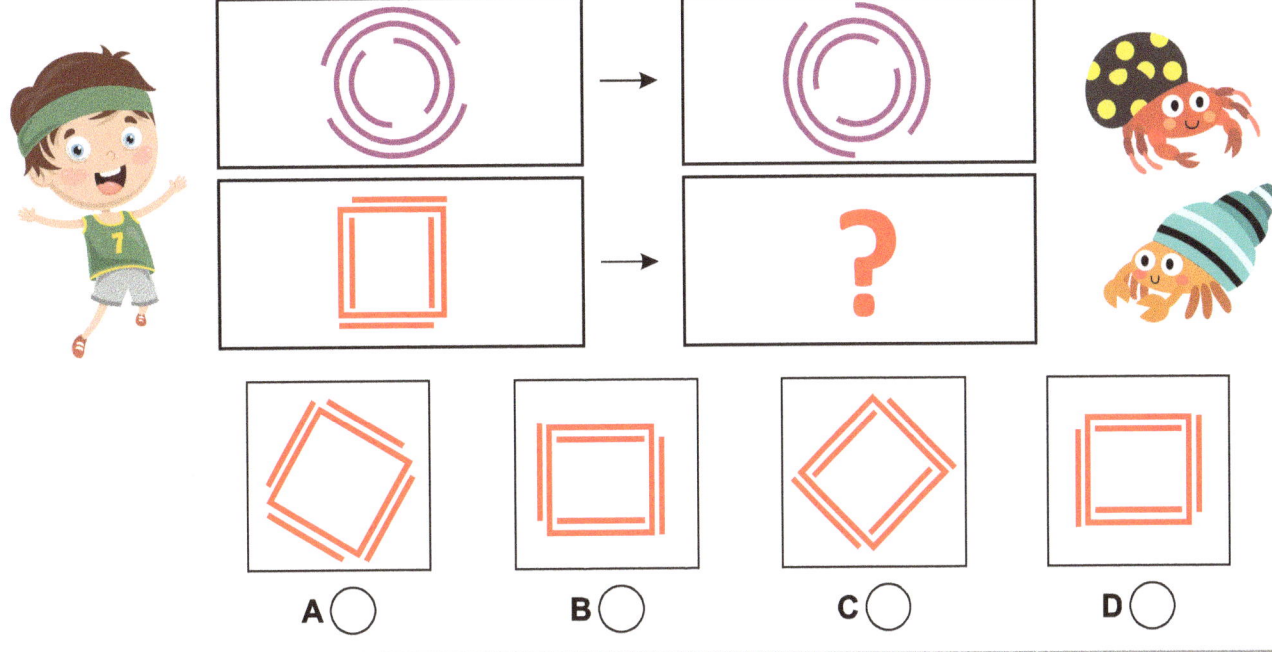

Q-10 Look at the question with the Manta Ray. The first row has some thing in common as the second row. Can you help Isha to identify what goes in the space of the question mark from the four given options A, B, C, and D. Choose the correct option.

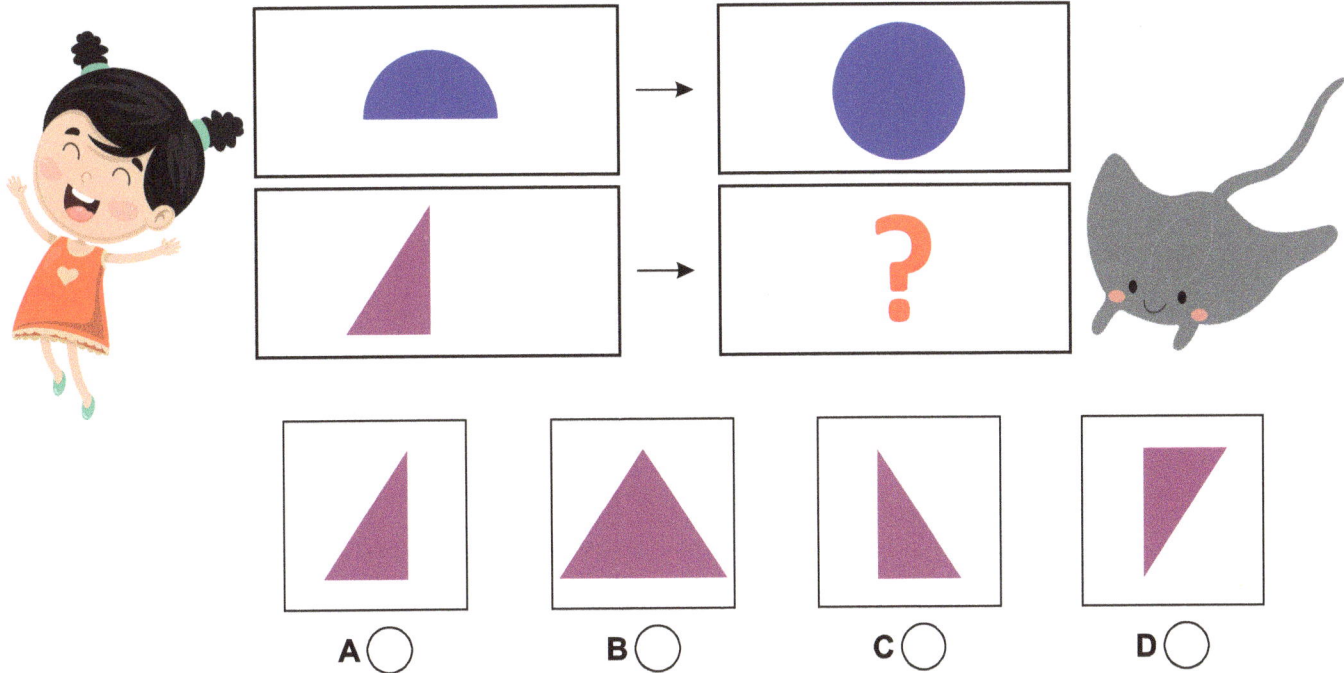

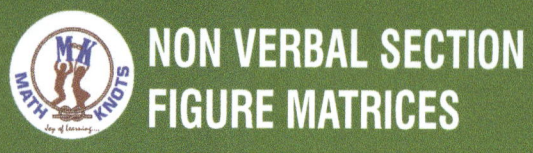

Q-11

Look at the question with the Mussel. The first row has some thing in common as the second row. Can you help Ava to identify what goes in the space of the question mark from the four given options A, B, C, and D. Choose the correct option.

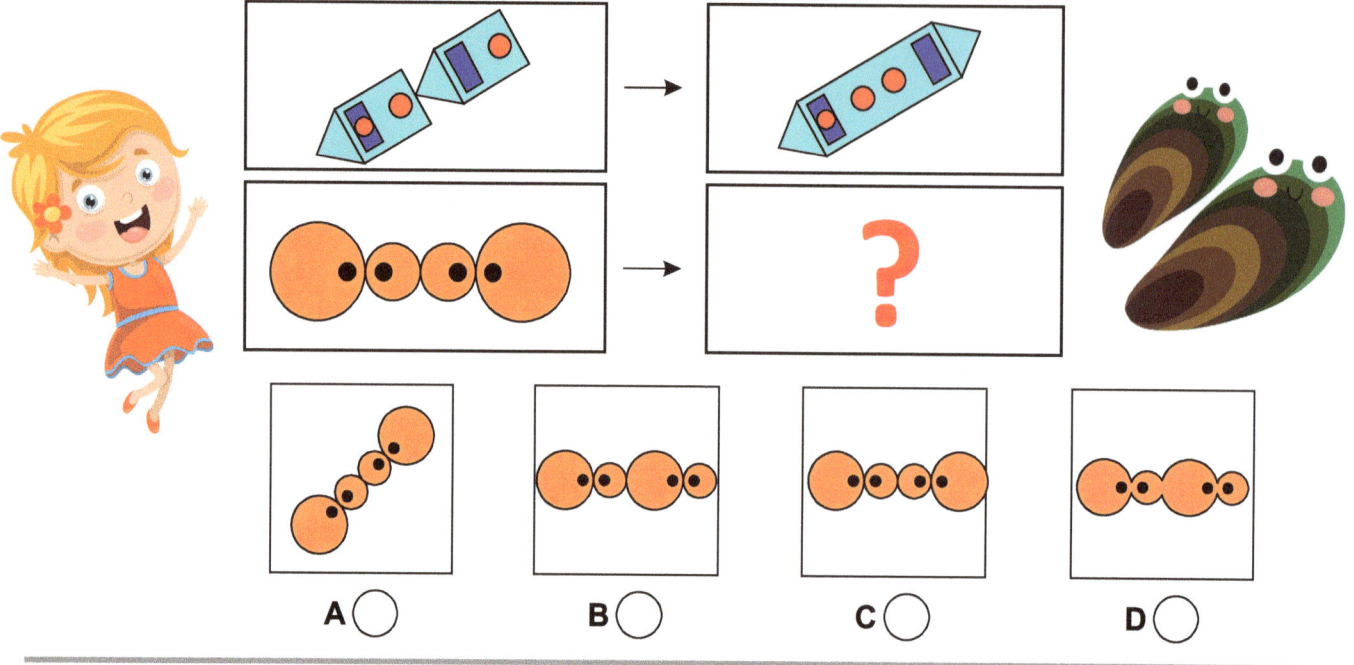

A ○ B ○ C ○ D ○

Q-12

Look at the question with the Zooplankton. The first row has some thing in common as the second row. Can you help William to identify what goes in the space of the question mark from the four given options A, B, C, and D. Choose the correct option.

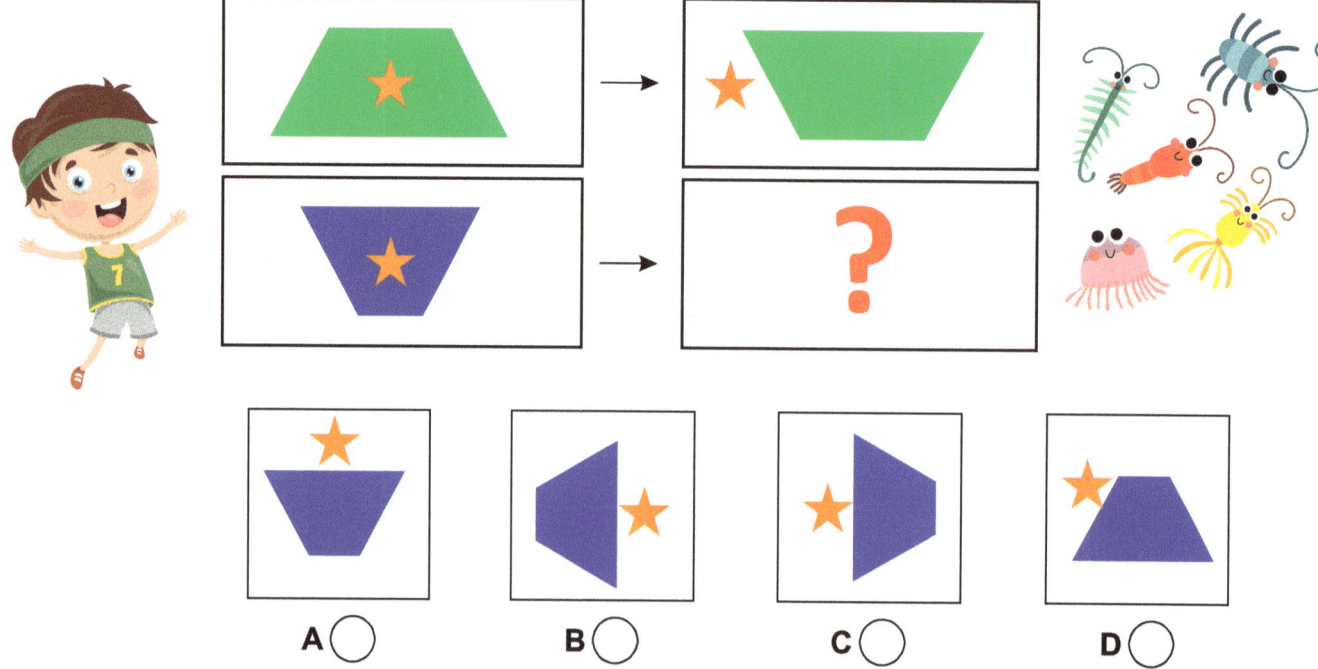

A ○ B ○ C ○ D ○

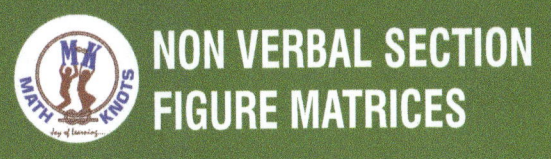
Q-13

Look at the question with the Sea horse. The first row has some thing in common as the second row. Can you help Thomas to identify what goes in the space of the question mark from the four given options A, B, C, and D. Choose the correct option.

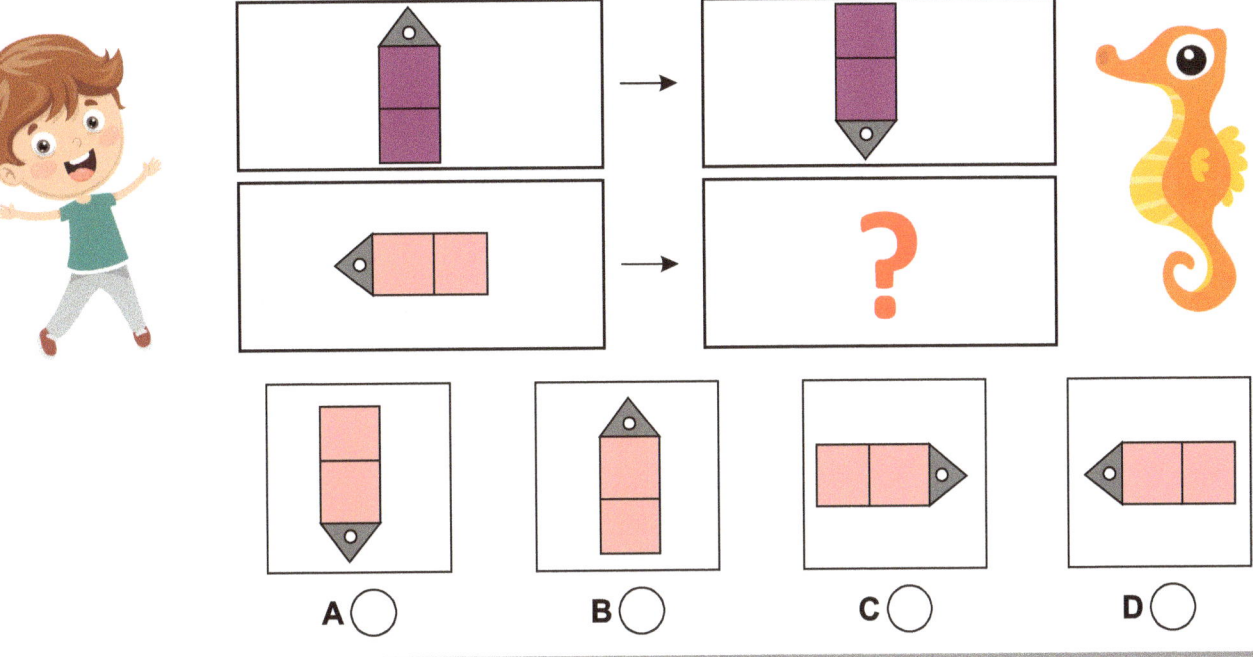

A ◯   B ◯   C ◯   D ◯

Q-14

Look at the question with the Tortoise. The first row has some thing in common as the second row. Can you help Olivia to identify what goes in the space of the question mark from the four given options A, B, C, and D. Choose the correct option.

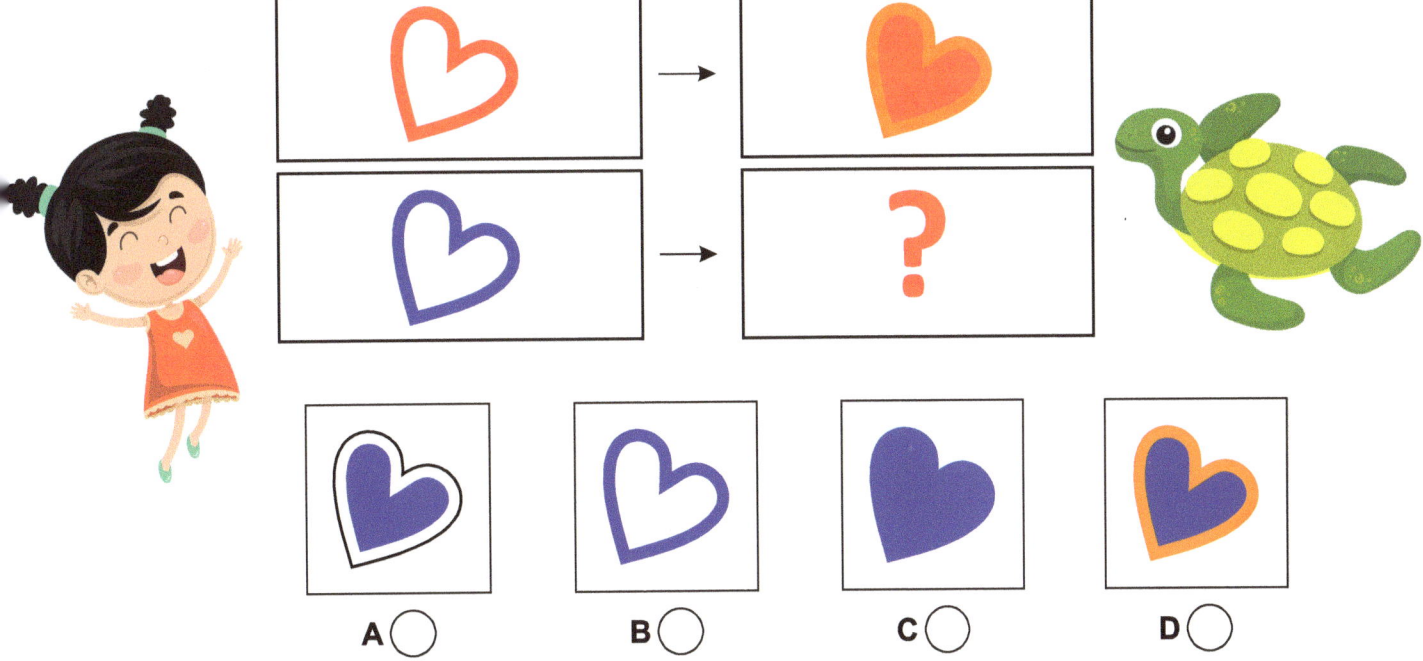

A ◯   B ◯   C ◯   D ◯

www.math-knots.com

Q-15

Look at the question with the Star Fish. The first row has some thing in common as the second row. Can you help Emily to identify what goes in the space of the question mark from the four given options A, B, C, and D. Choose the correct option.

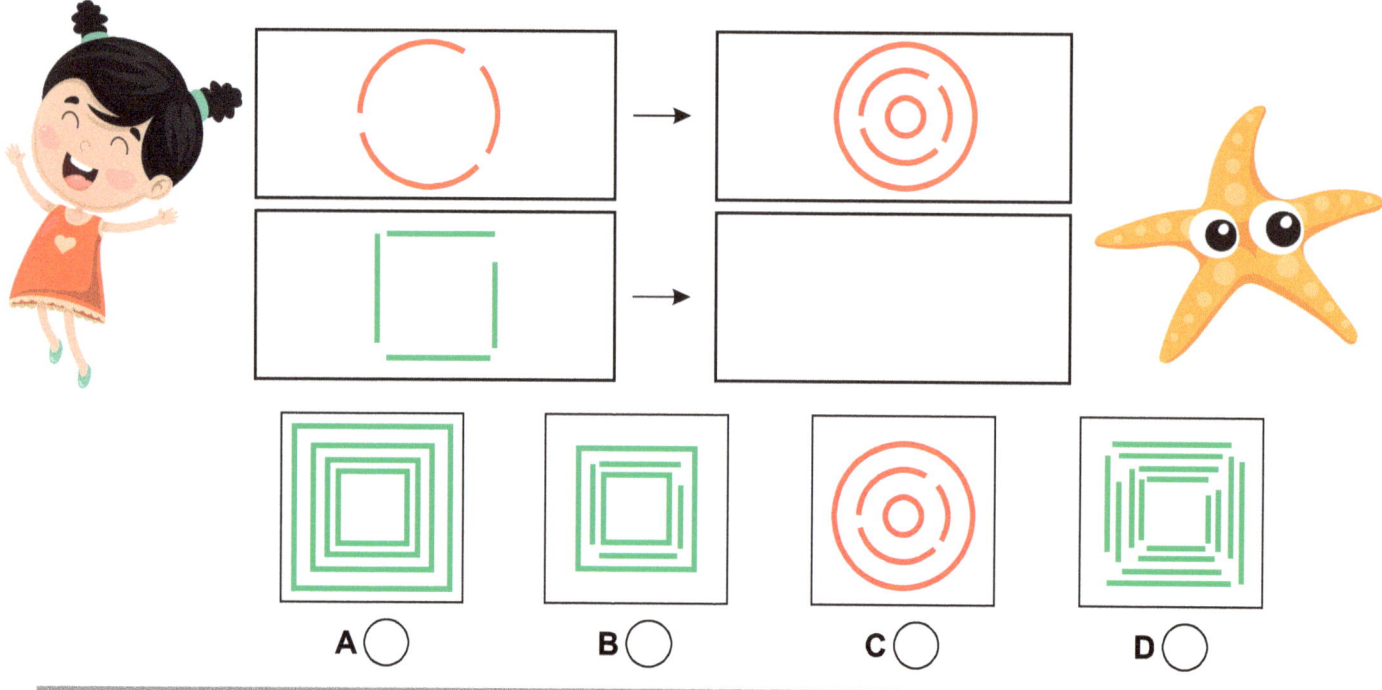

A◯　　B◯　　C◯　　D◯

Q-16

Look at the question with the Gold Fish. The first row has some thing in common as the second row. Can you help Lily to identify what goes in the space of the question mark from the four given options A, B, C, and D. Choose the correct option.

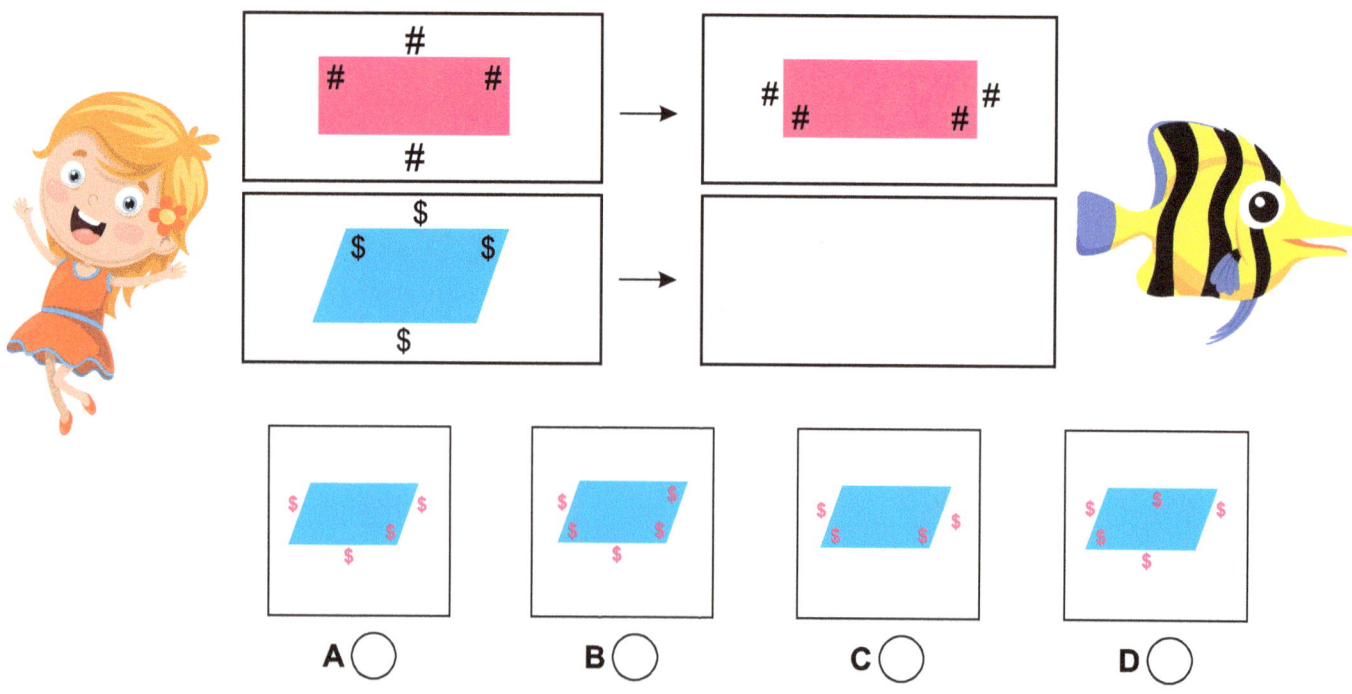

A◯　　B◯　　C◯　　D◯

www.math-knots.com

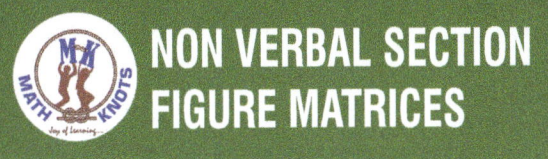
Q-17 Look at the question with the Crab. The first row has some thing in common as the second row. Can you help Jacob to identify what goes in the space of the question mark from the four given options A, B, C, and D. Choose the correct option.

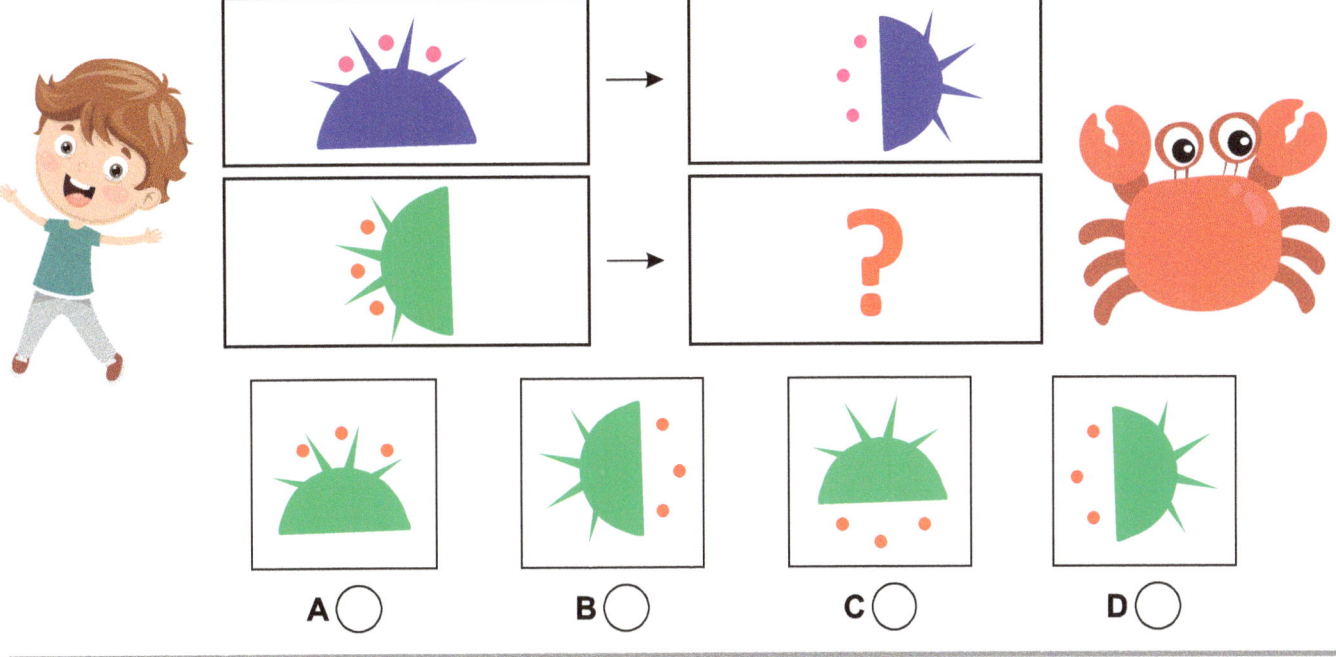

Q-18 Look at the question with the Blob Fish. The first row has some thing in common as the second row. Can you help Noah to identify what goes in the space of the question mark from the four given options A, B, C, and D. Choose the correct option.

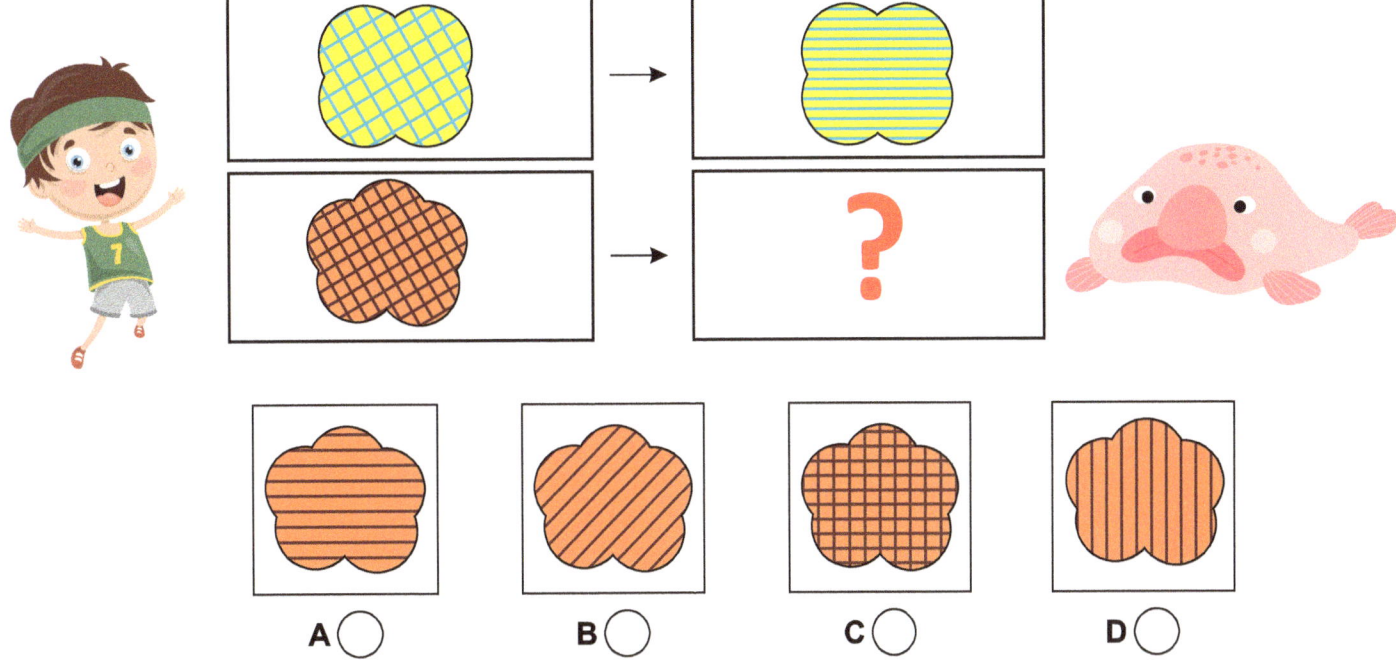

TEST - 1

NON VERBAL SECTION

PAPER FOLDING

Lets Start the Test...

www.math-knots.com

www.math-knots.com

Sample

Look at the question and put your finger on Bee. Amy folded the paper and made holes to it as shown. When the paper is unfolded how does it look? Help her bubble the right option.

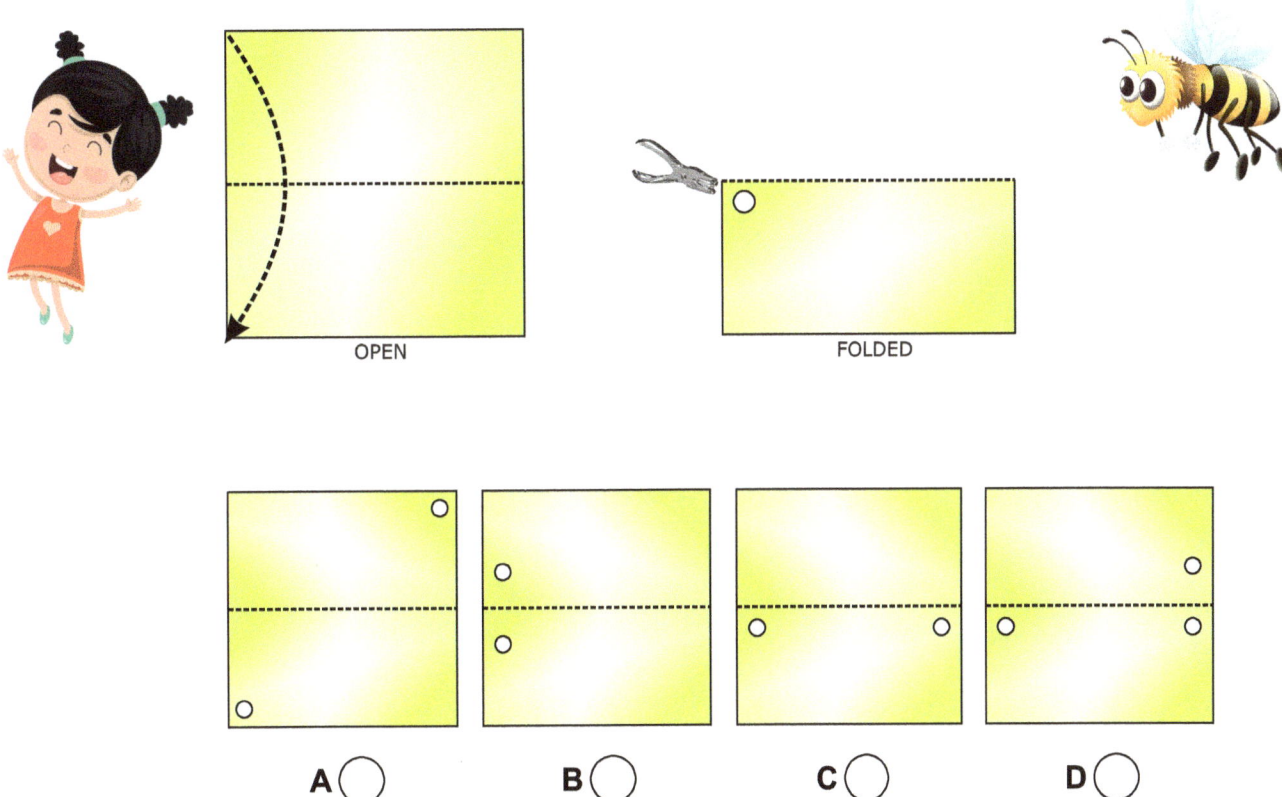

OPEN

FOLDED

A ◯ B ◯ C ◯ D ◯

Solution : B

A rectangle is folded once and hole is punched on top left corner. After punching the figure is unfolded the holes are shown in the middle left corner as shown in option B. Student choses the right option and fills the bubble completely.

www.math-knots.com

Q-1

Look at the question and put your finger on Alligator. Brianna folded the paper and made hole to it as shown. When the paper is unfolded how does it look? Help her bubble the right option.

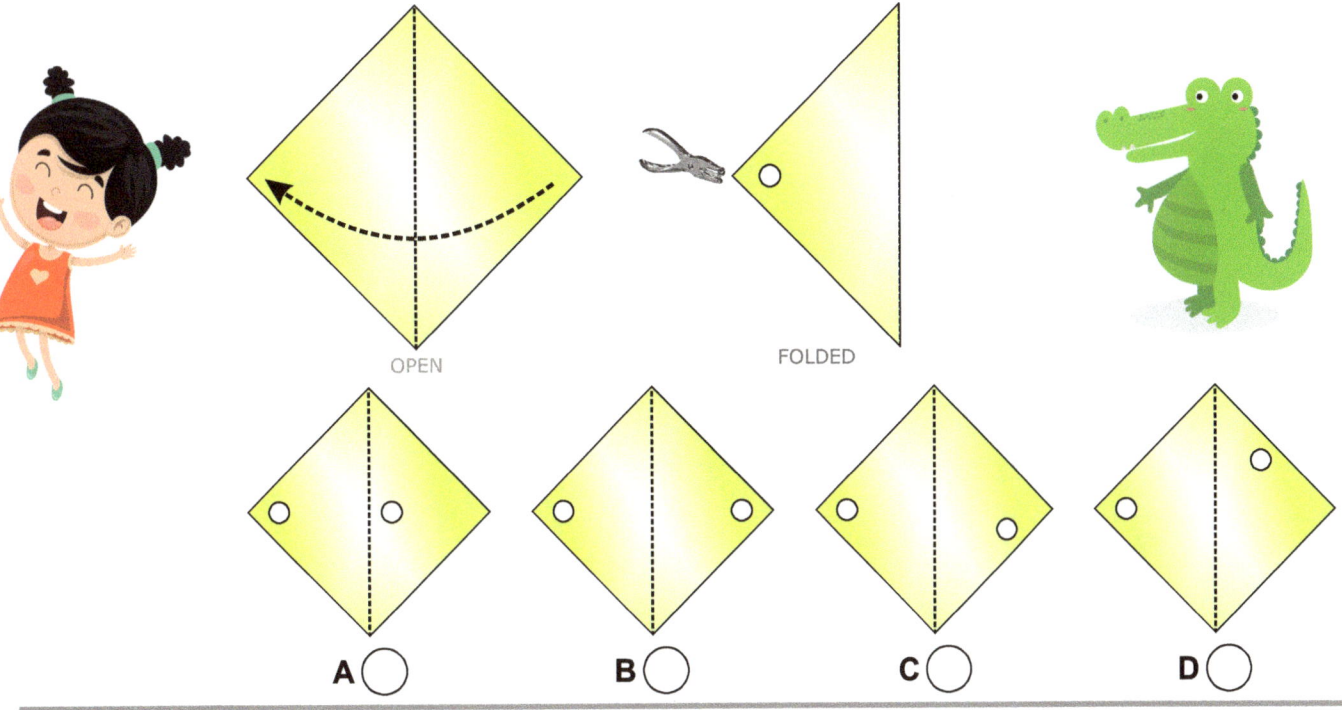

OPEN   FOLDED

A◯   B◯   C◯   D◯

Q-2

Look at the question and put your finger on Sparrow. Samuel folded the paper and made holes to it as shown. When the paper is unfolded how does it look? Help him bubble the right option.

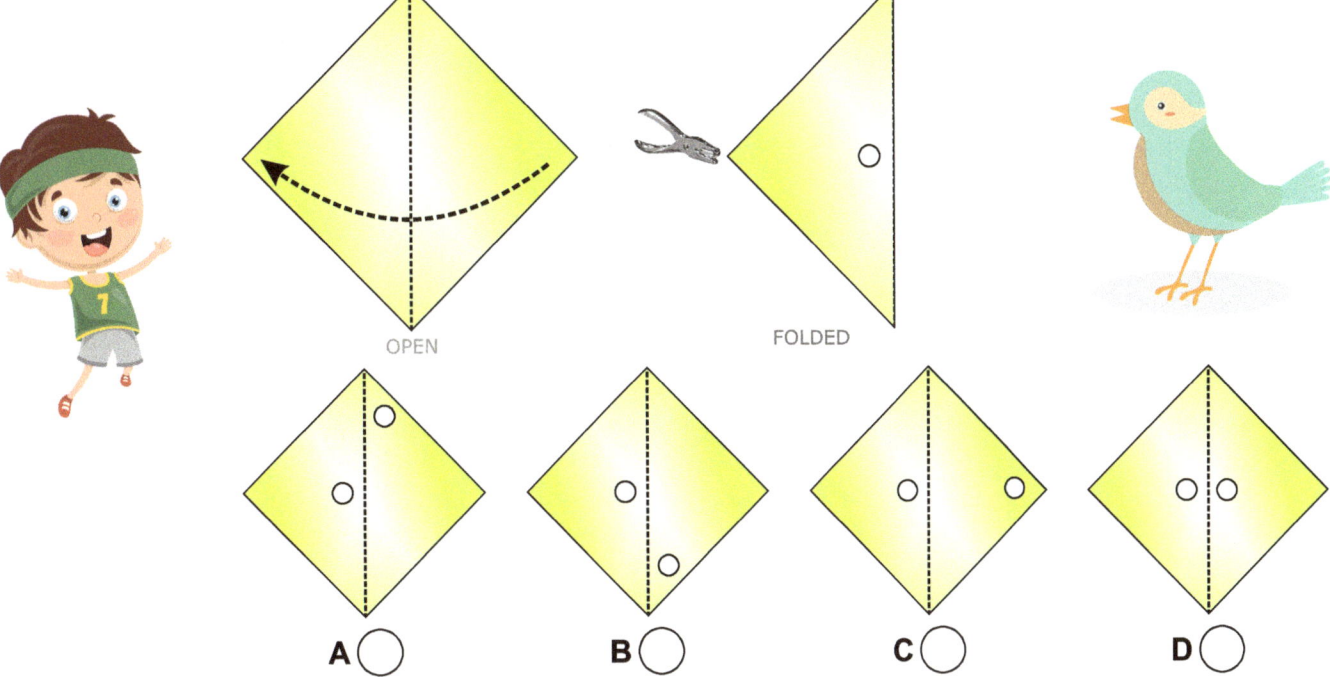

OPEN   FOLDED

A◯   B◯   C◯   D◯

www.math-knots.com

Q-3

Look at the question and put your finger on Dolphin. Hailey folded the paper and made holes to it as shown. When the paper is unfolded how does it look? Help him bubble the right option.

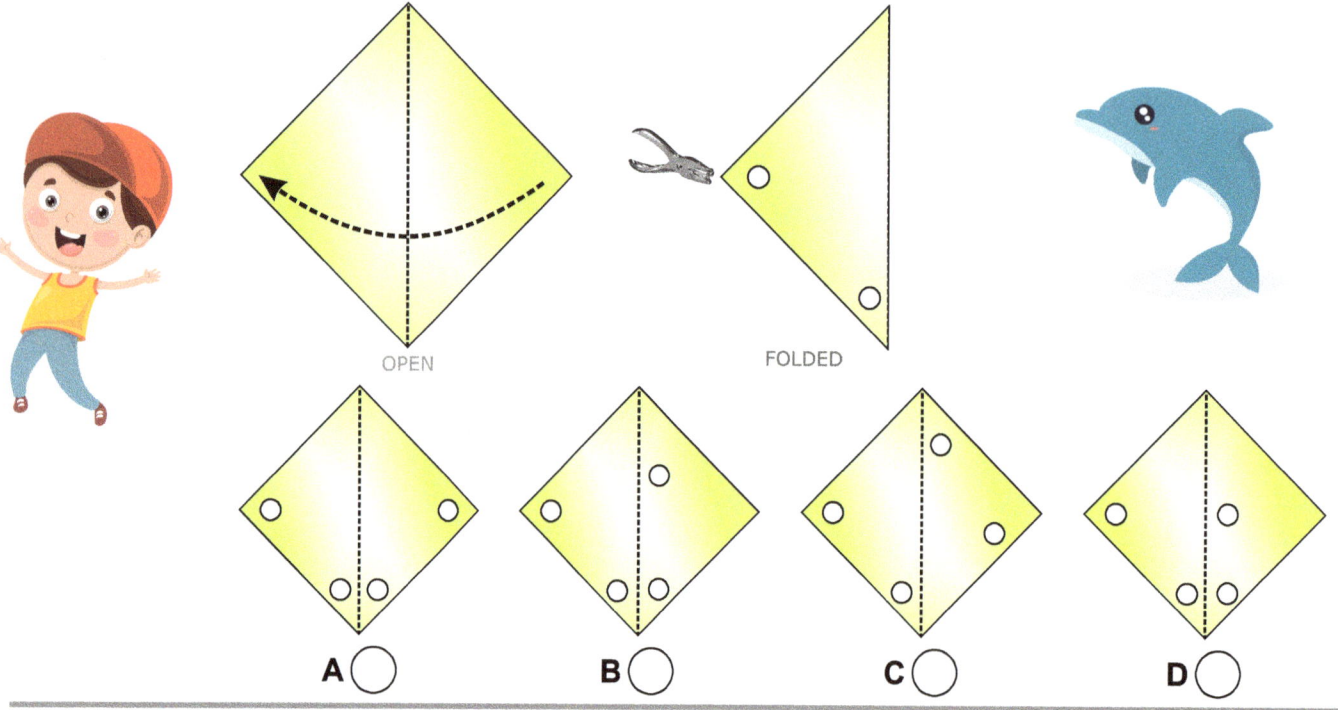

OPEN   FOLDED

A ⬤   B ⬤   C ⬤   D ⬤

Q-4

Look at the question and put your finger on JellyFish. Victoria folded the paper and made holes to it as shown. When the paper is unfolded how does it look? Help her bubble the right option.

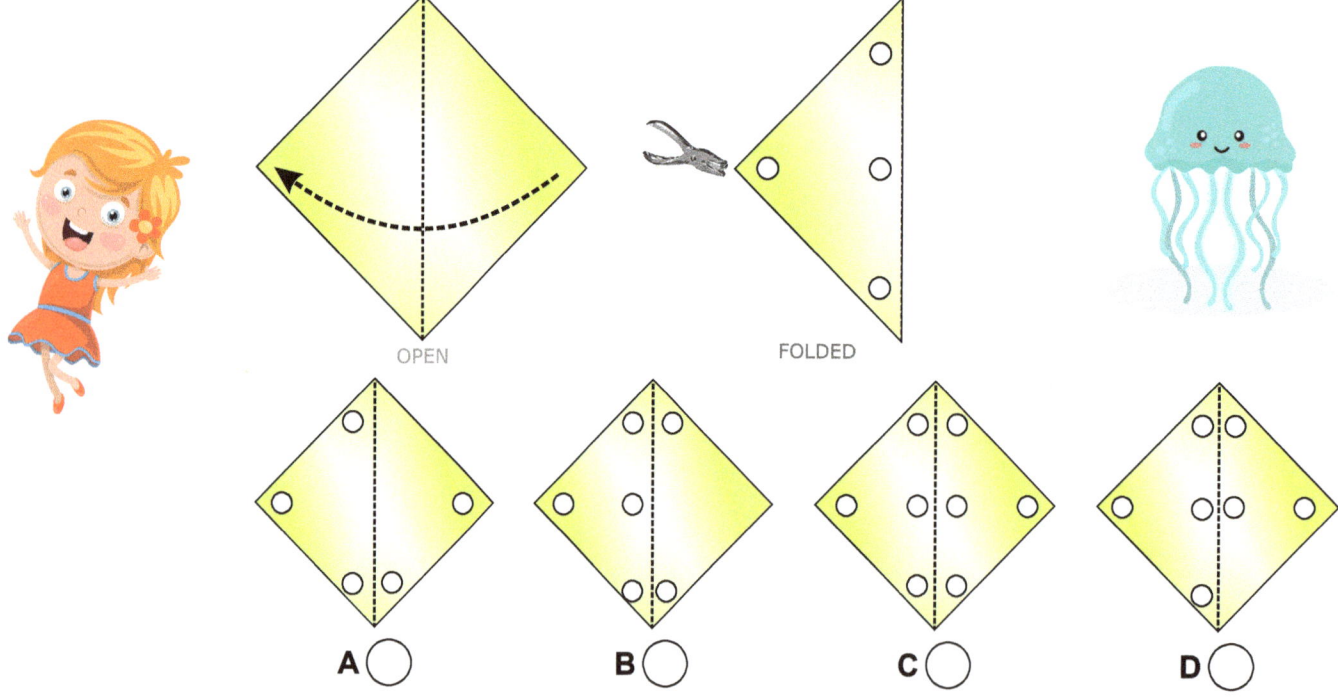

OPEN   FOLDED

A ⬤   B ⬤   C ⬤   D ⬤

www.math-knots.com

Q-5

Look at the question and put your finger on Fox. Noah folded the paper and made holes to it as shown. When the paper is unfolded how does it look? Help him bubble the right option.

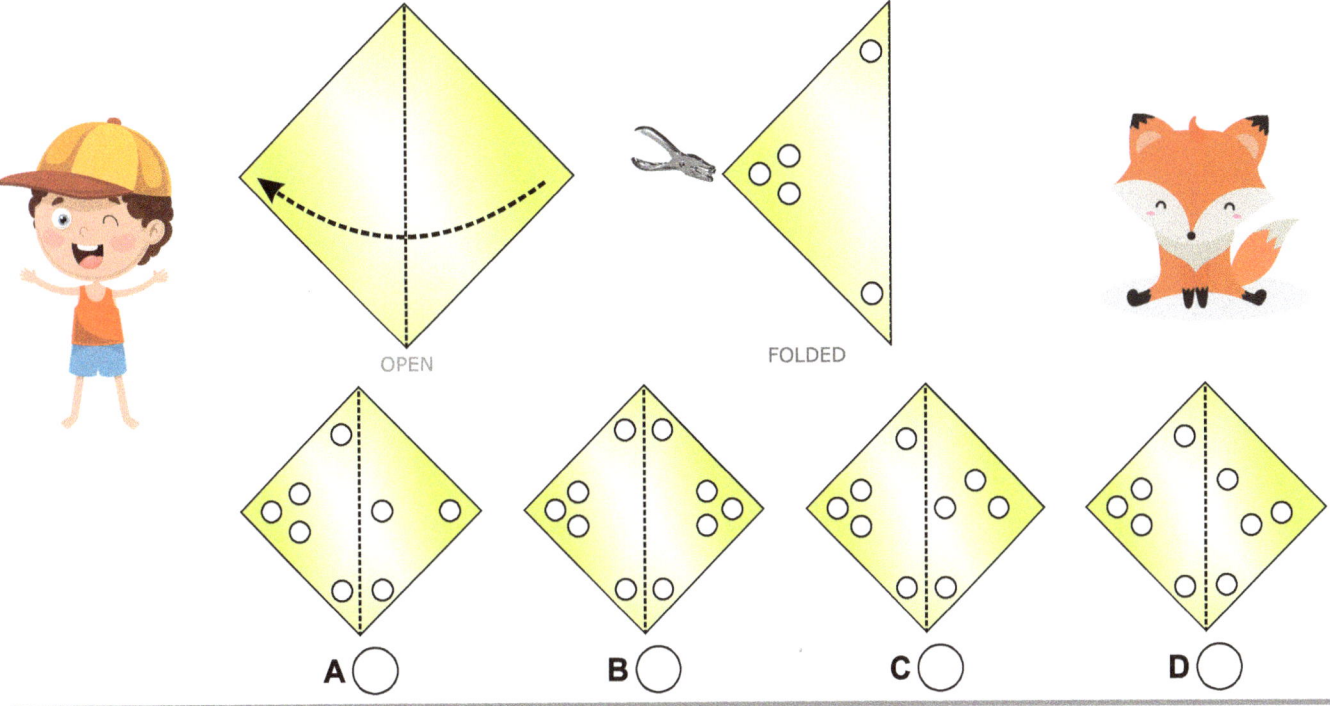

OPEN   FOLDED

A◯   B◯   C◯   D◯

Q-6

Look at the question and put your finger on Giraffe. Zachary folded the paper and made holes to it as shown. When the paper is unfolded how does it look? Help him bubble the right option.

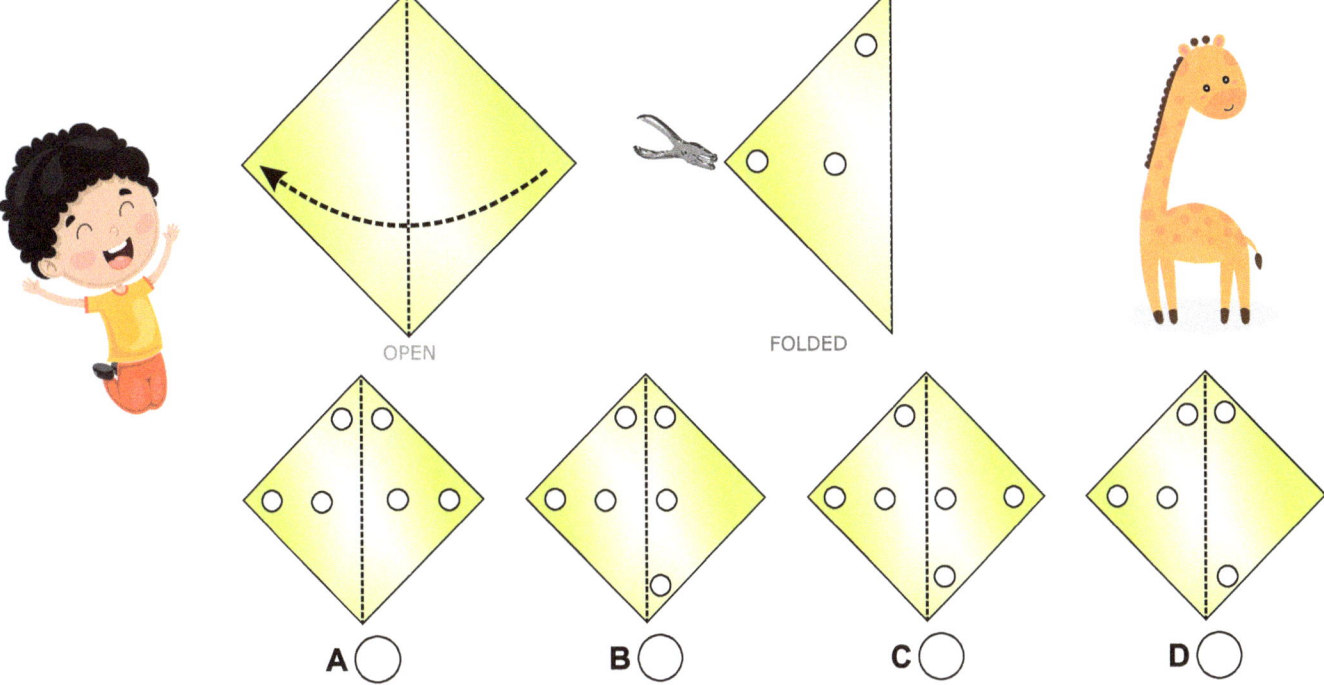

OPEN   FOLDED

A◯   B◯   C◯   D◯

www.math-knots.com

Q-7

Look at the question and put your finger on Iguana. Rita folded the paper and made holes to it as shown. When the paper is unfolded how does it look? Help her bubble the right option.

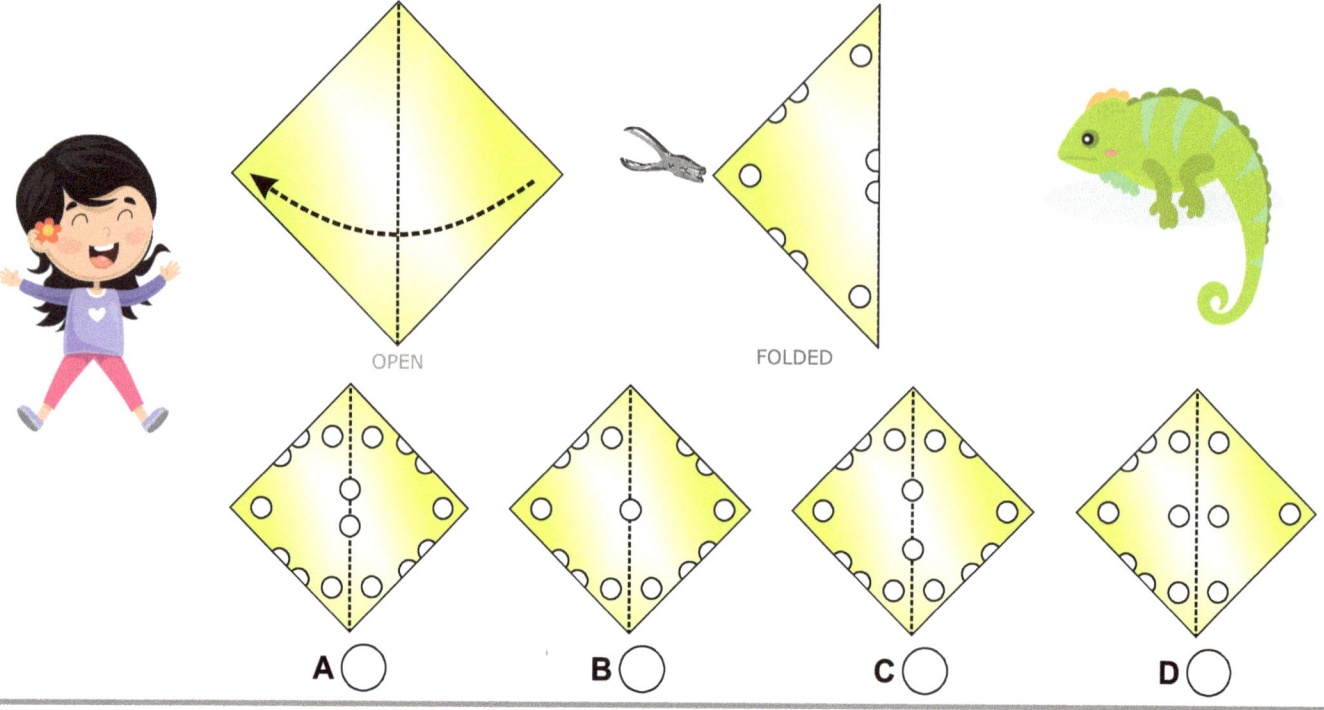

OPEN   FOLDED

A ○   B ○   C ○   D ○

Q-8

Look at the question and put your finger on Monkey. Devin folded the paper and made holes to it as shown. When the paper is unfolded how does it look? Help him bubble the right option.

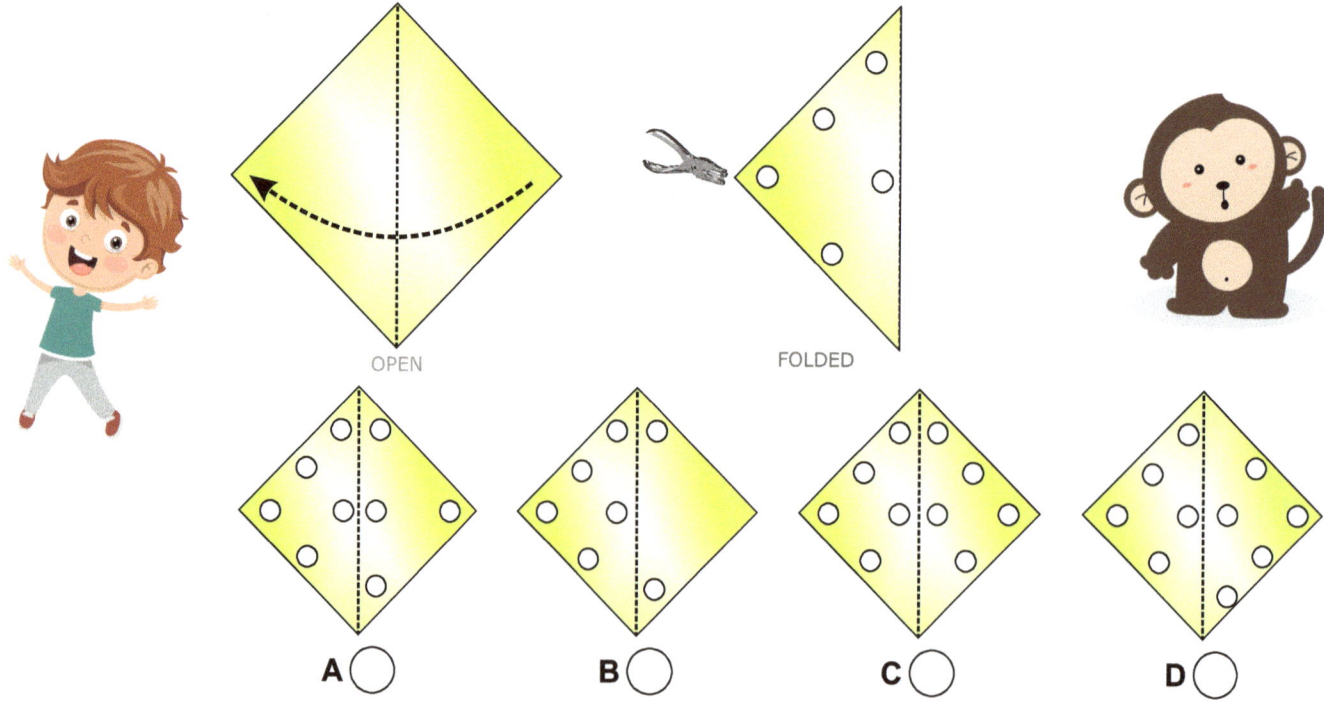

OPEN   FOLDED

A ○   B ○   C ○   D ○

www.math-knots.com

Q-9 Look at the question and put your finger on Koala Bear. Ashton folded the paper and made holes to it as shown. When the paper is unfolded how does it look? Help him bubble the right option.

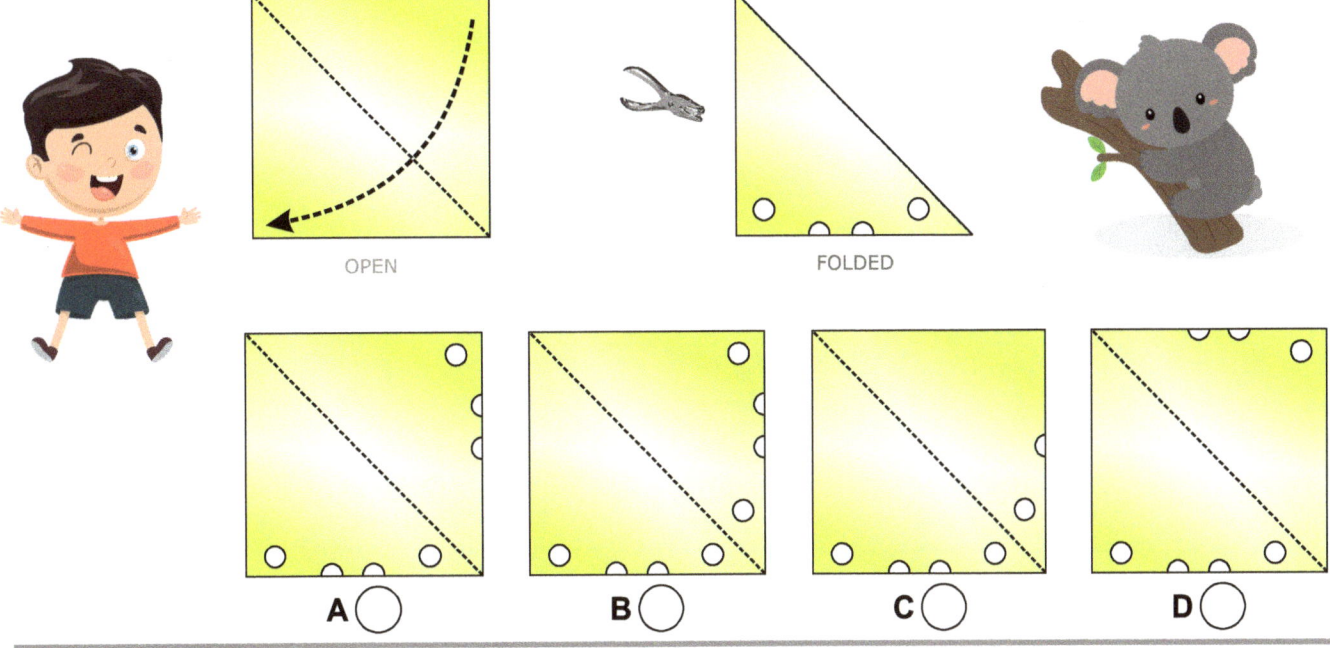

Q-10 Look at the question and put your finger on Pig. Sierra folded the paper and made holes to it as shown. When the paper is unfolded how does it look? Help her bubble the right option.

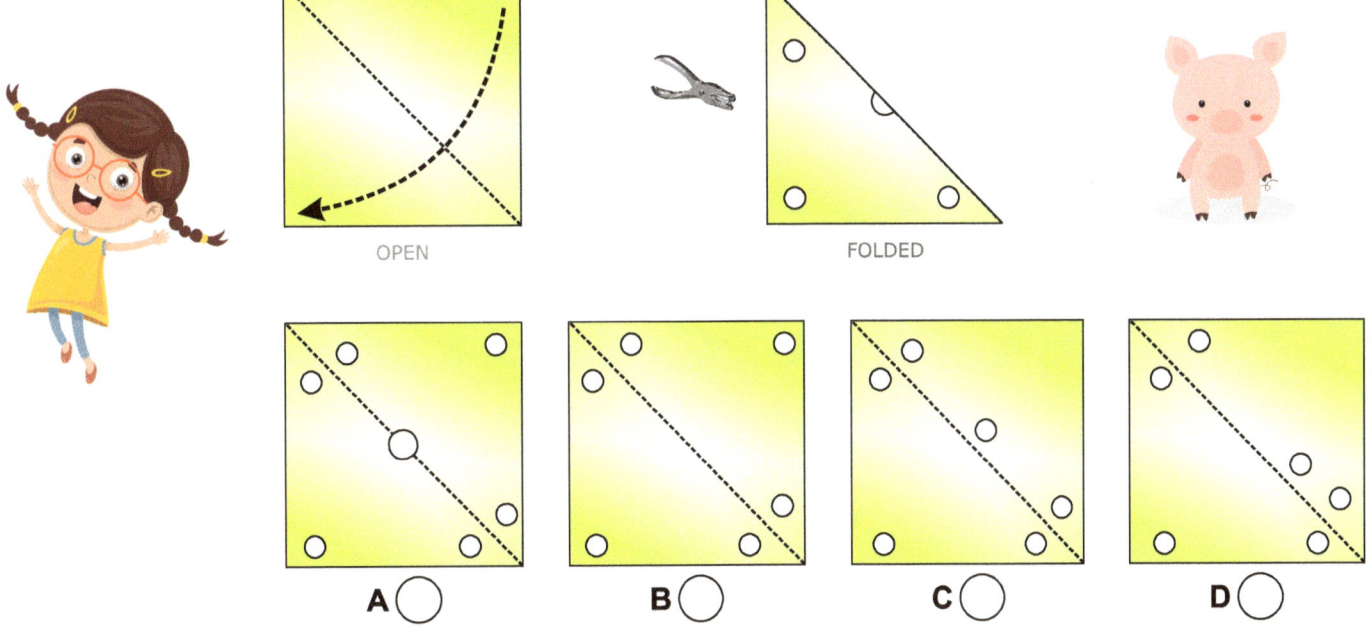

www.math-knots.com

Q-11

Look at the question and put your finger on Quail. Kathryn folded the paper and made holes to it as shown. When the paper is unfolded how does it look? Help her bubble the right option.

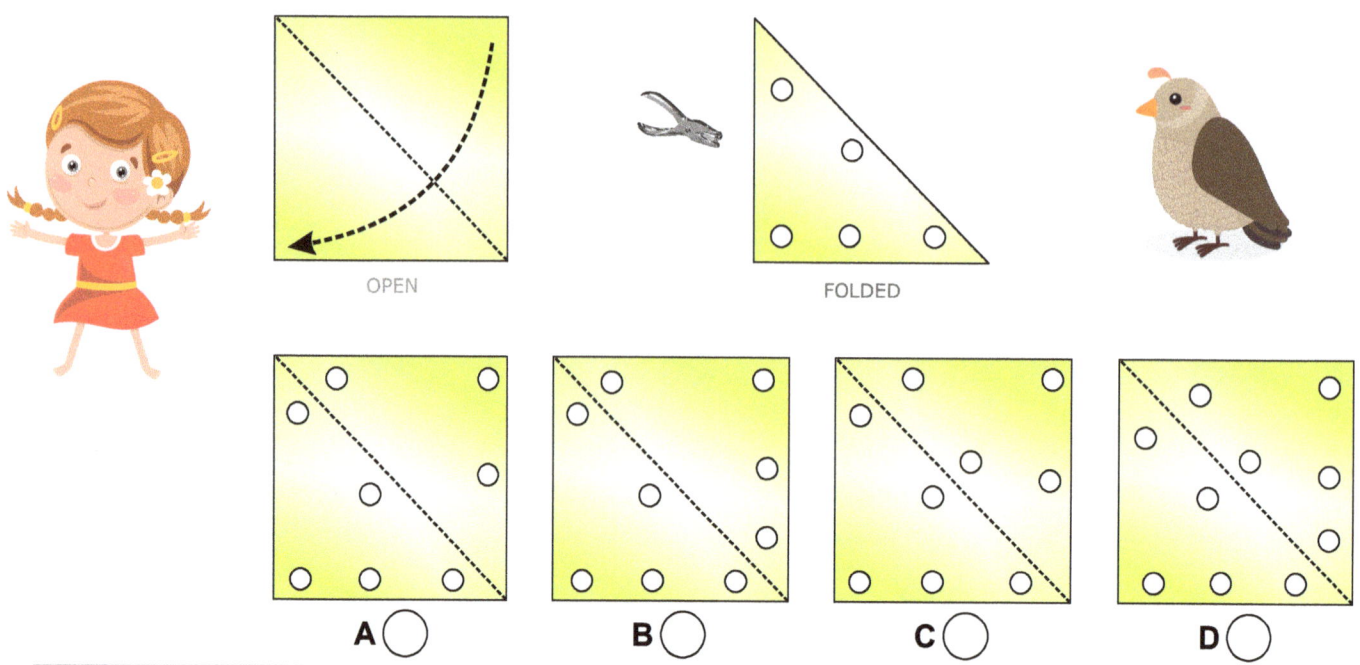

OPEN   FOLDED

A◯   B◯   C◯   D◯

Q-12

Look at the question and put your finger on Vampires Bat. Skylar folded the paper and made holes to it as shown. When the paper is unfolded how does it look? Help her bubble the right option.

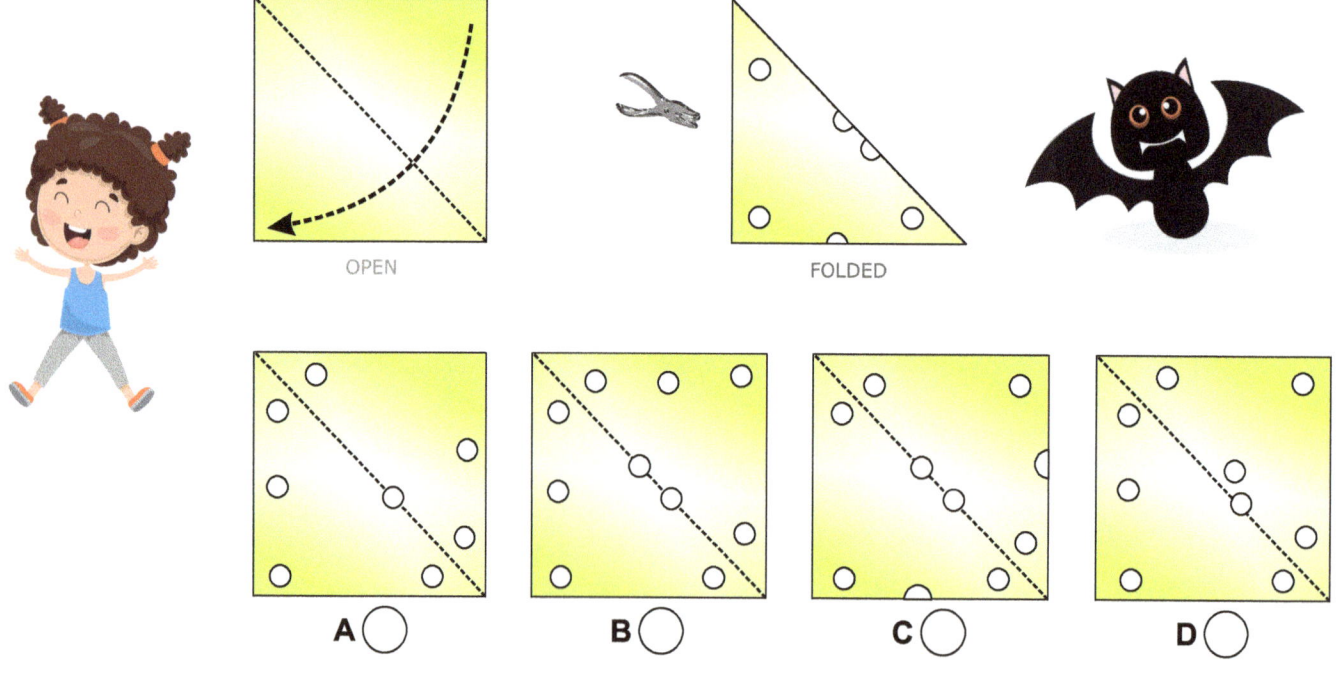

OPEN   FOLDED

A◯   B◯   C◯   D◯

www.math-knots.com

Q-13

Look at the question and put your finger on Lion. Rose folded the paper and made holes to it as shown. When the paper is unfolded how does it look? Help her bubble the right option.

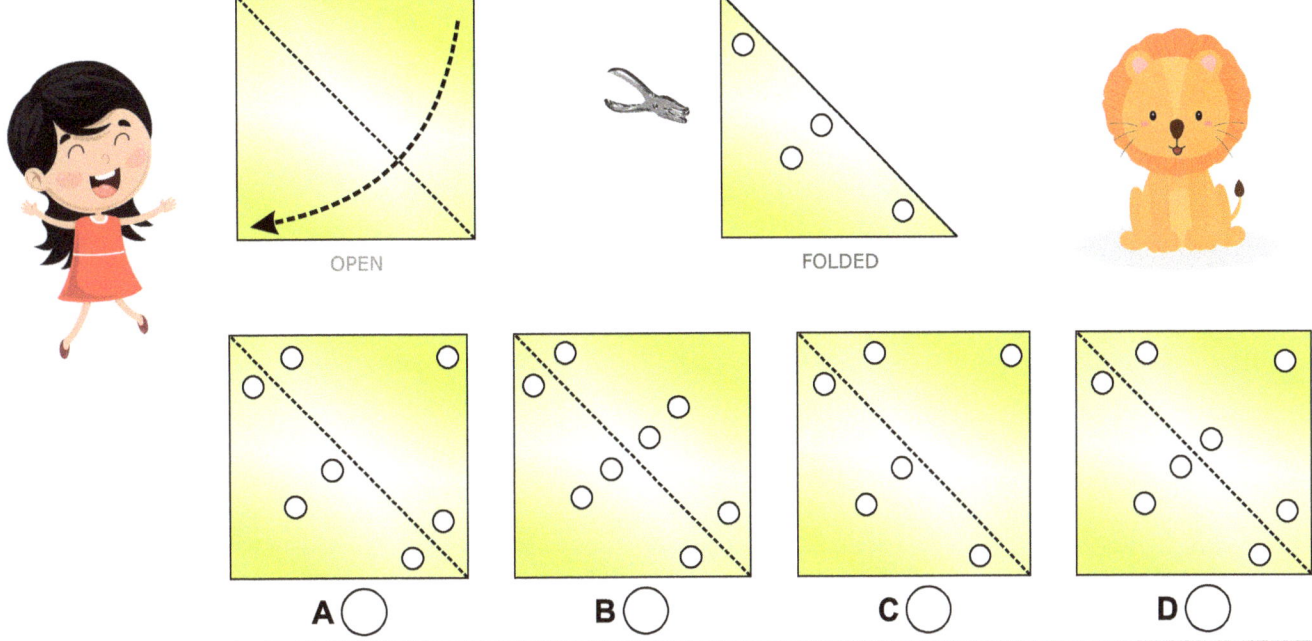

Q-14

Look at the question and put your finger on Raccoon. Matt folded the paper and made holes to it as shown. When the paper is unfolded how does it look? Help him bubble the right option.

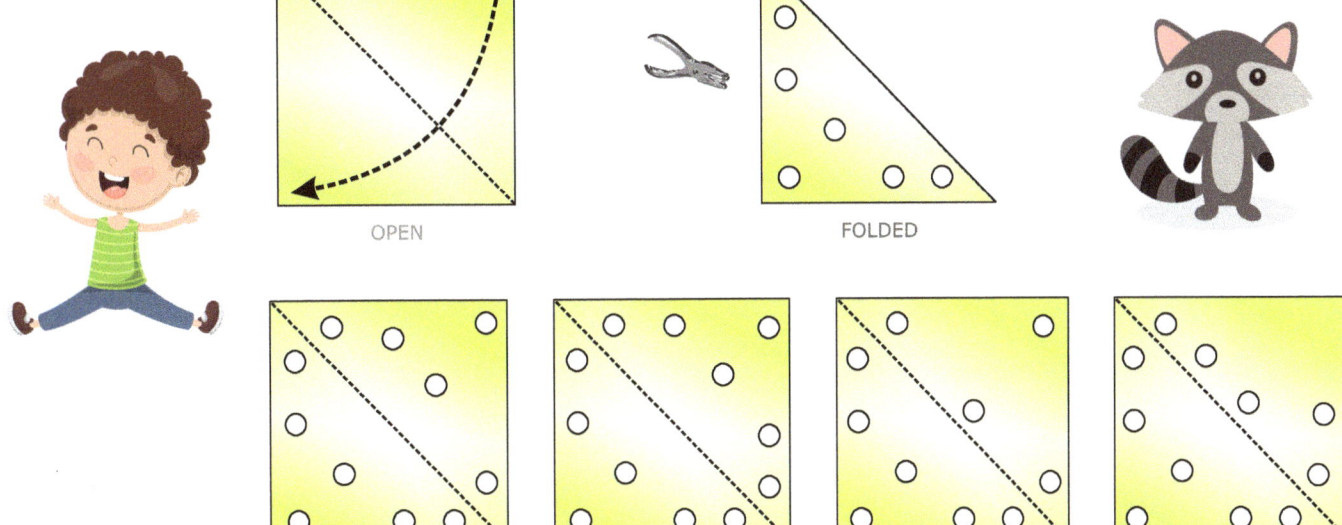

Q-15

Look at the question and put your finger on Octopus. Bryan folded the paper and made holes to it as shown. When the paper is unfolded how does it look? Help him bubble the right option.

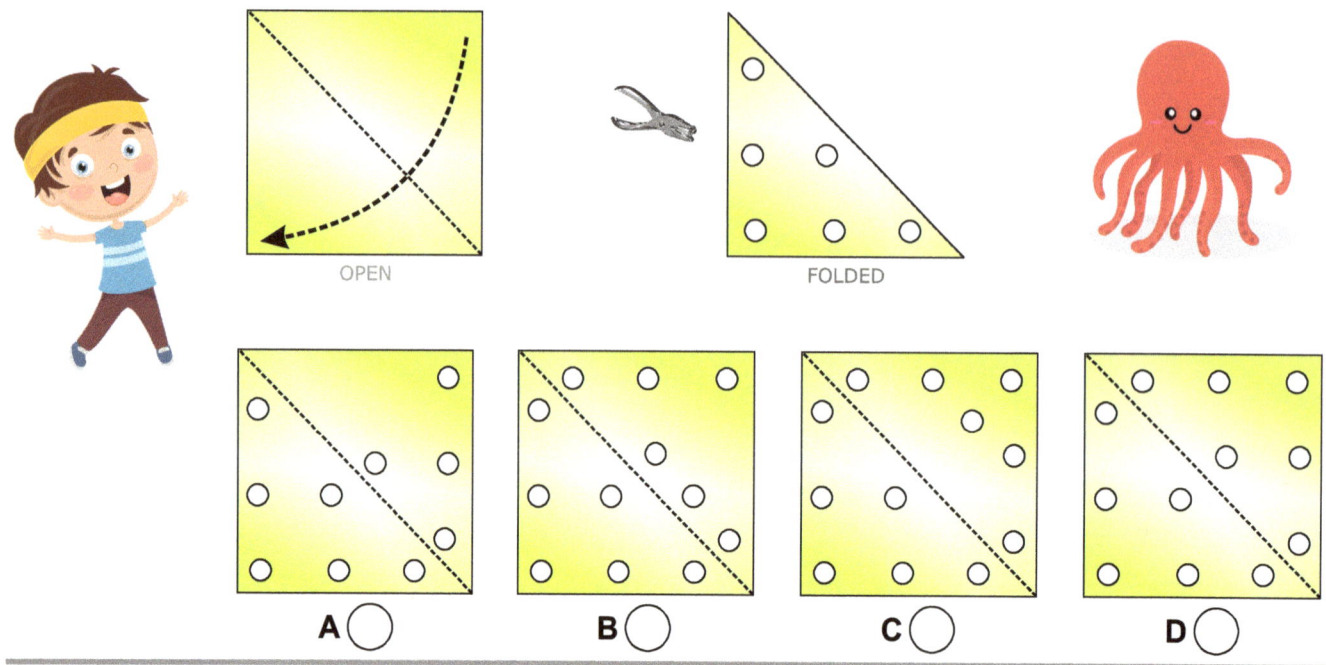

OPEN

FOLDED

A ◯   B ◯   C ◯   D ◯

Q-16

Look at the question and put your finger on Narwhal. Paige folded the paper and made holes to it as shown. When the paper is unfolded how does it look? Help her bubble the right option.

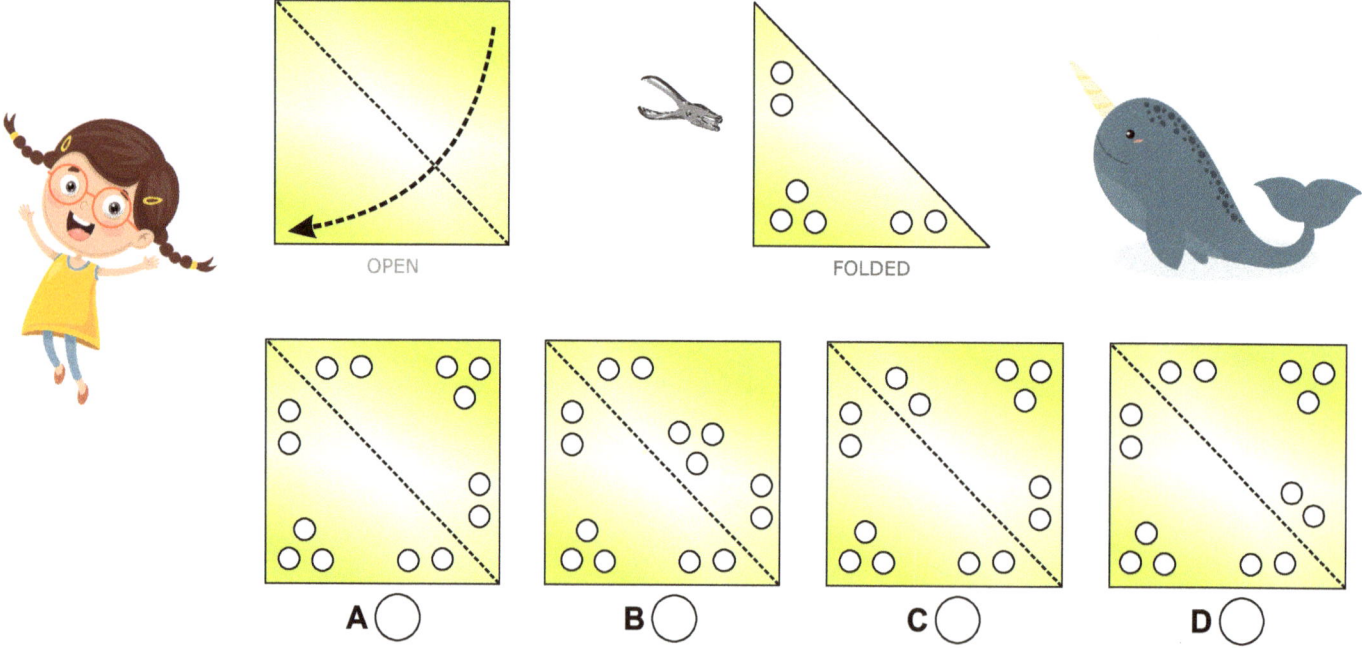

OPEN

FOLDED

A ◯   B ◯   C ◯   D ◯

www.math-knots.com

MATH-KNOTS CHALLENGE

Q-17

Look at the question and put your finger on Turtle. Seth folded the paper and made holes to it as shown. When the paper is unfolded how does it look? Help him bubble the right option.

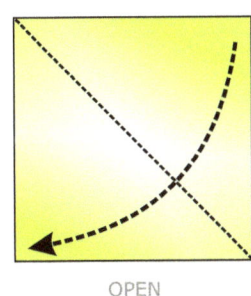

OPEN

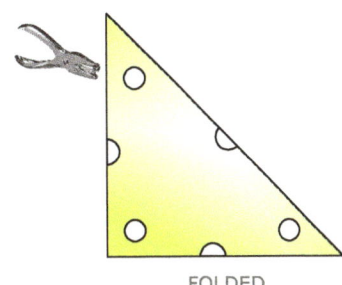

FOLDED

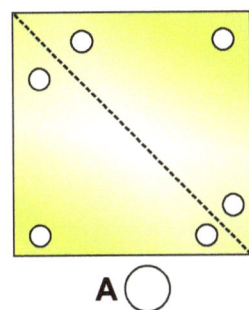 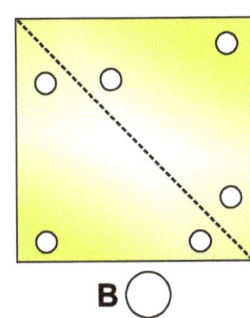 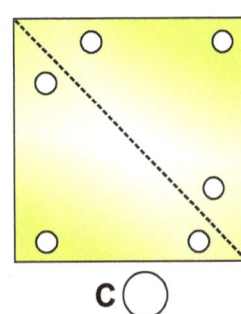 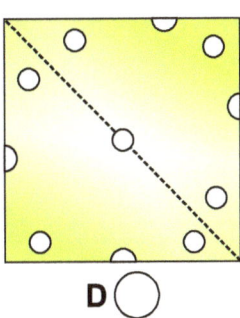

A ◯   B ◯   C ◯   D ◯

MATH-KNOTS CHALLENGE

Q-18

Look at the question and put your finger on X-Ray Fish. Diana folded the paper and made holes to it as shown. When the paper is unfolded how does it look? Help her bubble the right option.

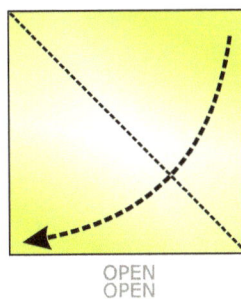

OPEN
OPEN

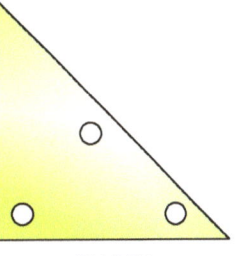

FOLDED

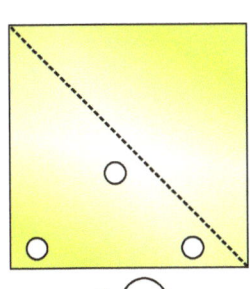 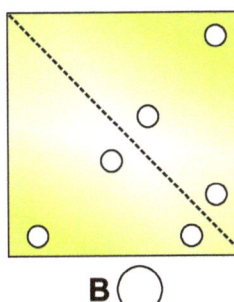 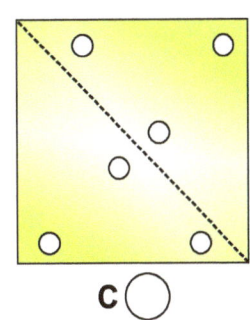 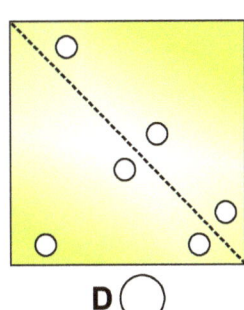

A ◯   B ◯   C ◯   D ◯

www.math-knots.com

MATH-KNOTS CHALLENGE

Q-19 Look at the question and put your finger on Yak. Maya folded the paper and made holes to it as shown. When the paper is unfolded how does it look? Help her bubble the right option.

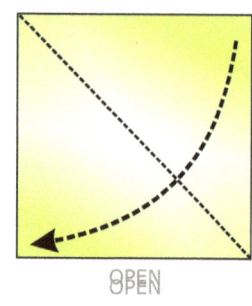

OPEN

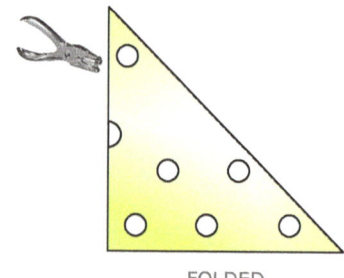

FOLDED

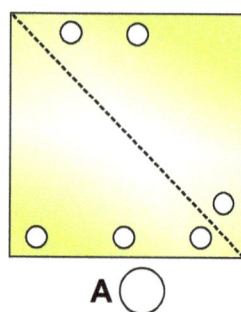
A ◯

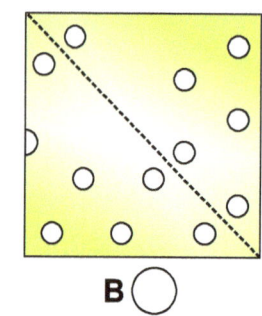
B ◯

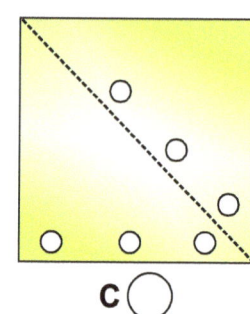
C ◯

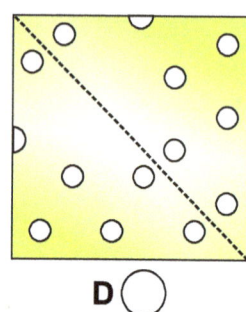
D ◯

MATH-KNOTS CHALLENGE

Q-20 Look at the question and put your finger on Walrus. Courtney folded the paper and made holes to it as shown. When the paper is unfolded how does it look? Help her bubble the right option.

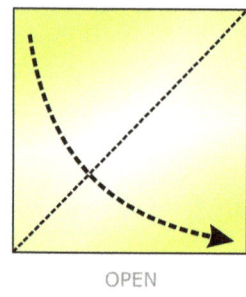

OPEN

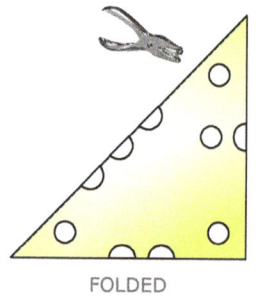

FOLDED

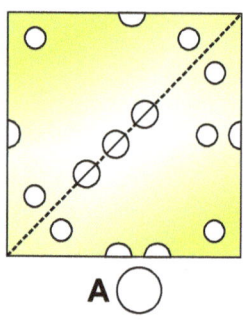
A ◯

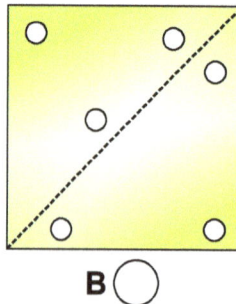
B ◯

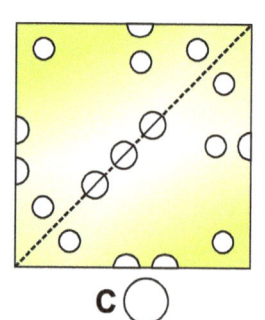
C ◯

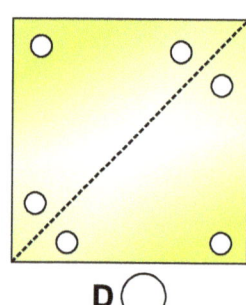
D ◯

www.math-knots.com

ANSWER KEYS

TEST - 1

Lets Start the Test...

131   www.math-knots.com

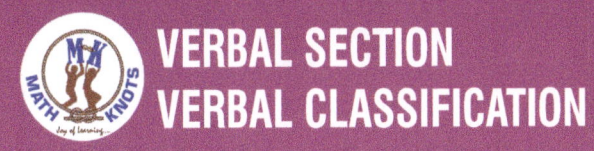
ANSWER KEY

1. B ;   Various continents

2. D ;   Types of houses

3. A ;   All are more than one in the human body

4. C ;   Branches of math

5. C ;   Various currencies

6. D ;   Same meaning

7. B ;   Shades of Yellow

8. A ;   Male animals

9. D ;   Solid figures

10. C ;   Types of looking; Wink is a momentary action

11. D ;   Various types of positive feelings

12. B ;   Things that girls wear on to their wrist / hand

13. D ;   Various performers in movies, plays, skits etc..

14. A ;   Milky way is a group of stars. All others are in sky as single entities

15. B ;   Various types of fruits

16. B ;   Various types of bugs not bug

17. C ;   Various types of tenses

18. D ;   Non-Metallic elements

ANSWER KEY

1.   C

Cereal is a processed food. Others are vegetables

2.   D

Sam < Tom < Tim so Tim weighs the most

3.   A

Bumble Bee is the only one that flies among given choices

4.   C

Option A is the figure, Option B is thermostat and Option D is showing weather forecast. Option C shows the thermometer which measures our body temperature

5.   D

Tennis players use a bat with mesh to play the sport

6.   D

Mia facing west when she makes a right turn she is facing North again a right turn means she is facing west

7.   B

Potatoes and carrots are few vegetables that grow underground. From the given choices option B potato is the right choice

8.   A

Option A shows weighing scale for the cookies or any grocery items including fruits and vegetables. Option B to measure length, Option C to measure liquids and option D is the weighing scale mostly used for larger weights

9.   D

All options belong to school supplies. We write in books but can't write with books. Hence Option D is the right choice

                                       www.math-knots.com

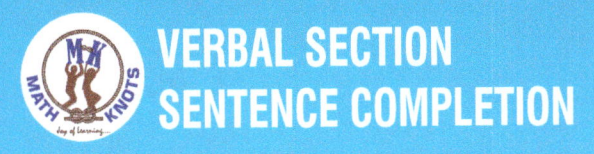
ANSWER KEY

10.   A

Zebra has black and white stripes. Only option showing black and white is option A

11.   C

A phone rings, Music plays,Drums make sound and finger rings doesn't ring. Right choice is Option C

12.   B

No of sides of Octagon > No of sides of Pentagon> No of sides of Square Octagon has more sides than other two figures

13.   D

Wind mill doesn't need electricity. It moves naturally in the direction of wind

14.   C

Urmi needs to brush her teeth. She needs a tooth brush and tooth paste. From the given choices tooth brush is the right choice

15.   A

To make a table we need to cut the wood. He needs a saw from the given choices

16.   B

Air modulation will be done through mouth. Only instrument that is played is through mouth is mouth organ

17.   D

Grapes doesn't belong to berries family

18.   A

Green represents St. Patrick's Day. Option is the only choice of red color

www.math-knots.com

ANSWER KEY

1. A

2. C

3. D

4. B

5. A

6. C

7. D

8. A

9. D

10. B

11. A

12. C

13. D

14. A

15. D

16. B

17. A

18. C

www.math-knots.com

ANSWER KEY

1.   B

         1 Whole --> Half

         1 Whole --> Half

2.   C

         5 --> 6 (Add 1)

         7 --> 8 (Add 1)

3.   A

         4 --> 2 (Half)

         2 --> 1 (Half)

4.   D

         8 --> 10 (Add 2)

         6 --> 8 (Add 2)

5.   B

         Half --> Full

         Half --> Ful

6.   D

         Color extends to next section

7.   A

         2 --> 7 (Add 5)

         5 --> 10 (Add 5)

ANSWER KEY

8.   C

6 --> 4 (Subtract 2)

9 --> 7 (Subtract 2)

9.   B

2 --> 9 (Add 7)

5 --> 12 (Subtract 7)

10.   D

1 --> 8 (Add 7)

3 --> 10 (Add 7)

11.   A

3 --> 2 (Subtract 1)

10 --> 9 (Subtract 1)

12.   C

1 Pair --> 2 Pairs

3 Pairs --> 6 Pairs

13.   B

4 --> 9 (Add 5)

1 --> 6 (Add 5)

14.   C

6 --> 12 (Double)

3 --> 6 (Double)

www.math-knots.com

ANSWER KEY

15.   D

10 --> 2 (Subtract 8)

8 --> 0 (Subtract 8)

16.   B

One Grape -->   Many Grapes

One Straw Berry -->   Many Straw Berries

17.   A

7 --> 4 (Subtract 3)

5 --> 2 (Subtract 3)

18.   C

1 --> 3 (Add 2)

4 --> 6 (Add 2)

ANSWER KEY

1.   B

2, 4, 2, 4, 2, 4; Numbers are increasing by 2

2.   D

5, 0, 5, 0, 5; Number sequence 5 ,0 is repeating

3.   C

1, 2, 3, 4; Each number is increasing by 1

4.   A

3, 3, 1, 1, 3, 3, 1, 1; Each number is repeating twice and then decreasing by 2 ,repeating and then increasing by 2

5.   D

4, 4, 6, 6, 8, 8; Each number is repeating twice and Numbers are increasing by 2 and then repeating again

6.   C

9, 7, 5, 3; Numbers are decreasing by 2

7.   A

5, 3, 1, 5, 3, 1, 5; Number sequence 5, 3, 1 is repeating.

8.   B

1, 2, 4, 7; Numbers are increasing by 1, 2, 3 ..etc
Pattern is like 1, 1 + 1, 2 + 2, 4 + 3

9.   A

1, 4, 7, 10; 1, 1 + 3, 4 + 3, 7 + 3; Starting with 1 Numbers are increasing by 3

www.math-knots.com

ANSWER KEY

10.   C

5, 4, 4, 5, 3, 6; First Alternate numbers are decreasing by 1 then next alternate numbers are increasing by 1

11.   B

3, 1, 5, 3, 1, 5, 3; Number sequence 3, 1, 5 is repeating

12.   C

2, 4, 2, 4, 2, 4; Number sequence 2, 4 is repeating

13.   D

4, 4, 4, 3, 3, 3, 2; Numbers are repeating three times and then decreasing by 1 ,repeat three times and so on

14.   B

10, 7, 4, 3, 0; Starting with number 10 and decreasing by 3

15.   A

5, 7, 7, 5, 7, 7, 5; Repeating sequence of 5, 7 and 7

16.   C

9, 8, 10, 9, 11 ; First Alternate numbers are increasing by 1 then next alternate numbers are increasing by 1

17.   D

6, 6, 5, 5, 6, 6, 5 ; Numbers are repeating twice and then decreasing by 1, repeating twice, then increasing by 1 and repeating. In other words 6, 6, 5, 5 is a repeating pattern

18.   A

4, 3, 2, 4, 3, 2; Repeating sequence of 4, 3 and 2

ANSWER KEY

1.   A

         $4 + 4 = 8$

2.   D

         $16 + 6 = 22$

3.   B

         $7 + 12 = 19$

4.   C

         $3 + 8 = 11$

5.   D

         $15 + 15 = 30$

6.   B

         $9 + 0 = 9$

7.   A

         $11 + 10 = 21$

8.   C

         $3 + 6 + 9 = 18$

9.   A

         $12 + 2 + 1 = 15$

10.   B

         $1 + 2 + 6 = 9$

www.math-knots.com

ANSWER KEY

11. B

$12 + 12 + 12 = 36$

12. C

$13 + 14 + 15 = 42$

13. A

$25 + 0 + 25 = 50$

14. C

$9 + 16 + 10 = 35$

15. D

$18 + 1 + 18 = 37$

16. B

$30 + 35 + 5 = 70$

17. D

$40 + 41 + 7 = 88$

18. C

$19 + 19 + 4 = 38 + 4 = 42$

19. D

$11 + 7 + 7 = 25$

20. B

$25 + 50 + 75 = 75 + 75 = 150$

ANSWER KEY

1. D   Crescent shape moon with yellow color more and blue color less

2. B   Fly with six antennas with same colors

3. B   Mango with a steam and two leaves

4. A   Star with # ,$ and @ next to each other in the same order

5. D   Triangle with two little square shapes attached to one side. Match the figure with same colors, shapes and sizes

6. C   Plant steam with 5 leaves in total

7. A   Rectangle with four little pictures in each corner, with two small curves on the side and a big curve in between

8. B   Leaf with a small stem and six lines inside of the same shade color

9. D   Figure with straight lines either horizontal, vertical or angular but not checks. They should have two different lines in each figure. So, A, B, and C are not right answers

10. C   Pencil divided into red ,blue and yellow colors in order with yellow color as tip

www.math-knots.com

ANSWER KEY

11.	A	Pot shaped picture with a yellow figure enclosed by a curve with three orange circles. Pay attention to options
12.	D	Circle with straight lines enclosed by a diamond shape. Outside diamond are 4 different figures and colors as well
13.	A	Figure with 6 diamonds, alternate yellow and red
14.	A	Each figure is divided into 4 equal areas or figures of same kind
15.	B	A line with Blue and orange squares on one side .Green and red squares on the other side
16.	D	A square divided into four sections .Each section has lines : 1,2,3 and 4 in order
17.	C	Different shapes of figures ,across the tear drop. Pay attention to colors and figure positions
18.	A	Circle enclosing a small circle(yellow) and a T shaped figure towards inside. Adjacent to T two green arrows originating from a point, pointing outwards

www.math-knots.com

ANSWER KEY

1. D

    Turning 90° to right side

2. A

    6 sides figure to 7 sides figure

    7 sides figure to 8 sides figure

3. B

    Turning into an angle

4. D

    Broken lines are connected

5. C

    Reducing size and switch the sides of outer figures
    (moving to the other sides)

6. D

    4 items --> 6 items

7. B

    1 item to 2 items; 2 items to 4 items by turning 90 degrees.

8. A

    Adding the same figure above the line in same direction in the
    bottom as well

9. C

    Turning to right side slightly

10. B

    Half to full

www.math-knots.com

ANSWER KEY

11.   B

Two pictures forming into a complete full picture.
One figure remains same, other one flips and joins.

12.   D

Big figure is flipped and inside object is outside.

13.   C

Flipping the figure top to bottom or right to left

14.   D

Outer border is filled

15.   B

One broken figure is enclosed by a closed figure of the same
and also includes the same figure inside

16.   C

Signs inside the figure are moving down.
outside figures are moving in clock wise direction.

17.   C

Turning the figure to right side (Clock wise) and circles are
moving to the flat side of figure.

18.   A

Checks are reduced to horizontal lines
(Vertical lines are deleted)

ANSWER KEY

1.   B ;

2.   D ;

3.   A ;

4.   C ;

5.   B ;

6.   A ;

7.   A ;

8.   C ;

9.   B ;

10.   A ;

11.   D ;

12.   C ;

13.   B ;

14.   B ;

15.   D ;

16.   A ;

BONUS CHALLENGE QUESTIONS

17.   D ;

18.   B ;

19.   D ;

20.   C ;

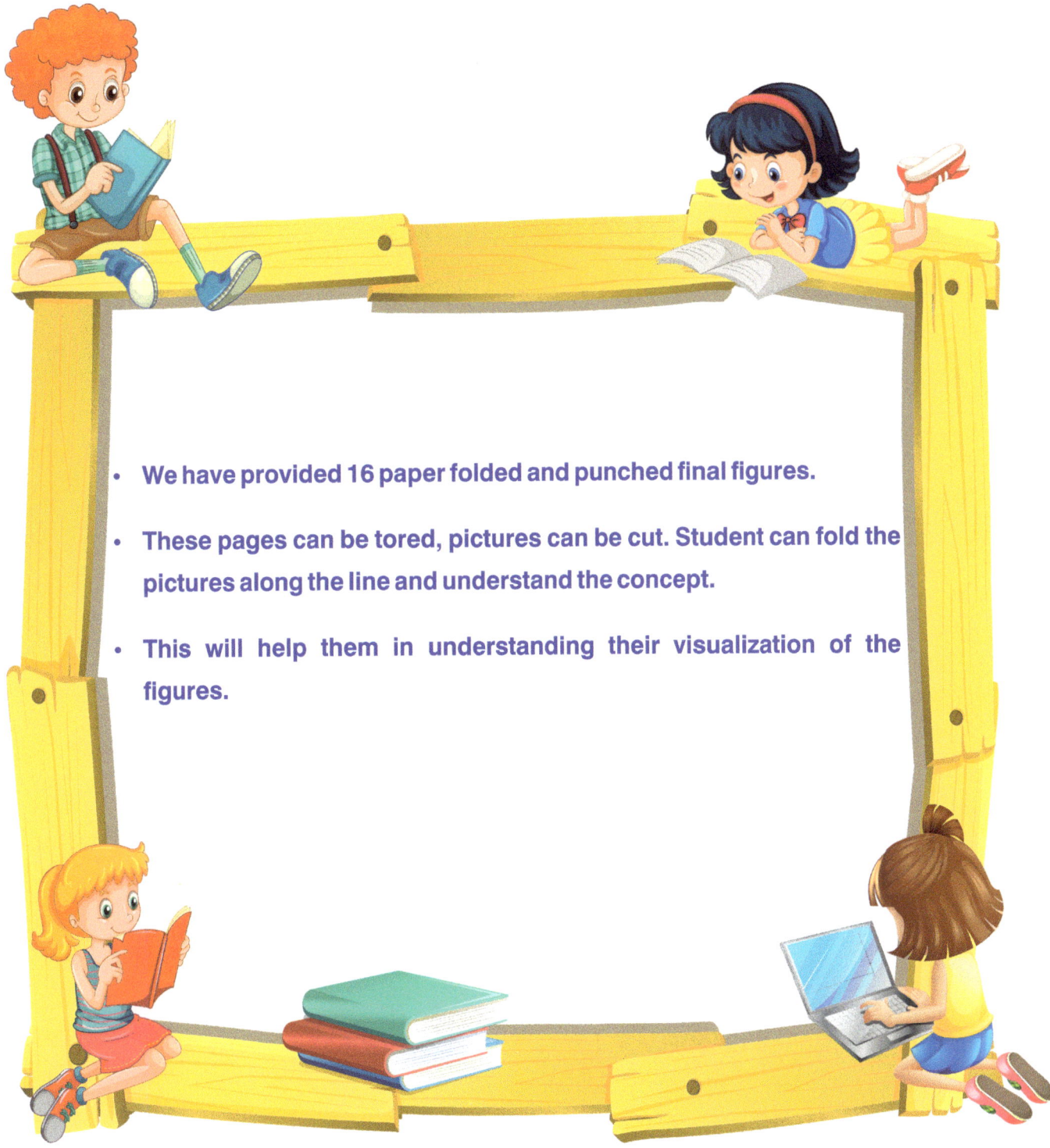

- We have provided 16 paper folded and punched final figures.

- These pages can be tored, pictures can be cut. Student can fold the pictures along the line and understand the concept.

- This will help them in understanding their visualization of the figures.

Q1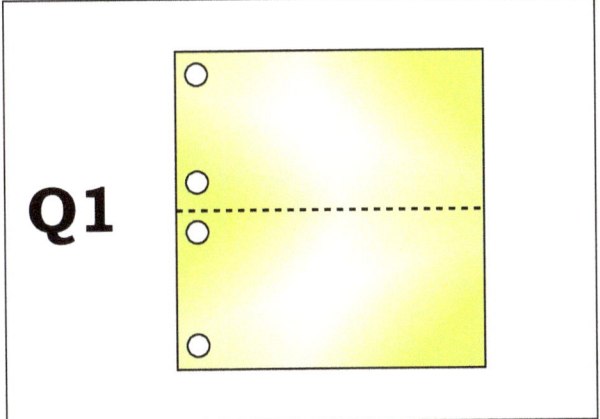

Q5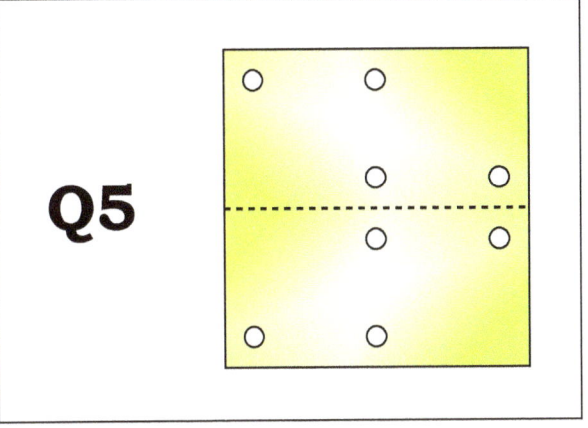

Q2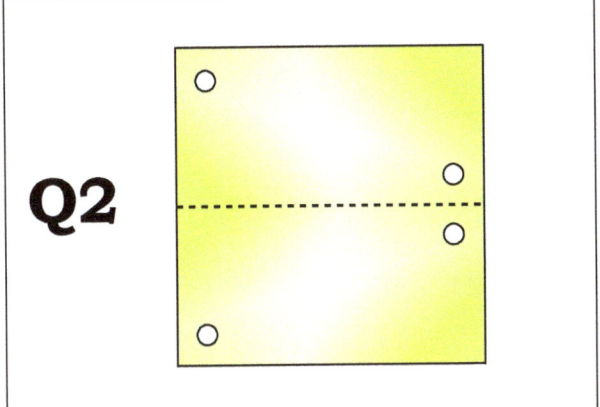

Q6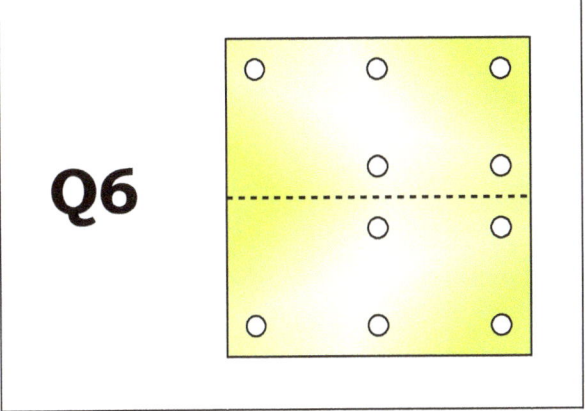

Q3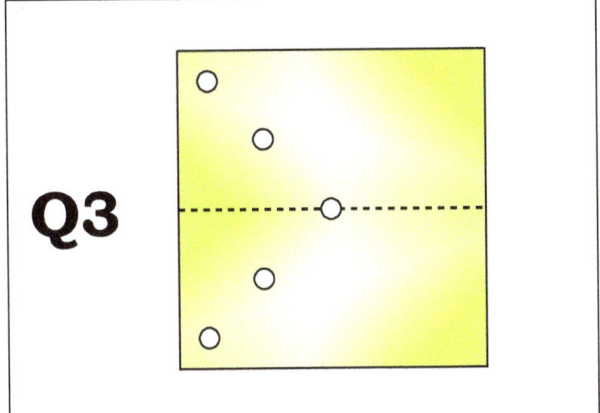

Q7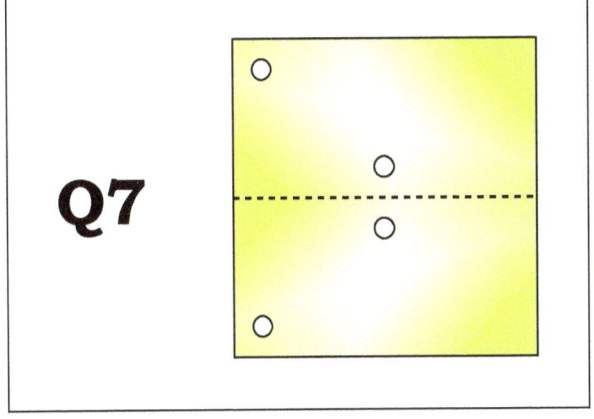

Q4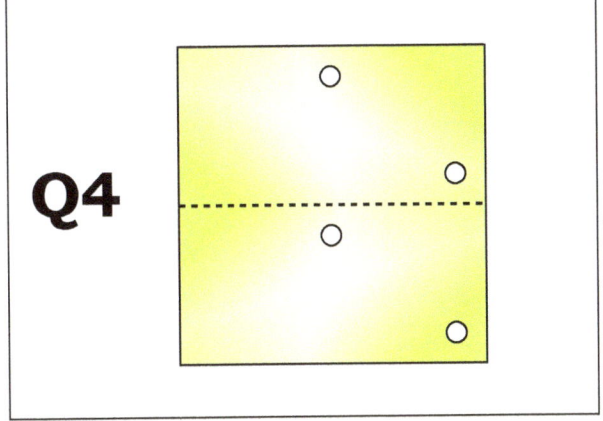

Q8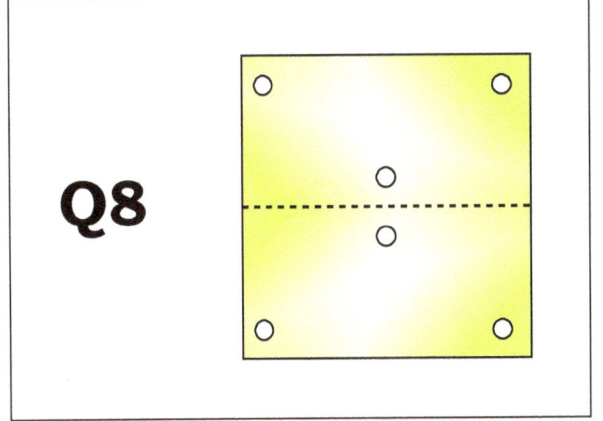

www.math-knots.com

Q9

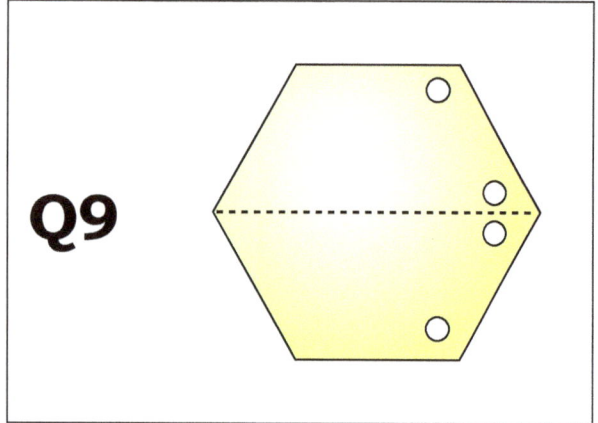

Q13

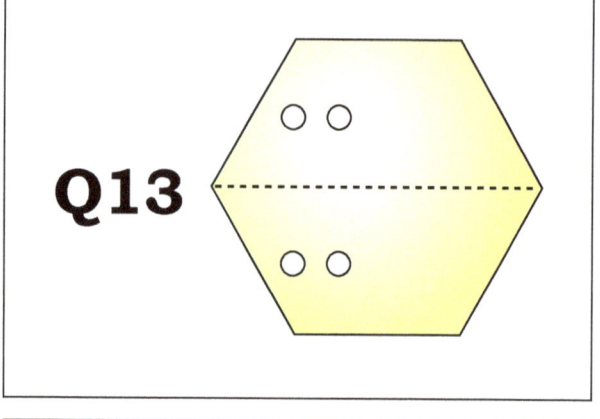

Q10

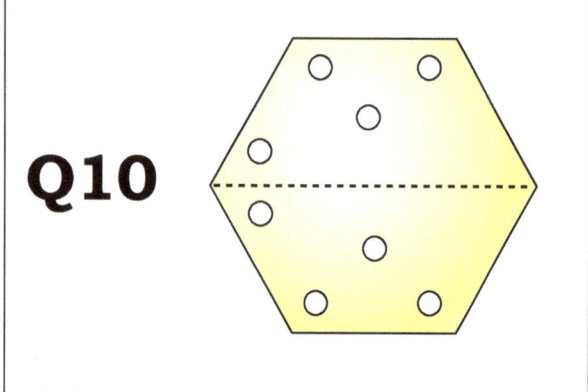

Q14

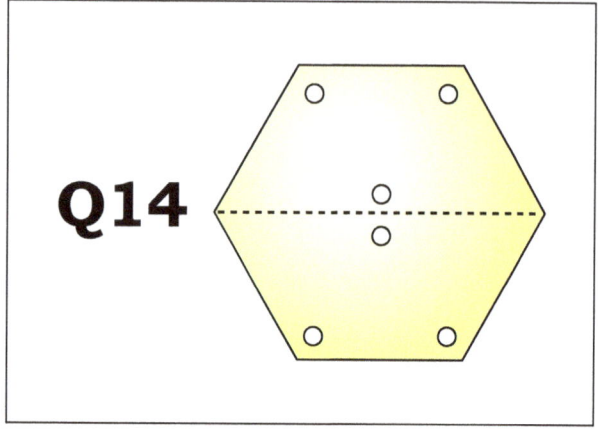

Q11

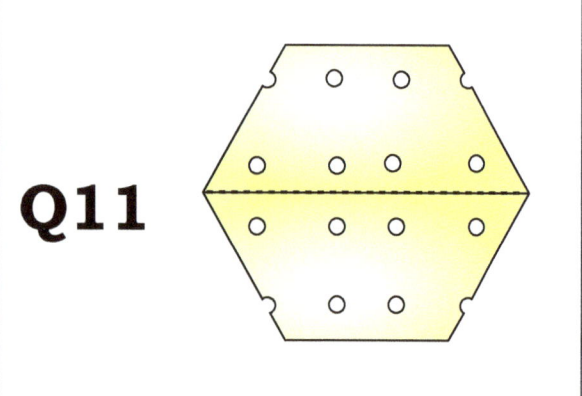

Q15

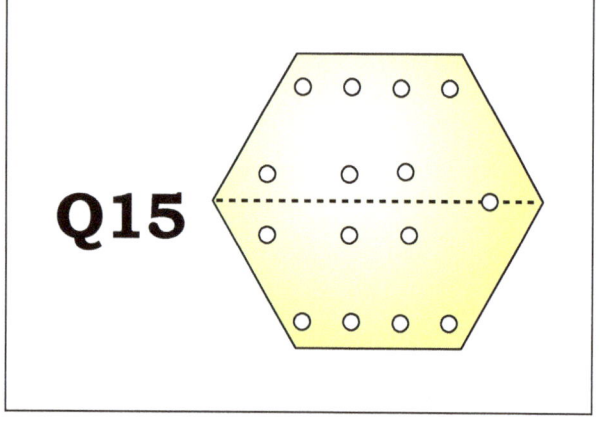

Q12

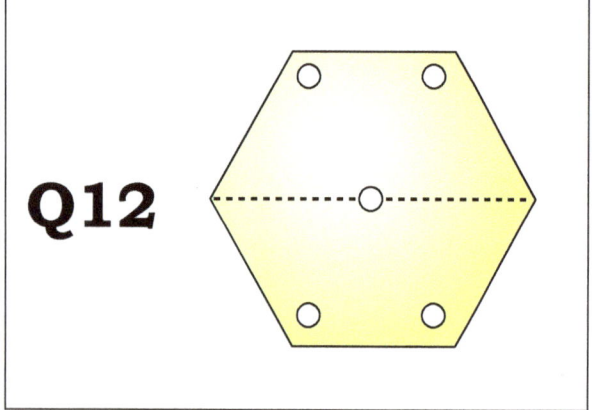

Q16

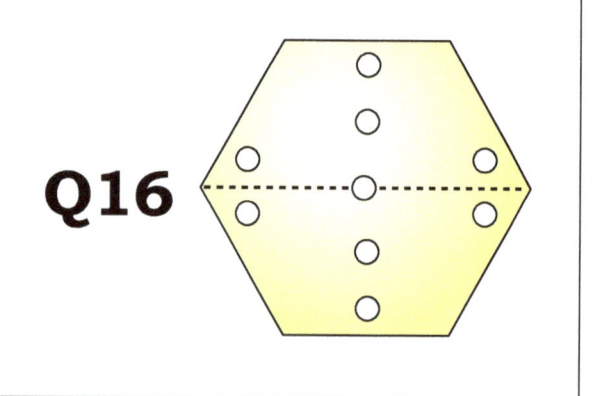

www.math-knots.com

	A	B	C	D
Q1.	○	○	○	○
Q2.	○	○	○	○
Q3.	○	○	○	○
Q4.	○	○	○	○
Q5.	○	○	○	○
Q6.	○	○	○	○
Q7.	○	○	○	○
Q8.	○	○	○	○
Q9.	○	○	○	○
Q10.	○	○	○	○
Q11.	○	○	○	○
Q12.	○	○	○	○
Q13.	○	○	○	○
Q14.	○	○	○	○
Q15.	○	○	○	○
Q16.	○	○	○	○
Q17.	○	○	○	○
Q 18.	○	○	○	○
Q 19.	○	○	○	○
Q 20.	○	○	○	○

www.math-knots.com

www.ingramcontent.com/pod-product-compliance
Lightning Source LLC
Chambersburg PA
CBHW041116120626
46547CB00019B/2729